Italy in the German Literary Imagination

Italy has long exerted a particular fascination on the Germans, and this has been reflected in German literature, most prominently in Goethe's *Italienische Reise* but also by numerous other writers who have returned to the topic. This book is concerned with two inextricably linked images — those of the German traveler in Italy and of Italy in German literature in the first third of the nineteenth century. Goethe's publication of his account nearly three decades after his actual journey was in some measure a vehicle to resist the challenge of a new generation of writers, who in turn would confront what they found to be a questionable, if not altogether false, representation. Hachmeister emphasizes the consequences of the disparity between the reality of Goethe's journey and his depiction of it, taking into consideration also his occasional discomfort with Italy's classical past. She shows how the German predilection for Italy is unique in the larger European cultural context of the Grand Tour, before moving on to chapters that contain readings of *Italienische Reise* and Goethe's *Römische Elegien*. Individual chapters follow on Eichendorff's *Aus dem Leben eines Taugenichts,* Platen's *Sonette aus Venedig,* and Heine's three Italian *Reisebilder,* each of which is to some degree a reaction to Goethe's work. These chapters investigate how the individual's reaction to Italy reflects his view of Germany and the author's role in early nineteenth-century German society. The conclusion offers a short glance at the continued evolution of the German fascination with Italy in the mid- and late nineteenth century.

Gretchen Hachmeister received her Ph.D. in German literature from Yale University.

Studies in German Literature, Linguistics, and Culture

Edited by James Hardin
(*South Carolina*)

Gretchen L. Hachmeister

Italy in the German Literary Imagination

Goethe's "Italian Journey" and Its Reception by Eichendorff, Platen, and Heine

☙ ☙ ☙ ☙

CAMDEN HOUSE

First published 2002
by Camden House

Camden House is an imprint of Boydell & Brewer Inc.
668 Mount Hope Ave., Rochester, NY 14620–2731 USA
and of Boydell & Brewer Limited
PO Box 9, Woodbridge, Suffolk IP12 3DF, UK

ISBN: 1–57113–226–0

Library of Congress Cataloging-in-Publication Data

Hachmeister, Gretchen L., 1964–
    Italy in the German literary imagination: Goethe's Italian journey and its
reception by Eichendorff, Platen, and Heine / Gretchen L. Hachmeister.
        p. cm. – (Studies in German literature, linguistics, and culture)
    Includes bibliographical references and index.
    ISBN 1–57113–226–0 (alk. paper)
        1. Goethe, Johann Wolfgang von, 1749–1832. Italienische Reise.
2. Italy — In literature. 3. German literature — Italian influences. 4. German
literature — 19th century — History and criticism.   5. Eichendorff, Joseph
Freiherr von, 1788–1857 — Criticism and interpretation.   6. Platen, August,
Graf von, 1796–1835 — Criticism and interpretation.   7. Heine, Heinrich,
1797–1856 — Criticism and interpretation.   I. Title. II. Studies in German
literature, linguistics, and culture (Unnumbered)

PT2001.C4 H33 2002
830.9'3245'09034—dc21

                                                                        2001059856

A catalogue record for this title is available from the British Library.

This publication is printed on acid-free paper.
Printed in the United States of America

For my fellow travelers, past and present.

Contents

List of Illustrations   viii

Acknowledgments   ix

List of Editions and Abbreviations
of Primary Works Cited   xi

Introduction   1

1: Goethe: Anticipation, Hesitation,
and Preparation for Italy   13

2: Rewriting the Journey: Goethe Remembers Italy   29

3: *Römische Elegien*   60

4: Eichendorff and the Romantic Return to Italy   77

5: Platen's *Sonette aus Venedig* and
the Post-Romantic Aestheticization of Italy   113

6: Subverting Tradition: Heine and
the German Myth of Italy   143

Conclusion   173

Appendix: *Sonette aus Venedig* —
Comparison of Editions   179

Works Cited   181

Notes   189

Index   213

Illustrations

Map of Goethe's journey   xiv

Goethe in der Campagna di Roma
  (Goethe in the Campagna, 1787)   12

Italia und Germania (Italy and Germany, 1811–1828)   76

Il Trionfo di Venezia (The Triumph of Venice, 1579–1582)   112

Engländer in der Campagna
  (The English in the Campagna, 1835–1836)   142

Acknowledgments

M Y INTEREST IN THE TOPIC OF GERMAN WRITERS in Italy sprang from both academic and personal circumstances, so both colleagues and family deserve special thanks.

First and foremost, I am indebted to Jeffrey L. Sammons of Yale University. As my dissertation advisor, he encouraged me with his insight and unceasing enthusiasm for the topic, which did not end with my graduation. Thanks also to Cyrus Hamlin of Yale and to my other teachers, including Ernesto Livorni, now of the University of Wisconsin, Madison, Italian Department, and my fellow graduate students. Early on, a summer fellowship allowed me to pursue research for this work at the Beinecke Rare Book and Manuscript Library. I am also grateful to Katharina von Hammerstein of the University of Connecticut and Waltraud Maierhofer of the University of Iowa.

James Hardin of Camden House has been enthusiastic from the start. I appreciate his patience and ongoing advice. It has been a pleasure to deal with Jim Walker on all aspects of the manuscript.

To my American, German, and Italian families and friends: many, many thanks, vielen Dank and Grazie mille. Randy, thanks for your ongoing love and encouragement.

G. H.
August 2001

Editions and Abbreviations of Primary Works Cited

Joseph von Eichendorff

Werke. Ed. Wolfgang Frühwald, Brigitte Schillbach, and Hartwig Schultz. 6 vols. Frankfurt am Main: Deutscher Klassiker Verlag, 1985–1893.

Abbreviations for texts from this edition:

ALT	*Aus dem Leben eines Taugenichts*
MB	*Das Marmorbild*

Johann Wolfgang von Goethe

Poetische Werke. Kunsttheoretische Schriften und Übersetzungen. Ed. Siegfried Seidel. 22 vols. Berlin: Aufbau, 1960–1978.

Werke. Ed. Erich Trunz. 14 vols. Munich: Beck, 1981.

Sämtliche Werke, Briefe, Tagebücher und Gespräche. Ed. Dieter Borchmeyer et al. 40 vols. Frankfurt am Main: Deutscher Klassiker Verlag, 1985–.

Abbreviations for texts from this edition:

IR	*Italienische Reise*
DW	*Dichtung und Wahrheit*

Heinrich Heine

Heinrich Heine Säkularausgabe. Ed. Nationalen Forschung- und Gedenkstätten der klassischen deutschen Literatur in Weimar and Centre National de la Recherche Scientifique in Paris. 27 vols. Berlin: Akademie, and Paris: Editions due Centre National de la Recherche Scientifique, 1970.

Historisch-kritische Gesamtausgabe der Werke. Ed. Manfred Windfuhr. 16 vols. Hamburg: Hoffmann und Campe, 1973–1997.

Abbreviations for texts from this edition:

R	*Reise von München nach Genua*
B	*Die Bäder von Lucca*
S	*Die Stadt Lucca*
RB	commentary, *Reisebilder*

August von Platen

Die Tagebücher des Grafen August von Platen: Aus der Handschrift des Dichters. Ed. G. von Laubmann and L. von Scheffler. 2 vols. Stuttgart: Cotta, 1896–1900.

Abbreviations for texts from this edition:
>   *PT*   Platen, *Tagebücher*

Lyrik. Ed. Kurt Wölfel and Jürgen Link. Munich: Winkler, 1982.

Abbreviations for texts from this edition:
>   *P*   Platen, *Lyrik*

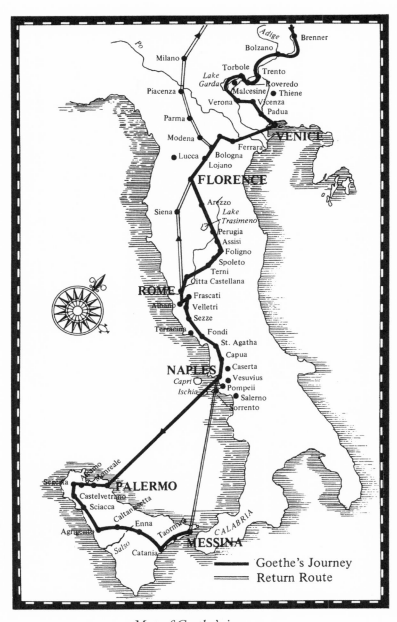

Map of Goethe's journey.
Copyright © 1989 by Suhrkamp Publishers and Princeton University
Press. Reprinted by permission of Princeton University Press.

Introduction

ITALY. THE NAME ALONE CONJURES UP COUNTLESS IMAGES in the minds of both those who have been there and those who have not. The twenty-first century reader's associations are by and large not so far removed from those of the late eighteenth- and early nineteenth-century northern European traveler. The circumstances, aims, modes, and speed of travel may have changed, but the attractions are much the same: pleasant climate; diverse and exotic landscape including active volcanoes; the ruins of ancient history; fine art culled from more than two thousand years; fresh fruit, vegetables, seafood, and fine cuisine; the Italian temperament; Italian music. The list goes on.

The story of German travelers to Italy hardly began with Goethe, but numerous factors conspired to project upon him the status of German traveler par excellence, including his own poetic choreography and his audience's sometimes premature, if not altogether false, assumptions. Goethe's work on Italy is inseparable from its multifaceted historical contexts. He journeyed on the eve of the French Revolution, departing Germany in 1786 and returning in 1788, but composed his *Italienische Reise* (Italian Journey, 1816, 1817, 1829) three to four decades later, at the end of the Age of Napoleon, throughout the early Restoration, and on the cusp of the Industrial Revolution and advent of mass tourism.

Italy has long occupied a privileged position in the German imagination, specifically in literature, the visual arts, and music. In the mid-eighteenth century, German travel to Italy expanded, both in the distances traversed and, in a broader representation, among the classes of travelers. It was also during the second half of the eighteenth century that a revolution began in the written representations of such journeys to the land we today refer to as Italy. Both of these developments, increased interest in travel to and changes in written portraits of Italy, occurred symbiotically, one not accounting for the other, but both resulting simultaneously from a changing European social, political, and cultural climate. During this time, it was surely the exception, rather than the rule, when a prominent or, for that matter, even lesser-known writer did not travel to the Italian peninsula. It should also be noted that this is not a singularly German phenomenon; the literary traditions of France and Great Britain exhibit a similar tendency. Nowhere else, though, is the tradition of literary representation so bound to one individual's experience as is the German to Goethe's. Within a short period of time, writers as diverse as Eichendorff, Platen, and Heine reacted to the Weimar poet's portrayal of Italy and elected to offer their own renderings.

The historical and psychological ties between the two countries in question had been established centuries before. As the Old German Empire was reunified in 919, the German emperor claimed sovereignty over Italy. Frederick II, German king and later Holy Roman Emperor, grew up in Sicily in the early thirteenth century: with the exception of two visits to his German kingdom, he spent his entire life in Italy. From the sixteenth century until its demise in 1806, a later incarnation of this empire was known as "Das Heilige Römische Reich Deutscher Nation" (Holy Roman Empire of the German Nation), a name that stresses the long and entangled history of these northern and southern Europeans. During the Middle Ages, travel was limited to German nobility, scholars, and some exceptional students. Religious and educational opportunities were then Italy's greatest assets: by the time of the establishment of the first German university in Prague in 1348, fifteen universities thrived in the Italian territories. In the early modern period the German image of Italy remained rather ambivalent: the great humanistic ideals of Italy stood in sharp contrast to the absolute power of the Roman Catholic Church. In the Renaissance numerous German artists, including Albrecht Dürer, worked or studied in the artistic centers of Italy. However, when it fell to Spanish rule in 1558, the increased political power of the Roman Catholic Church provincialized much of Italy. The resulting image of Italy as a downtrodden land led for a while to a lack of interest in the country, as the culture of the German Enlightenment was simultaneously oriented on French and English models. Subsequently, the closest ties in post-Reformation Europe developed between Germany and the Netherlands. Although travel between Germany and Italy never completely ceased, it did not reemerge with powerful cultural significance until the early eighteenth century: in 1748 the Treaty of Aix-la-Chapelle resulted in a renewed period of peace and political stability. Rome became the ultimate goal of the Grand Tour, the finishing touch to the education of many privileged young British, and of the *Kavaliersreise,* a similar German tradition.

Italy, as both a destination and a highly charged cultural symbol, reached a new apex at mid-century with the rediscovery and preliminary excavations of Herculaneum in 1737 and Pompeii in 1748, and the publication of Winckelmann's *Geschichte der Kunst des Altertums* (History of Ancient Art) in 1764. By the time of Goethe's departure for Italy in 1786, he was but one of many artists and writers who turned to the South for inspiration and renewal. Shortly after Goethe's return to Weimar, the French Revolution and its aftermath, including the Napoleonic Wars (1803–1815), would interrupt the free flow of northern Europeans to Italy. By the time of the Restoration (1815–1830), a new generation would embark for Italy, but they often traveled not only with a revised itinerary, but also with completely altered motivations and goals. Thus, the first third of the nineteenth century marks a time of drastic turmoil in the dominant German image of Italy: the model of the *Kavaliersreise* slowly gave way to the development of modern tourism. It is this period of transition that is the main focus of this study.

No other geographic location outside of Germany itself plays such a large role in the annals of German literature than does Italy. To this day German writers and tourists continue to visit, flee to, and write about Italy. Whether they reconstruct Italy in the pages of their diaries or novels, or in the lines of their poetry, authors participate in and engage with a long tradition of writers before them. One cannot speak of a singular, individual German image of Italy, but rather must investigate the variant images prevalent not only in the work of a variety of writers, but that may also coexist within one individual's oeuvre. Representations of the people, places, customs, culture, and history of Italy, fictional as well as ostensibly factual ones, have illuminated and clouded the views of subsequent generations.

During the last third of the twentieth century, the literary genre of travel writing slowly gained a position on the tables of contents of many scholarly publications, as well as the respect of increasing numbers of literary critics. Changes precipitated in the 1960s and 1970s in German literary studies led to the expansion of the canon to include the less traditional genres, besides poetry, drama, and fictional prose. The resulting new orientation facilitated a more prominent discussion of autobiographical writings, legitimizing such texts as the *Reisebericht* (travel report).

French and American comparatists carried out an abstract, theoretical, and highly charged debate in the 1960s over the admissibility of the study of national images into the accepted course of study of comparative literature. In the early 1950s, René Wellek resolutely challenged the project of French scholars Jean-Marie Carré and Marius-François Guyard, who strongly advocated the inclusion of the study of one nation's images of another within the field of literary studies. Wellek's prominence among American comparatists assured that national images in literature would remain relatively unexplored during the 1960s and 1970s as he pronounced the study of such national images best left for historians, sociologists, and psychologists.[1]

In 1966, the Belgian comparatist Hugo Dyserinck refuted Wellek, arguing that the study of national images and mirages can indeed be a successful strategy in literary scholarship. Dyserinck established the inherent importance of such images in literature outside of sociological, psychological, historical, or political agendas, and stressed the significance of confronting literary national images that might serve to reinforce accurate stereotypes and ideologies.[2]

It is not until the 1970s that critics begin to examine specific texts in light of these theories. Peter Boerner demonstrated the importance of imagology to the study of literature through an analysis of the influence of the French and English reading public on the exceptional ascent of German letters in eighteenth-century Europe.[3] Above all, imagology deals with perception and the limits thereof: the perception of self, or one's own nation, the auto-image, and that of the other, the hetero-image. These terms are synonymous with the ethnocentric and the exotic, and the interplay between self and other is not to be underestimated. The foreign observer confronts the limits of his own perception: the representation is always just that, a representation and not reality. Equally challenging is the frequent propagation of mythical images. Writers often privilege a fictional idealization of a place over more realistic representations, but what happens when foreign readers perceive the image of a particular nation as fact, in such seemingly diverse works as a novel set in Italy and a supposed autobiographical account of a journey? As Manfred S. Fischer points out, such fictional images, which lack an objective reality, can influence the reading public's notion of reality. In a sort of domino effect, these revised images of another nation can in turn influence new written images of the other place.[4] Whereas Dyserinck views imagology as part of a strategy of de-ideologization, by the 1980s, critics, including Fischer, stress the applicability of a reading of national images as a politicized project (263). As these examples attest, the large debate gradually developed into a sustained defense of the anti-Wellek position. Although the more contentious aspects of this debate had blown over by the mid-seventies, little advance was made in actually studying these more abstractly discussed national images. Gradually, and partly as a reaction to the Wellek debate, critics opened the canon to include texts rife with national images, those of travel literature. Exceptional texts such as Goethe's *Italienische*

Reise, which certainly had been the focus of many thousands of pages of research before this time, would attract new interest and approaches in the seventies and eighties.

Peter J. Brenner's work is the most prominent research in the genre of nonfiction German-language travel literature.[5] Employing a multidisciplinary strategy, Brenner attempts to define exactly what he means by *Reiseliteratur,* as well as the problems and challenges inherent in any critical approach to it. Any reading of an account of a traveler's encounter with the foreign requires an investigation into the interchange between the *Wahrnehmungsform* and the *Darstellungsform* of the individual account: the form of the author's perception is of equal importance to the author's presentation. Brenner expands his discussion of authenticity and contemplates the close relation of *Reisebericht* and *Fiktion:*

> Reisende genießen seit je einen schlechten Ruf. Nicht nur Reisende lügen, aber ihr Verhältnis zur Wahrheit wurde stets im besonderen Maße angezweifelt. Der Reisende als Lügner und der Reisebericht als eine Gattung, deren Wahrheitsgehalt wenig Vertrauen verdient, gehören zu den Topoi, welche die Reiseliteratur seit ihren antiken Anfängen begleitet haben.[6]

The relationship of perception to representation mirrors the endeavor of reading travel literature: it is that of understanding the dichotomy of and confrontation between that which is foreign and that which is one's own. The traveler and the reader both experience the foreign, though the traveler only does so from a distance. Brenner astutely explicates the gradual change that such a contrast underwent, especially in the centuries associated with voyages of discovery and the Enlightenment. The sharp conflict between one's perception of the self and the other began to give way to a new way of witnessing foreign places and concepts; the image of *das Fremde* became more inclusive, making way for a more homogenous view of the world. The other would soon be seen as part of the entirety of the world along with that which is familiar: two different parts of the same, all-encompassing earth (20–23). The heavily quantitative reports of the early and mid-eighteenth century gave way to the aestheticization of experience. In the face of the extreme changes in Europe around 1800, the personal and subjective gained primacy, allowing for a greater multiplicity of views than ever before. And finally, according to Brenner, the advent of mass tourism eliminates the question of the traveler as liar and anticipates the wide use of standardized guidebooks:

Die Standardisierung der Gegenstände seiner Erfahrung läßt ihm keine Wahl, als die Wahrheit zu sagen — eine Wahrheit freilich, die keiner mehr hören will, weil sie jeder schon kennt. (39)

Wolfgang Neuber articulates the most fundamental concern in reading these texts, the question of authenticity and its reconciliation with the literary status and implied fictionality of such works. Such a definition of fictionality as that which a particular society accepts as believable at a specific historical moment and place, is useful; it recognizes the impossibility of purely mimetic representation and accommodates the power of literary suggestion and influence.[7] Critics studying travelers and the literary perceptions of their journeys today adopt many different perspectives, embracing the concerns of the historian, and literary and cultural critic alike.

Although I do not posit a purely psychoanalytic reading of the literary works in question, I believe that the genre of travel literature is particularly well suited for some of that theory's interpretive tools. The attraction to and fear of the exotic; the desire to flee or escape the familiar; the role of fantasy and imagination; and the compulsion to overcome obstacles, to exceed, indeed transgress, previously delineated borders inform all the works, both fiction and nonfiction, read here. Dennis Porter promotes a psychoanalytic reading of selected European travel writings from the past two centuries, via the work of Lacan and Foucault back to Freud, largely because of the inherent role of the self-exploration within the genre. The priority of desire, both conscious and unconscious, to psychoanalysis is especially applicable to the works discussed:

> Most forms of travel at least cater to desire: they seem to promise or allow us to fantasize the satisfaction of drives that for one reason or another is denied us at home. As a result, not only is travel typically fueled by desire, it also embodies powerful transgressive impulses.[8]

Porter sees these frequently visited lands as haunted territory. "A sense of belatedness" forces the traveling writer to respond to his encounters in a unique way and to live up to the "reputation of a hallowed site: To the anxiety of travel is added the anxiety of travel writing" (12). One need only think of Goethe's motto, "Auch ich in Arcadien!" Harold Bloom's tenet of the anxiety of influence is largely derived from Freudian principles:

> Poetic Influence — when it involves two strong, authentic poets, — always proceeds by a misreading of the prior poet, an act of creative correction that is actually and necessarily a misinterpretation. The

history of fruitful poetic influence, which is to say the main tradition of Western poetry since the Renaissance, is a history of anxiety and self-saving caricature, of distortion, of perverse, willful revisionism without which modern poetry as such could not exist.[9]

Although developed as a theory of poetry, I would venture to apply it to Goethe's status in the field of German-language travel literature.[10]

The work of many of these critics, like the broader projects of cultural studies, has certainly been influenced by Edward Said's *Orientalism*. His model of western perceptions and construction of the Orient is at least in part analogous to the German relationship to Italy; many of the defining statements he posits in *Orientalism* are equally reflective of the German predilection for Italy. One need only substitute German for European and Italy for the Orient in the following: "European culture gained in strength and identity by setting itself off against the Orient as a sort of surrogate and even underground self."[11] Similarly, my primary concern is the German cultural appropriation of Italy. The writing of the journey seals this appropriation through interpretation, itself a creative act like travel. Much as the geographic destinations become a stage for the foreign traveler to act out his fantasies: "travel writing provided a stage on which they [travelers] could act out their desires for authority and importance."[12] Where do the author and reader draw the line between homage and imitation, praise and repetition? And how do new, younger generations free themselves from the long shadows cast by their predecessors, especially well-established cultural icons, such as Italy, the image, or Goethe, the traveler?

An entire subspecialty in British literary and art historical studies, known as "Grand Tour Studies," began to emerge in the 1980s and investigates the issues related to the eighteenth-century tradition of British travel to Italy.[13] This scholarship situates the "[Grand] Tour within a larger network of international travel and exchange that involved the circulation of bodies and luxury goods. . . ."[14] Recent interests have included the influence of the decorative arts on British domestic architecture and design; the practice of acquisition and collection; an ongoing fascination with Emma Hart and Lord Hamilton in Naples; and the sometimes debilitating effect of Rome on the health of its artistic visitors. Chloe Chard cites the "primary pleasure" of travel as "the pleasure of experiencing various forms of difference and alterity."[15] The traveler is obligated:

> to derive from the topography of foreignness not only enjoyment but also the form of cultural benefit that Yorick, the traveller-narrator of Sterne's *Sentimental Journey*, terms "knowledge and improvements." (8)

Chard distinguishes between the slower, deliberate travel of the Grand Tour, "a series of static confrontations with sights, wonders, curiosities, and other objects of observation" and the nearly perpetual motion associated with tourism, where velocity is of the utmost importance (25). Her description aptly applies to the development we will see from Goethe through Eichendorff to Heine. In her recent book, Chard drafts a list of the potential components and devices of travel literature of the Grand Tour. These include the use of hyperbole; expressions of shock and wonder; details of excitement and danger; curiosity, which often leads to digression and promotes dilettantism; comparisons between home and abroad; a tendency to catalogue; and expressions of pleasure and frivolity.[16] Many of these are clearly employed as part of the authorial strategies in the works investigated here: they become the very media for rewriting and challenging Goethe's Italian experiences. A bifurcation in the forms of travel parallels the evolution of the literary representations of those journeys in the late eighteenth and early nineteenth centuries. As Eichendorff, Platen, and Heine all struggle to come to terms with the status of Italy and German travel to Italy between 1819 and 1831, they respond nearly simultaneously and in vastly different ways to a grand concept of travel, the influence of Goethe, and the changing European social and political climates.

All of these strategies and responses are equally applicable to the examples of the less-traditional genre of travel narrative presented herein. Although I am concerned with the cultural reception of a national literary image, my work is not largely derivative of reception theory, or the closely related reader-response school of literary theory. These analytic approaches are, in general, concerned with the response of group readership to texts and the role of the reader in the construction of meaning. In contrast, I trace the ways in which individual readers (authors) are influenced by and respond to Goethe's *Italienische Reise* and *Römische Elegien* within their own texts.

The creative reconstruction of the memory produced the well-endowed cultural icon of Italy within German society. In the mid-eighteenth century, literary travel became a highly invested unit of cultural currency within German social and intellectual exchange. The resulting images of Italy acquired a great value, just like the sculptures, engravings, and relics collected along the way. Above all, it would be the acquisition of the experience of Italy that could determine the futures of these writers. Their use of the *Kavaliersreise,* in one form or another, granted them entry into a growing but still elite circle of Germans and, most importantly, provided them with fodder for their literary endeavors. The travelers themselves could become cultural monuments, frozen in the collective memory, as evidenced by the status of the image of Goethe in Italy.[17] It is this ongoing process, coupled with the changes brought about by the French Revolution, Napoleonic Wars, and the Restoration, that endowed the voyage to Italy as a means to achieve literary notoriety, if not critical success.

My investigation focuses on the intersection of the German images of Italy created during the second and third decades of the nineteenth century and the reception by younger writers of Goethe's powerful figurations of Italy, both poetic and autobiographical; in other words, I am interested in the intersection of image and influence in each individual writer's quest for originality. In addition, I uphold the primacy of home within a discussion of travel narrative. Van Den Abbeele hopes to go beyond the semiotic interpretations of travel prevalent in the 1970s, for example the work of Jonathan Culler and Dean MacCannell, to establish what he calls throughout his study "the economy of travel." In addition to the accepted idea that travel involves the potential of gain, whether economic, political, social or personal, he posits the equal possibility of loss. The existence of a home, or homeland, from which the traveler departs and to which he will eventually return, serves as a point of reference throughout the journey, thus completing the model of the economy of travel.[18] Although the works in question are set in Italy, both the authors and narrators, when not identical, are focused on the differences between home and abroad. Italy is privileged precisely because it is not Germany, because it is exotic. The implied focus then becomes, if not always as drastic as how to change Germany to be more like Italy, then at least a contemplation of how one's Italian experiences can enhance life, both personal and public, after the return home. Therefore, the perception of the self is closely linked to the construction of the other.

Although bound by their apparent interest in Italy, the works discussed diverge greatly on the spectrums of genre, tone, style, and authorial intent. Of the texts considered in this study, one postures itself as autobiography; another parodies that mimetic autobiographical tradition within the structure of a fictional narrative; two are formal, poetic cycles derivative of various traditions; and three self-consciously and ironically integrate fictional elements within the framework of prose nonfiction. All are bound by the priority of Italy as object and the German traveler in that foreign environment as subject. I argue that Eichendorff in *Aus dem Leben eines Taugenichts* (From the Life of a Good-for-Nothing, 1826), Platen in his *Sonette aus Venedig* (Sonnets from Venice, 1825), and Heine in his three Italian *Reisebilder* (Travel Pictures, 1829, 1830, 1831) consciously respond to the presence of Goethe in the early nineteenth-century conception of Italy. Goethe's comments regarding his lengthy stay in Italy in his correspondence, the *Römische Elegien* (Roman Elegies, 1795), the *Venezianische Epigramme* (Venetian Epigrams, 1796), and, much later, the *Italienische Reise* (1816, 1817, 1829) clearly inform the responses of those other authors, who in turn write for an audience already steeped in the mythos of Goethe in the South. The propagation of the myth of Goethe's Italy was initially as much a result of his audience's expectations as his own determination. It is in this context that the almost thirty-year lapse between his journey and the publication of the *Italienische Reise* is invested with import. It is worth bearing in mind, however, that, by publishing the first part of his travel report in 1816, Goethe reestablishes his view of a pre-revolutionary Italy. The uncertain future of Europe catapulted Goethe backward in time. The defeat of Napoleon in 1814, and ultimately in 1815, impacted the Weimar poet immeasurably; in the same year, he abruptly stopped work on his autobiography and turned to his most exotic work, the *West-östlicher Divan* (West-Eastern Divan), which would appear in 1819. His wife Christiane died in 1816. Within a few days of her burial on 8 June, it seems that Goethe returned to his editing on the section of Naples and Sicily. The journey to Italy can be read as a journey that lead Goethe home to Christiane, as it ended just days before they first met. During this period of poetic Persian fantasy, his thoughts eventually turned to the most foreign of his own life experiences, his two-year visit to Italy of 1786 to 1788. All of these historical and biographical details motivated Goethe's decision to edit, complete, and publish his travel memoirs much later in life. In them he responds to the intervening tumultuous thirty-year period of revolution and war as well as to the concurrently emerging younger German perceptions of Italy.

The actual window of time in which these primary texts (excluding Goethe's two poetic cycles) included here were published is remarkably limited. Spanning from 1816 to 1831, these works each reveal a tremendous individuality of approach, strategy, aim, and spirit. Because the *Italienische Reise* clearly impacts on all the other works and authors covered, it is the focus of the first three chapters. Chapter 1 offers the factual and theoretical background to Goethe's actual journey. A detailed reading of the *Italienische Reise* follows in chapter 2. The image of Italy emergent from the *Römische Elegien* comprises the third chapter. Chapters 4, 5, and 6 reveal the great extent to which Eichendorff,

Platen, and Heine, respectively, respond to Goethe's work as Italy took on the role of valued cultural currency and became a potential ticket to literary success.

Figure 1. Goethe in der Campagna di Roma *(1787)*
by Johann Heinrich Wilhelm Tischbein.
Reproduced with the permission of the Städelsches Kunstinstitut,
Frankfurt am Main. Photograph © Ursula Edelmann,
Frankfurt am Main.

1: Goethe: Anticipation, Hesitation, and Preparation for Italy

WHEN GOETHE SET FOOT IN ITALY in 1786, he followed in the footsteps of countless Germans, both prominent and anonymous, famous and infamous, including Winckelmann, Lessing, and his own father. The poet finally traveled south in an effort both to participate in and break with the traditions of his family and the larger society. During his absence from the courtly culture of Weimar and in the years between his return to Germany and the publication of the *Italienische Reise*, he expertly molded his own image as traveler to Italy in part to secure his place in the lengthy German tradition. Yet it is his journey that mobilized the German imagination in a way that Italy had never done before or has since.

Johann Wolfgang von Goethe's nearly two-year visit to Italy remains the most celebrated portion of his long, meticulously documented life and, more than two hundred years hence, still pervades much of the German mythos of Italy. A response to almost forty years of education, preparation, and expectation, the poet's mere presence in the South galvanized those left behind in Weimar and resulted in a convoluted loop of influence. Consequently, the culture he returned to in 1788, exceedingly receptive to new currents, would also project back upon the writer its own conception of Italy, itself fed by Goethe's carefully crafted correspondence from abroad. The ongoing and significantly unchallenged prominence of the journey in the writer's biography also stems from the literary and cultural canonization of Goethe as the epitome of German Classicism, normally explained as a direct offshoot of the Italian experience, and therefore unthinkable without it.

The most persistent visual image of Goethe remains J. H. W. Tischbein's *Goethe in der Campagna* of 1787 (see figure 1), which the painter began while sharing quarters with the writer in Rome. This larger-than-life-size portrait depicts Goethe, dressed in typical clothing of the time, draped with a toga-like garment, reclining on fragments of fallen ancient ruins somewhere in the Roman countryside. The poet looks serious but relaxed and gazes far into the distance. An ancient bas-relief represents the recognition scene from *Iphigenie auf Tauris* (Iphigenia: A Tragedy, 1787). Nearly every illustrated book on Goethe includes this painting; it has graced numerous book jackets as well, including the first volume of Nicholas Boyles's biography. His comments about the painting evidence the continued prominence of this two-year period within the poet's biography:

> The painting is dominated by the head and the right hand, the writing hand, which between them have summoned up in poetry an immortal image, that of Iphigenia and Orestes, out of the ruinous fragments of the past — an achievement which, the dimensions of the painting suggest, has something of the superhuman about it.[1]

Not only has the author achieved immortal status within the painting, but this depiction has become the canonical image of its subject. Visually, it anticipates the cultural reception of the poet by future generations of readers and critics. Upon seeing the work in progress on 29 December 1786, however, Goethe underestimated his own status and cast the portrait in a dismissive light:

> Es gibt ein schönes Bild, nur zu groß für unsere nordischen Wohnungen. Ich werde wohl wieder dort unterkriechen, das Portrait aber wird keinen Platz finden.[2]

As the painting was not displayed in Germany until well after Goethe's life, it is interesting to contemplate the painting's own role in the canonization of the Italian Goethe in the German mind.[3]

Much like the powerful influence of that painting on Goethe's readers today, Mignon's song from *Wilhelm Meisters Lehrjahre* (Wilhelm Meister's Apprenticeship, 1795–1796), strongly colored the expectations of Goethe's contemporaneous public and remains the German poetic reference to Italy par excellence:

> Kennst du das Land, wo die Zitronen blühn,
> Im dunkeln Laub die Goldorangen glühn,
> Ein sanfter Wind vom blauen Himmel weht,
> Die Myrte still und hoch der Lorbeer steht,
> Kennst du es wohl?
>   Dahin! Dahin
> Möcht' ich mit dir, o mein Geliebter, ziehn![4]

The opening question quickly became clichéd, as the repetition of its common emblematic images easily identified the unnamed subject as Italy. Goethe composed Mignon's song at least three years before he himself departed for Italy. Despite this strong testimony of the power and expectation of Italy in Goethe's own imagination, there is but a weak link between Mignon's song, the reality of Goethe's journey, and his *Italienische Reise*. The verses, included in the earlier *Wilhelm Meisters theatralische Sendung* (Wilhelm Meister's Theatrical Mission, 1777–1785), open the first chapter of the third book of the *Lehrjahre* and conform to the prominent nineteenth-century attributes ascribed to Italy by northern cultures. It is interesting to note that in the seventh chapter of the second book of *Wilhelm Meisters Wanderjahre* (Wilhelm Meister's Travels; or the Renunciants, 1821) Wilhelm travels to the Lago Maggiore in search of Mignon's home, in the hopes of clarifying his perception and memories of her. Goethe wrote this novel in the years immediately following the publication of the first two volumes of the *Italienische Reise*. Wilhelm's first journey to Italy, recalls the restorative character of Goethe's own travels, although the poet did not visit the Lago Maggiore. Wilhelm befriends a traveling painter, reminiscent of Goethe's own incognito, already in the region expressly to paint Mignon's home and hopes to aid the artist in his accuracy through his stories and descriptions of her. Interestingly, the most moving and honest depiction of Mignon was created before the painter met Wilhelm. He strives to learn to appreciate nature through artistic representation during this period of his travels. In contrast, Goethe, who never lacked for enthusiasm and understanding of the natural world, struggled throughout his southern sojourn with the meaning of the visual arts and their place in his own future. The artist's attempt to sing Mignon's song "Kennst du das Land" though is a step too far and must be abandoned.

When he finally embarked for Italy in 1786, Goethe found a place vastly different than his dreams had conjured up. The poet produced a number of texts in reaction to his lengthy sojourn including his problematic, reconstructed travel diary, now commonly referred to as the *Italienische Reise,* and two poetic cycles, the *Römische Elegien* and the *Venezianische Epigramme*. My readings of the *Italienische Reise* and the *Römische Elegien,* in particular, will illustrate the extent to which Goethe experiences, represents, and appropriates multiple Italies, all in an attempt to define his relationship to his contemporary Germany.

Goethe's lifelong fascination with Italy originated in his early childhood and within his poetic choreography it is presented as a natural offshoot of his father's own affinity for the South. In the opening pages of the first book of *Aus meinem Leben. Dichtung und Wahrheit* (From my Life. Poetry and Truth, 1811), the younger Goethe underscores the presence and important influence of Italian culture in his parents' home:

Innerhalb des Hauses zog meinen Blick am meisten eine Reihe römischer Prospekte auf sich, mit welchen der Vater einen Vorsaal ausgeschmückt hatte, gestochen von einigen geschickten Vorgängern des Piranesi, die sich auf Architektur und Perspektive wohl verstanden, und deren Nadel sehr deutlich und schätzbar ist. Hier sah ich täglich die Piazza del Popolo, das Coliseo, den Petersplatz, die Peterskirche von außen und innen, die Engelsburg und so manches andere. Diese Gestalten drückten sich tief bei mir ein, und der sonst sehr lakonische Vater hatte wohl manchmal die Gefälligkeit, eine Beschreibung des Gegenstandes vernehmen zu lassen. Seine Vorliebe für die italienische Sprache und für alles, was sich auf jenes Land bezieht, war sehr ausgesprochen. Eine kleine Marmor- und Naturaliensammlung, die er von dorther mitgebracht, zeigte er uns auch manchmal vor, und einen großen Teil seiner Zeit verwendete er auf seine italienische verfaßte Reisebeschreibung, deren Abschrift und Redaktion er eigenhändig, heftweise, langsam und genau ausfertigte. Ein alter heiterer italienischer Sprachmeister, Giovinazzi genannt, war ihm daran behülflich. Auch sang der Alte nicht übel, und meine Mutter mußte sich bequemen, ihn und sich selbst mit dem Klaviere täglich zu akkompagnieren; da ich denn das "Solitario bosco ombroso" bald kennen lernte, und auswendig wußte, ehe ich es verstand.[5]

The atmosphere in the Goethe household in Frankfurt ensured, indeed presaged, the son's own formative journey south. Italian was the first modern foreign language to which Goethe was exposed: his skills in both written and spoken Italian remained sharp throughout his long life, culminating in his translation of Benvenuto Cellini's autobiography from the Italian in 1803. He reported to Eckermann in 1829 that he practiced the language with the Italian artisans working in the ducal palace of Weimar.[6] The elder Goethe, Johann Caspar, set out for Italy as a thirty-year-old bachelor in December of 1739 and remained there through the summer of 1740; he visited the main attractions of early eighteenth-century Italy, adhering to the typical itinerary starting in Venice, proceeding through Tuscany to Rome, then further south to Naples. It is remarkable that the middle-class Goethe senior made such an extensive trip: the privilege of such a *Bildungsreise* was generally reserved at that time for young aristocrats.[7] As his son described years later in his own autobiography, the elder Goethe would present his Italian experience as his life's most important act. In his own, astonishingly Italian-language, travel report, *Viaggio per l'Italia* (Journey through Italy), not only did Caspar Goethe recount his daily adventures, but he also copied and translated many hundreds of inscriptions on the ancient monuments he viewed. He died in 1780 without the satisfaction that his son had also made the same pivotal journey upon which he had insisted for so long. In 1794, the father's 1,096 page manuscript passed into the hands of the son in Weimar, where it eventually made its way to the archives until its first publication in 1932.[8] Caspar Goethe's purpose was clear, as he explained upon his arrival in Venice:

> Ich bitte Sie, keinen Anstoß daran zu nehmen, denn es gehört schließlich zu den Hauptabsichten der Reisenden, die Eigenarten der verschiedenen Nationen und ihre unterschiedlichen Lebensweisen und Sitten kennenzulernen; dies kann aber nur geschehen, wenn man sich damit auch bei solchen Gelegenheiten vertraut macht.[9]

His stated intention is typical for his generation of traveler, although much would change in the nearly fifty years between the two Goethes' visits and even more in the eight decades between Caspar's journey and the publication of the first volume of his son's *Italienische Reise*. The writer's father, clearly responsible for his son's early link to Italian, plays a looming, yet subtle role in the *Italienische Reise*. The assumed trip eventually became a generational point of contention.[10] Goethe would postpone his journey, in part to defy his father, and would eventually surpass the boundaries of his father's earlier trip. This literary oedipal complex anticipates a similar response on the part of younger writers to Goethe's own patriarchal literary status.

Although the seeds of interest were planted in early childhood, Goethe struggled with both his own desires and his father's expectations regarding an Italian visit during adolescence and the first two decades of adulthood. On 29 April 1770 Goethe wrote in a letter from Strasbourg to his school friend in Leipzig, Ernst Theodor Langer:

> Nach Italien Langer! Nach Italien! Nur nicht über's Jahr. Das ist mir zu früh; ich habe die Kenntniße noch nicht die ich brauche, es fehlt mir noch viel. Paris soll meine Schule seyn. Rom meine Universität. Denn es ist eine wahre Universität; und wenn man's gesehen hat, hat man alles gesehen. Drum eil ich nicht hinein.[11]

The sense of urgency is countered by the desire to delay an event seen as life's culmination, to be undertaken seriously, with adequate preparation, as to maximize the benefit. Five years later Goethe would twice abort such a tour: in June 1775 Goethe was in Switzerland with friends and on the twenty-first ascended via Göschenen to Andermatt. From there Goethe was afforded a view into the Italian territories on the other side; however, he chose to return to Frankfurt. He did so only after having sketched a picture he called *Scheide-Blick nach Italien*

(Parting Glance at Italy). Later that same year, with his future still un-
decided, the elder Goethe urged his son finally to make the necessary
Italian pilgrimage instead of taking up a post in Weimar. As is well
known, the poet's father was not in favor of his son allying himself with
the aristocracy. The younger Goethe waited without definite news from
Weimar until the end of the month and then on 30 October set out for
Italy with his manservant, Philipp Seidel, noting in his diary: "Ich
packte für Norden, und ziehe nach Süden, ich sagte zu, und komme
nicht, ich sagte ab und komme" (*VFW*, 489).[12] As it turns out, the
Duke of Weimar's messenger, von Kalb, was delayed and eventually
intercepted Goethe in Heidelberg, where von Kalb convinced him to
change his plans and move to Weimar. One additional opportunity to
travel to Italy presented itself during Goethe's second tour of Switzerland, this time while accompanying Duke Carl August in the autumn
and winter of 1779/1780. It would have been fairly straightforward to
follow the Simplon Pass to Italy for a brief tour of the Lake Maggiore.
Having served for less than one year in Weimar, Goethe felt that he had
much yet to prove in that capacity. Above all, a journey to Italy was a
journey he meant to make himself (*BI*, 310).

   Italy permeated the air in Weimar during the course of the 1780s.
Dowager Duchess Anna Amalia called Christian Joseph Jagemann to
the court, where he served as Italianist, language tutor, literary scholar,
librarian, translator, and general consultant on all things Italian from
1775 until his death in 1804. Goethe consulted him on questions regarding language; Jagemann translated *Hermann und Dorothea* (*Her-
man and Dorothy*, 1797) into Italian. He edited and published many
books on Italian literature and culture and contributed countless articles to Wieland's *Teutschen Merkur* (German Mercury). He published
the eight-volume anthology, *Magazin der Italienischen Litteratur und
Künste* (Magazine of Italian Literature and Arts), from 1780 to 1785.[13]

   Goethe would not head to Italy until the end of his first decade in
the service of Carl August and six years after his father's death. After
spending the month of August with Carl August, Charlotte von Stein,
and other Weimar friends in Karlsbad, Goethe left early on 3 September 1786 (significantly, the Duke's birthday): only Philipp Seidel, his
private servant and secretary, knew of his plans. His eventual departure
for Italy is generally viewed as a flight from personal and professional
constraints experienced within the close-knit courtly society of Weimar,
a judgment that Goethe himself did much to establish:

denn ich muß gestehen, da meine Reise eigentlich eine Flucht war vor allen den Unbilden, die ich unter dem einundfünfzigsten Grad erlitten, daß ich Hoffnung hatte, unter dem achtundvierzigsten ein wahres Gosen zu betreten. (*IR*, 21)

Here, just five days after his departure, Goethe colors his Italian journey as a self-imposed, voluntary exile. The preparation of the first collected works, the first four volumes of which were published by Göschen during Goethe's prolonged absence from Weimar, informed his decision to leave for Italy. In the months preceding his departure, Goethe, ordering and editing his earlier work, saw the tangible evidence of scant literary production for his first Weimar decade. He departed with the intention of returning to his writing, carrying with him a number of manuscripts ripe for completion. He seems to have considered these packages and the literary creations they contained as traveling companions; like the poet they were in need of a transformation, but at the same time served as a link to those left behind. They became a common topic of conversation in the poet's correspondence and a bond to his new-found circle in Rome.

Italienische Reise: Genesis, Composition, and Form

The *Italienische Reise* poses many challenges due to its, at least at first, seemingly complex structure and evolution as a complete text. What readers today commonly refer to as the *Italienische Reise* was actually published in three parts over the course of thirteen years, the first volume of which did not appear until thirty years after Goethe's original departure for Italy.[14] Almost immediately upon leaving Karlsbad, Goethe began to keep a diary of his journey, intended, he originally claimed, exclusively for Charlotte von Stein. In these five epistolary *Reisetagebücher* (Travel Diaries), Goethe recounts at length his travels to Rome, ending with his arrival there on 29 October 1786. By mid-December Goethe sent the final volume to Weimar.

These *Tagebücher,* extant today, later served as Goethe's main source for a large part of what he would call *Italienische Reise I,* published in 1816 as a continuation of his autobiography titled, *Aus meinem Leben. Zweyter Abteilung. Erster Teil* (From My Life. Second Section. First Part). In this volume Goethe recounts his journey from Karlsbad and his first stay in Rome, spanning the period from 3 September 1786 to 21 February 1787. The Roman portion of the book is based on correspondence to Carl August, Frau von Stein, Herder, and others in Weimar. *Italienische Reise II,* published in 1817 as *Aus meinem Leben.*

Zweyter Abteilung. Zweyter Theil (From My Life. Second Section. Second Part), chronicles Goethe's journey from Rome to Naples, his stay in Naples, his trip to Sicily, and eventual return to Rome (22 February to 6 June 1787). For this second volume Goethe again culled his correspondence as well as a diary he kept during his Neapolitan stay. Although Goethe destroyed all these sources after editing, critical consensus corroborates the accuracy and objectivity of these first two volumes. Much philological, text-based research specifically compares the original *Reisetagebücher*, his correspondence, and the first volume of *Italienische Reise*, and reveals that the editorial process altered the tone far more than the content of the reports. The original form of address was changed from *Du* or *Sie* to the collective idea of *die Freunde.* As a result, Stefan Oswald concludes, a more anonymous monologue replaces the personal dialogue of the original correspondence:

> Es entsteht dadurch der Eindruck, als seien die Mitteilungen aus Italien von vornherein an ein Publikum gerichtet, das in der von Goethe suggierten Gestalt der Lesergemeinde die wohlwollende und verständnissvolle Aufnahme garantierte, die er nach seiner Rückkehr nach Weimar bei den tatsächlichen Adressaten nicht fand.[15]

During the editorial process, in a letter to Zelter dated 17 May 1815, Goethe stresses the importance of his original sources as well as the recollections of his friend Meyer. The poet emphasizes his attempt to regain the immediacy of the long past journey and imposes on the reconstruction of the journey the imperative of clarity, unity, and purpose:

> Ich beschäftige mich jetzt mit meiner *italienischen Reise* und besonders mit *Rom*. Ich habe glücklicherweise noch Tagebücher, Briefe, Bemerkungen und allerlei Papiere daher, so daß ich zugleich völlig wahrhaft und ein anmutiges Märchen schreiben kann. Hiezu hilft mir denn höchlich Meyers Teilnahme, da dieser mich ankommen und abreisen gesehen, auch die ganze Zeit, die ich in Neapel und Sicilien zubrachte, in Rom blieb. Hätte ich jene Papiere und diesen Freund nicht, so dürft ich diese Arbeit gar nicht unternehmen: denn wie soll man, zur Klarheit gelangt, sich des liebenswürdigen Irrtums erinnern, in welchem man, wie im Nebel, hoffte und suchte, ohne zu wissen was man erlangen oder finden würde.[16]

Goethe upholds the possibility of the coexistence of truthfulness and "ein anmutiges Märchen," a combination not unlike his autobiographical program formulated in the title *Dichtung und Wahrheit.*

The objectivity and veracity of autobiographical representation in the remainder of the *Italienische Reise* remains a more contentious issue. This final installment was published twelve years later in 1829 as the twenty-ninth volume of the *Ausgabe letzter Hand* and is generally referred to as the *Zweiter Römischer Aufenthalt* (Second Roman Stay). Notably, this final portion lacks a subtitle connecting it to his earlier autobiography. This portion of Goethe's work details the period from June 1787 through his departure from Rome in the following April, but he leaves no account of his actual return to Weimar. The events of the second Roman stay thus stand alone: in Goethe's arrangement these are the most crucial months of his tour, a time seriously devoted to *Selbstbildung*. The structure of the *Zweiter Römischer Aufenthalt* is itself unique and less cohesive than the first two volumes. Goethe divided the material by month, subdivided further into sections titled *Korrespondenz* (Correspondence) and *Bericht* (Report), which in most cases summarizes the correspondence, but from the retrospective distance of forty years. Goethe also included a number of loosely related texts, some of which he had published independently in the first years after his return to Weimar from Italy, in addition to an excerpt from a text by Karl Philipp Moritz. Robert Gould locates a skepticism in the distinct voice of the autobiographer of the *Bericht*, when compared to the voice of the much earlier *Korrespondenz*, a pessimism that in turn calls into question the feasibility of artistic and linguistic communication.[17] The text itself, through the selective editing of actual letters and the retrospective voice of the reports, becomes a demonstration of the process of literary reception (75). Because of the long lapse in time between Goethe's preparation of the various volumes of the *Italienische Reise* and the fact that the source letters and notes are no longer extant, scholars agree that the *Zweiter Römischer Aufenthalt* lacks the mimetic status of the two earlier volumes. Italo Michele Battafarano, attempting a useful and accurate definition of the genre of the *Italienische Reise*, a work which defies classification as a simple travel report, describes the text as a "literarisches Erzählwerk in Form einer poetisierten Autobiographie, die eine Realreise durch die Brief- bzw. Tagebuchform thematisiert."[18] In this way Goethe has broken with the tradition of the reporting eighteenth-century travelers before him, injecting the text with a radical new subjectivity. Despite the extent of the elderly Goethe's editing of his manuscripts from Italy, there remains in the pages of the *Italienische Reise*, at times, surprising candor. He confesses his indecision and conflicts, his competing desires. This honesty should not be overlooked or discounted. Yet the fragmentariness stands in contrast to Goethe's finding of self in Italy.

In terms of thematic organization within the *Italienische Reise,* Jochen Schütze recognizes the preponderance of dichotomies or polarities, beyond being a handy sort of organizing principle, as one way Goethe maintained an orientation or direction within his conception of travel. Emphasized contrasts, often between Germany and Italy, contribute to his method of feeling at home while abroad.[19] Thus, in Schütze's eyes, we have two volcanoes, Vesuvius and Etna; two painters, Tischbein and Hackert (but what of Angelika Kaufmann?); two Italian beauties, *die schöne Mailänderin* and *die schöne Römerin;* two different cities, Rome and Naples. Although the constant mirroring of and dialogue between home and abroad, native and foreigner, cannot be overemphasized in my reading of the *Italienische Reise,* Schütze's insistence on the prevalence of contrasting pairs is perhaps too strong. In the very least, it should be viewed first and foremost as a principle imposed upon the elderly Goethe's memories of a distant past.

Autobiography and Fiction

Goethe's *Dichtung und Wahrheit* is usually considered in conjunction with the works of St. Augustine and Rousseau in the classification of dominant "seminal" autobiographers repeatedly cited in the criticism,[20] or with Rousseau and sometimes Wordsworth in a definition of the "classical age of autobiography."[21] Goethe carefully designed his autobiography to reveal his development as a writer, and in this context the absence of the first decade in Weimar from that narrative assumes its import: that period confounded more than contributed to Goethe's oeuvre. The Italian experience will redirect the course toward literary fame.

Strangely, few critics include the *Italienische Reise* as part of their discussion of the author's autobiography. By extrapolation, Goethe's understanding of the autobiography's title sheds light on his intent in the travel report as well:

> Diese Deutung — aus der Sicht des Alters — nannte [Goethe] *Dichtung.* Die Tatsächlichkeit der Einzelheiten nannte er *Wahrheit.* Der Titel *Wahrheit und Dichtung* bedeutet also: die Tatsachen und ihr Zusammenhang; oder: die Richtigkeit der Einzelheiten und die verbindende Schau und künstlerische Form.[22]

Research on the *Italienische Reise* must necessarily confront critical concerns of both autobiography and travel literature, genres both bound by the role of subjectivity and the viability of mimetic representation. *Dichtung und Wahrheit* has been called a major stumbling block to the study of autobiography.[23] For many critics of autobiography, "Goethe marks both a beginning, a zenith and, in some sense, an end" (167). Such remarks could easily apply to the canonical standing of the *Italienische Reise* and explain, at least in part, why many aspects of the work have been overlooked and underexplored.

Theory and Criticism

The magnitude of the critical attention paid to the *Italienische Reise* makes its overwhelming consensus all the more striking. The privileged status of both writer and text has to a great degree shielded the *Italienische Reise* from further investigation. Not surprisingly, products of the recent Goethe year 1999 contributed for the most part to the established views. Two earlier sources in particular are extremely helpful in sorting out and dealing with the vast number and wide array of approaches to Goethe's travel literature. Both Peter Boerner and Peter J. Brenner convincingly document that despite the vast literature on Goethe, a surprising amount of work remains undone. Also invaluable are the commentaries to two editions of the *Italienische Reise:* Herbert von Einem's remarks accompanying the 1981 publication of the twelfth edition of the *Hamburger Ausgabe,* and especially the more recent and in many ways more comprehensive commentary to the *Frankfurter Ausgabe* of 1993, compiled by Christoph Michel and Hans-George Dewitz.

Peter Boerner calls for renewed and original investigations of Goethe's text in a short article of 1985, part literature review, part interpretation, and introduces a number of neglected aspects and approaches as suggestions and encouragement for further research. Boerner calls to task the astonishing fact that most aspects of Goethe's own self-representation in the *Italienische Reise* have been accepted part and parcel into the standard biography of the poet's life; since the text's original publication, the *Italienische Reise* has enjoyed almost continual success. It is the most readily cited example of the genre of travel writing, a great irony itself considering its structure and genesis. It bears little if any resemblance to many other representatives of the class. Boerner attributes the relative scarcity of full-length, comprehensive interpretations to the text's mixed constitution,[24] a property that I argue makes the text so interesting, challenging, and inviting for further study. In light of several rather hesitant and negative observations made by Goethe in the *Italienische Reise* and continually ignored in scholarship, Boerner suggests a welcome alternative to the overwhelmingly prevalent critical reading of Goethe's Italian journey as *Wiedergeburt*. Indeed the darker tone of select portions of the text has perhaps only accentuated the brighter, more optimistic passages associated with rebirth (361).

Brenner situates Goethe's *Italienische Reise* as a pivotal point in the development of the genre and explains that at the beginning of the nineteenth century the status of the *Reisebericht* undergoes a serious and important transformation: travel reportage assumed to be of a factual nature evolved toward a more subjective interpretation of the individual experience, entering the territory of fiction as the traveling writer poetizes his experiences.[25] Brenner rightly points out that Goethe is not alone in these changes. Winckelmann did much to shift the focus from the Baroque to the Classical. Herder, Moritz, and others traveled south in the wake of renewed interest in the classical roots of their tradition. However, no one else had yet stylized his or her Italian experiences in the way Goethe would (276).

Hans Mayer's reading of Goethe's texts, despite its age, serves as a good example of the traditional approach followed by many critics. In light of Goethe's new-found poetic productivity after his return to Weimar, Mayer celebrates Goethe in his full glory and displays the poet's journey south as the decisive event of Goethe's writing life. In this interpretation, the first ten years in Weimar culminate in a life crisis for which there is but one resolution, the Italian journey. A number of his observations bear repeating, including the often overlooked fact (perhaps because it is actually rather obvious) that Goethe blatantly avoided treating the early Weimar years, 1775–1786, in any part of his autobiography. In *Dichtung und Wahrheit,* Goethe recounted his childhood and maturation through his departure for Weimar. Mayer points out the lack of contemporary historical interest on Goethe's part and underscores the view that Goethe went to Italy with the desire and goal to confirm his expectations, privileging insight over opinion.[26] What awaited the poet in Italy had the potential of either fulfilling or shattering those dreams. Mayer also locates numerous affinities between the text of the *Metamorphose der Pflanzen* (Metamorphosis of Plants, 1790) and the *Italienische Reise:* the analogous laws of nature and art underscore the unity of the world (70–72). He describes Goethe's journey as a turning away, both aesthetically and socially, from all that the *Sturm und Drang* represented (75).

Many readings of the text from the 1980s, a period of renewed interest in such nontraditional genres, continue to promote the theme of *Wiedergeburt*, specifically in Rome. Strategically, Stefan Oswald situates Goethe chronologically after the German Romantics, by ordering Goethe's texts by publication dates and not by the actual dates of the travel. He situates Goethe contemporaneous with the Romantics, not as their predecessor, and in doing so emphasizes the extremely programmatic nature of the *Zweiter Römischer Aufenthalt,* especially in Goethe's critique of the German Romantic painters in Italy, known as the Nazarenes (*O,* 98). Although many critics and editors have commented on Goethe's single reference to these German painters in Rome in the final portion of the text, Oswald develops more fully and convincingly what he sees as Goethe's implicit anti-romantic strategy. The Nazarenes, however, did not settle in Rome until 1810; thus Oswald concludes:

> Eine Ursache für die Veränderung wird in dem Umstand zu suchen sein, daß die Auseinandersetzung mit der neudeutschen Schule, die der *Italienischen Reise* weitgehend implizit sind, in der Schilderung des römischen Aufenthalts explizit geführt werden. . . . In ihr stellt Goethe dem Leben der romantischen Künstler in Rom seine eigene damalige Existenz modellhaft entgegen. . . . So gewaltsam wie der Einschub in den Kontext ist die Argumentation Goethes; er verlegt das Erscheinen der nazarenischen Schule in Rom um zwanzig Jahre vor, um seinen Angriff gegen deren Hochschätzung des frühen Raffael zu legitimieren. (*O,* 104)[27]

The book-length study *"Ein Gefühl von freierem Leben": Deutsche Dichter in Italien* ("A Feeling of a Freer Life": German Writers in Italy, 1990), by Gunter E. Grimm, Ursula Breymayer, and Walter Erhard, attempts to offer a literary-historical overview of the entire span of German writers traveling to Italy. For the most part, they accept his departure as a flight from a personal and professional crisis. Uniquely among most publications concerning the *Italienische Reise,* they offer many interesting technical details of his trip, culled from the more sociologically based research of the history of travel and tourism, thereby highlighting the commonalities and differences between Goethe and his contemporary travelers.[28]

Heinrich Niederer rejuvenates the critical discourse on the *Italienische Reise* through the introduction of some radically new interpretative ideas. Although he adheres to the majority view of the rejuvenative aspect of the journey and the priority of the act of seeing during Goethe's journey, Niederer maintains that Goethe's departure from Karlsbad in the late summer of 1786 was deliberate, premeditated, and long contemplated. Thus, Niederer does much to counter the seemingly unanimous view of Goethe's trip as flight. Niederer unmasks the significance of many seemingly banal details of the trip, assembling a fairly comprehensive picture of Goethe's *Reisekunst*. Most importantly for his argument, Niederer stresses the necessity and import of his return, even in Goethe's own conception of his trip before its onset.[29] Weimar will serve as the constant reference point for Goethe during his absence: in other words, the entire journey can be read as a deeply concerted effort to make himself understood at home, that is by his circle in Weimar, as well as by Germany at large (92). Despite is strengths, Niederer's analysis fails to consider the impact of Christiane Vulpius in Goethe's life almost immediately upon his return from Italy, makes no distinction between Goethe's first and second stays in Rome, and typical of many critics, dismisses Goethe's trips to Naples and Sicily as relatively unimportant.

Nicholas Boyle supports Niederer's idea of a premeditated, planned departure for Italy, but he goes further to hypothesize that Goethe began contemplating a journey to Italy as early as May 1786 (*B1*, 396). Boyle unmasks the irony in Goethe's decision to leave the country at exactly the time that he is trying to reestablish a connection with his German reading public, through the planned publication of the collected works (*B1*, 397). The cover of leaving from a working vacation in Karlsbad concealed Goethe's long-time preparations (*B1*, 395). In the preceding months his workload had lightened and he had organized his responsibilities in Weimar public affairs in such a way that his colleagues could easily assume them. All personal documents and copies of his work were left in the ducal archives. Seidel would organize the poet's correspondence in his absence; banking details were left up to J. J. H. Paulsen, in Jena (*B1*, 396). Although Goethe's trip as a whole may appear to be a desperate escape from various circumstances, the poet did everything he could to be prepared and organized. This meticulous attention would color not only the actual technical details of travel, but Goethe's own changing conception of his journey while underway and later in his own literary representation of it.

Foremost in any discussion of Goethe and his text is a clear understanding of the multiple roles Goethe plays, not only as the protagonist of the text, but also as a historical figure. On the one hand, Goethe exists as the traveler who experienced the events described in the travel report as well as the writer and editor who created that report, the *Italienische Reise*. On the other hand, there exists Goethe, the protagonist of the text, a construct of the other, writing self. Like all writers of travel prose, he is at once both representer and represented, subject and object. As Oswald astutely observes:

> Durch Ausblendung bzw. Retuschierung seiner persönlichen Situation entzieht der Autor der *Italienischen Reise* den Goethe jener italienischen Jahre den Augen des Publikums, indem er an seine Stelle eine Kunstfigur 'Goethe' setzt. Diese ist nicht fiktional im Sinne einer Romanfigur, ebensowenig läßt sich aber Goethe, wie er aus dem Tagebuch und den Briefen entgegentritt, mit dem Protagonisten der Autobiographie zur Deckung bringen. Das Verhältnis von historisch realer zu literarisch gestalteter Figur kommt dabei weniger in den völlig unterdrückten oder neu hinzugefügten Partien zum Ausdruck, als vielmehr in der Überarbeitung authentischen Materials. (*O*, 96)

Authorial intention maintains a high priority throughout.

In 1815 Goethe began a short poetic requiem for an Austrian field marshal, Karl Joseph Fürsten von Ligne. Goethe's work on this piece is contemporaneous with the editing of the first volume of the *Italienische Reise*. Parts are assigned to a chorus, various natural spirits, and foreign lands. The penultimate speaker is the personified Italy to be sung by a soprano, who extols her own virtues:

> Das Wehn der Himmelslüfte,
> Dem Paradiese gleich,
> Des Blumenfelds Gedüfte,
> Das ist mein weites Reich.
>
> Das Leben aus dem Grabe
> Jahrhunderte beschließt;
> Das ist der Schatz, die Habe,
> Die man mit mir genießt.[30]

These characteristics are not far from those of Mignon's earlier song. For the public honor of a deceased friend, Goethe maintained the prototypical attributes of an Italy rich in natural wonder and classical connotation. Eternity seems almost promised to be attainable through firsthand experience with the enduring Roman ruins of the South. The poet's strategy here clearly challenges the prevalent Romantic program and does not accommodate the more uncomfortable, if not entirely negative, reaction that occasionally surfaces in the simultaneously evolving travel narrative. This piece, although only an unpublished fragment, propagates a culturally accepted version of Italy, both a response to and potential cause of the audience's expectations for Goethe.

Central to my reevaluation of Goethe's *Italienische Reise* and its resulting *Italienbilder* is Goethe's perception of himself as a traveler. Surprisingly few scholars have gone beyond the more familiar topoi to look closely at how Goethe, within the text of the *Italienische Reise*, may have viewed his journey in relation to his predecessors and his contemporaries. Goethe's self-perception as a traveler clearly shapes his various *Italienbilder*. As the epigraph of the book implies, this would be Goethe's opportunity to show his Italy: "Auch ich in Arcadien!"[31] This choice clearly aligns the author in 1816 with the classical tradition of ancient Greece and Rome, in opposition to the Romantic movement that had gained popularity in the decades since his return from Italy. It also calls the reader's attention to the lengthy tradition of the pastoral, both literary and visual. To what extent do Goethe's earlier memories refute subsequent cultural developments? Chapter 2 offers a chronological close reading of Goethe's travel narrative precisely because of the import of its overall structure and evolving authorial intent. This detailed attention will facilitate close readings of the works of Eichendorff, Platen, and Heine. How does Goethe, the editor, confront the very authors who in their own works challenge the public's expectation of Goethe, the traveler, in Italy?

2: Rewriting the Journey:
Goethe Remembers Italy

Italienische Reise I: **Toward Rome**

THE POET'S EASE IN ASSUMING THE ROLE of traveler reflects his long, clandestine mental preparation for the journey; the steps taken are at once new and strangely familiar; the experience, a dream and simultaneously the fulfillment of that dream. Throughout the *Italienische Reise,* Goethe's self-depictions shift as he assumes the various roles of German, artist, poet, student, and traveler. Although the poet's own descriptions of the first leg of his journey range in emotion and tone, they are blanketed by an overriding sense of impatient haste to reach his destination. His prose installments exhibit an enthusiasm that is sometimes ecstatic and at other times intentionally subdued or repressed. In the first portion of the *Italienische Reise,* Goethe's self-portraiture is largely informed by his comments on his incognito, the consulted guidebooks, and fellow foreigners he meets along the way.

Goethe's incognito went unchallenged throughout his journey to Rome, and upon his arrival there Goethe appreciated the many benefits it offered; indeed, most of the Germans in Tischbein's circle suspected his true identity, even if they were not certain of the famous poet's presence in Rome. The willing complicity of Tischbein and a few other prominent members of German society in Rome protected Goethe's semi-incognito. On 11 November 1786, Goethe relishes the apparent anonymity, something long since impossible in Germany:

> Mein wunderliches und vielleicht grillenhaftes Halbinkognito, bringt mir Vorteile, an die ich nicht denken konnte. Da sich jedermann verpflichtet, zu ignorieren wer ich sei, und also auch niemand mit mir von mir reden darf, so bleibt den Menschen nichts übrig als von sich selbst oder von Gegenständen zu sprechen, die ihnen interessant sind, dadurch erfahr' ich nun umständlich, womit sich ein jeder beschäftigt oder was irgend merkwürdiges entsteht und hervorgeht. . . . Genug, ich habe meinen Willen und entgehe der unendlichen Unbequemlichkeit, von mir und meinen Arbeiten Rechenschaft geben zu müssen. (*IR,* 143)

Ironically though, it is through his diary and these letters home that Goethe does account for himself and his work; however, by silencing, or at least delaying the other half of the dialogue through the post, he minimizes confrontation and maintains his own self-confidence.

Roberto Zapperi devotes much consideration to the motivations and details of Goethe's incognito. Amazingly, even the Weimar circle did not know Goethe's assumed identity. Seidel kept the secret, forwarding correspondence on to Italy. Eventually Goethe shared his address with a select few, who were advised to send their correspondence sealed in an envelope, which in turn was to be enclosed in another envelope addressed to Tischbein.[1] As Goethe implied above, had the poet traveled as a minister and member of the cabinet of the Duchy of Weimar, his trip would have assumed a markedly different character. Accompanied with a small entourage of servants, he would have been obliged to make the diplomatic rounds in all the major stops along the way. Had Goethe traveled under his own name as the established poet, he would have been identified solely as the famous author of *Die Leiden des jungen Werthers* (The Sorrows of Young Werther, 1774) and subject to the expectations of the public: a completed man, not a work-in-progress. A simple traveler, without guise or calling card, would have aroused suspicion of espionage. Thus, the guise of a German painter from Leipzig named Jean Philipp Möller forced Goethe to travel by less comfortable means, forgoing the private coach. Instead Goethe traveled alone, without servants, by postal coach, the usual public means of transport of the time.[2] Such conveyance demanded independence, flexibility, patience, and time, but on the other hand, it assured optimum opportunity to observe and interact with the changing landscape and local residents.

Jochen Schütze underlines the power established by maintaining an incognito, which thrives on uncertainty and mystery. Goethe, he argues, ultimately traveled under a pseudonym, not in order to conceal his true identity, but rather precisely so that his real name would eventually be uncovered.[3] In much the same way, his absence from Weimar is equally controlled: the traveler can only stay away as long as he remains the center of the Weimar circle's attention (*GR*, 32). Both strategies uphold his self-assured indispensability, explaining, at least in part, his constant preoccupation with the problem of making the Italian experience relevant to life in Germany after his return. Jane Brown posits a deeper motivation for the incognito, a motivation specifically related to Goethe's identity as a writer:

The decision to travel incognito, whatever more obvious functions it may have had, represents in this context a stripping away of Goethe's own subjectivity for the purposes of the journey. The suppression of the *Subjekt* allows objects to become more visible. . . . Thus the incognito even allows Goethe to merge with the object of observation. The goal of such self-immersion in objects is not escape from subjectivity, but rather a new view of the self.[4]

Brown does not completely distinguish between Goethe, the writer and editor, and Goethe, the traveler. Since the decision to travel under an assumed identity had consequences not only for the traveling self, Brown's comments suggest that the incognito was, at least in part, a strategy of the writer as well; she posits a sort of internal incognito within his mind. Lilian Furst corroborates, identifying a marked difference between Goethe's work and the work of his contemporary travelers, Smollett, Stendhal, Hazlitt, and Chateaubriand, in the objectification of the traveler's self:

> The distance that [Goethe] interjects in the *Italienische Reise* between the traveler and the writer may well stem in part from the temporal gap between his journey and its final literary format, but more fundamentally it testifies to Goethe's recoil from the contemporary tendency to cultivate an idiosyncratic self that is allowed to dominate the discourse. As a result of his eschewal of an inflated role for the persona of the traveler, the orientation of the *Italienische Reise*, despite its individualistic tone and flavor, remains firmly set towards the object of contemplation and the audience.[5]

Contrary to Furst, I would argue that Goethe's occasional remarks concerning other travelers and the act of travel itself should not be discounted. Throughout his vacillation between embrace and rejection of the status of traveler, the writer fine-tunes his own role.

Most prominent in Goethe's remarks regarding the reference works he consulted either before or during his trip is the multivolume *Historisch-kritischen Nachrichten von Italien* (Historical-Critical Report from Italy) by Johann Jacob Volkmann, the first edition of which was published from 1770 to 1772. Certainly the most popular "guidebook" of its time, it is comprised not only of Volkmann's own observations, but also of excerpts from contemporary French and English sources. Goethe's correspondents vicariously joined him in his sightseeing by paging through their own copies of Volkmann. Although Goethe occasionally berates Volkmann as a model for how not to travel in Italy, the poet reserves his harshest criticism for the ignorant Archenholz's *England und Italien* of 1785, in which all things British are far preferred to

those Italian (*IR*, 155). Such remarks give fodder to Goethe's own latent desire to write about Italy and justify his attempts in the already
crowded field, even elevating letter above book.

However important these guidebooks may have been to Goethe,
especially before his trip, it is undoubtedly his father who serves as
Goethe's most significant predecessor to Italy.[6] The son, in part, charts
his course based on Johann Caspar's earlier trip and delimits his own
self-image in reference to the father, beginning in Venice, the first major stop on his journey:

> Ich gedachte dabei meines guten Vaters in Ehren, der nichts besseres
> wußte, als von diesen Dingen zu erzählen. Wird mir's nicht auch so ge-
> hen? (*IR*, 74)

Again, both ambivalence and anxiety coexist. The younger Goethe in-
sinuates a greater purpose than simply recounting his journey. Goethe
meets a wide variety of foreigners traveling to or through Italy, none of
whom escape his glance.[7] On the canal from Padua to Venice on 28
September 1786, Goethe encounters two religious pilgrims from
Paderborn. He volunteers his services as a translator, thus enabling the
Italian helmsman to converse with them, while reminding his corre-
spondent and later, reader, of his linguistic abilities. Goethe allies himself with his fellow Germans and chooses to sit with them in the
exposed stern. Part of a different circle of traveling Germans, these religious pilgrims will not publicize Goethe's presence in Italy and thus
represent a benign interaction for the poet. In other instances Goethe
shies away from his countrymen, but their religiosity somehow Italian-
izes them for Goethe as if this is one of his first encounters with Italians. Goethe identifies with the pilgrims' need to belong in Italy, to
escape the sense of outsider at home. Likewise, his pilgrimage exhibits
aspects of both exile and nomadism.

Goethe's next encounters with foreign travelers leave him with a far
less favorable impression: in Venice he meets a Frenchman who travels
quickly and obliviously. Goethe is amazed that a seemingly well-
educated, upstanding Frenchman could be so undemanding of his
travel experience (*IR*, 103, 11 October 1786). Again his comments
bolster the narrator's constructed journey, both physical and literary,
and validate his superior point of view. Eleven days later, while on the
road to Rome, Goethe recalls an English pair, remarkable solely for
their offensive, negative attitude (*IR*, 120, 22 October 1786). Once in
Rome the poet will cite the British as the most knowledgeable tour
guides (*IR*, 142–43, 7 November 1786).

Goethe seldom complains of the often primitive and substandard condition of his accommodations as did many of his contemporaries.[8] One must wonder if Goethe astonished his correspondents by presenting himself as an open and flexible tourist, relishing the independence and self-responsibility that comes with the role:

> Schon jetzt, daß ich mich selbst bediene, immer aufmerksam, immer gegenwärtig sein muß, gibt mir diese wenigen Tage her eine ganz andere Elastizität des Geistes; ich muß mich um den Geldcours bekümmern, wechseln, bezahlen, notieren, schreiben, anstatt daß ich sonst nur dachte, wollte, sann, befahl und diktierte. (*IR*, 28, 11 September 1786)

The everyday minutiae of travel, instead of becoming a burden, serve a liberating function. From early on Goethe wishes to blend in as much as possible. For example, in Verona he trades his typically north European boots for shoes and socks (*IR*, 55, 17 September 1786). Roberto Zapperi has recently discovered that, parallel to his diary, Goethe religiously maintained a record of all expenditures during his absence from Weimar (42).[9]

Goethe delights in the role of traveler, as he works toward the destination of Rome, with overwhelmingly positive remarks. Notwithstanding their importance, Goethe's account of his journey reveals, upon closer examination, his own discomfort with his highly charged emotional response to the fulfillment of a long-held dream. Outer calm masks inner turmoil: as a result, the poet frequently, especially in the first two published portions of the *Italienische Reise*, assumes the viewpoint of another, an almost third-person strategy for coming to terms with these unfamiliar sensations:

> da fühlt man sich doch einmal in der Welt zu Hause, und nicht wie geborgt, oder im Exil. Ich lasse mirs gefallen als wenn ich hier geboren und erzogen wäre, und nun von einer Grönlandsfahrt, von einem Wallfischfange zurückkäme. Auch der vaterländische Staub der manchmal den Wagen umwirbelt, von dem ich so lange nichts erfahren habe, wird begrüßt. (*IR*, 29, 11 September 1786)

He imposes a familiarity on a place he has never seen before. Roger Cardinal describes Goethe's "[anticipation of] a major theme of Romanticism, [as he] rewrites his journey as a myth of return — a return to origins."[10] His emotions are at times so overpowering that he must temper them with other tangential observations. As the journey proceeds, Goethe repeatedly attempts to define the specific purpose of this trip; unable to acknowledge or accept the act of taking this long-wished-for trip as being meaningful enough, he constantly searches for, evaluates, and redefines his intentions:

> Ich mache diese wunderbare Reise nicht um mich selbst zu betrügen, sondern um mich an den Gegenständen kennen zu lernen. . . . (*IR*, 49, 17 September 1786)

Such purposeful statements contrast repeatedly with his dreamlike descriptions of Italy, which, in turn, although freshly set on paper, have a reminiscent, memory-like quality to them. This frequent modulation in tone is visible throughout the text. For Goethe, not long removed from his duties as minister in Weimar, everything must have a clear purpose. The almost childlike innocence with which Goethe approaches much of his early Italian experiences is at odds with the writer's ambitions and diligence. As Goethe winds up his stay in Venice, he prepares the first volume of his diary to send back to Weimar, and his perusal of these recent pages incites deeper reflection:

> Schon jetzt finde ich manches in diesen Blättern, das ich näher bestimmen, erweitern und verbessern könnte; es mag stehen als Denkmal des ersten Eindrucks, der, wenn er auch nicht immer wahr wäre, uns doch köstlich und wert bleibt. (*IR*, 104, 12 October 1786)

Already, editorial impulses surface in the writer nearly thirty years before publication of the words in question. First impressions remain the strongest and most authentic representation of emotion, yet their very integrity disarms the seasoned writer, who describes perfectly the dilemma of the autobiographical writer.

Goethe's own impatience for Rome combats the increasing pressure from within to create something out of multitudinous new experiences. Suddenly, as the traveler moves further south, inching closer to Rome, the text resonates with a crescendo of testimonies of the deep, repressed pain of recent years. Goethe introduces the metaphor of the long-suffered illness, which the present journey is meant to cure. He confesses both physical and mental weakness brought on by the mere thought of Italy. The recent affliction would surely have proved fatal had he not set out on his travels. Again Goethe represses his ardor sufficiently by concentrating on the sensation of reliving a past impression (*IR*, 105–6, 12 October 1786). Approaching the outskirts of Rome, he envisions the historical past before him:

> Mit dem was man klassischen Boden nennt, hat es eine andere Bewandnis. Wenn man hier nicht fantastisch verfährt, sondern die Gegend real nimmt, wie sie daliegt, so ist sie doch immer der entscheidende Schauplatz, der die größten Taten bedingt, und so habe ich immer bis-

her den geologischen und landschaftlichen Blick benutzt, um Einbildungskraft und Empfindung zu unterdrücken, und mir ein freies klares
Anschauen der Lokalität zu erhalten. Da schließt sich denn auf eine
wundersame Weise die Geschichte lebendig an, und man begreift nicht
wie einem geschieht, und ich fühle die größte Sehnsucht den Tacitus in
Rom zu lesen. (*IR*, 130–31, 27 October 1786)

The sensations of old and new thus mingle with heightened expectation as he reigns in his own imagination. The reader feels the distance
between the writer and his subject/object, the traveler. Goethe expresses the repression exercised by the traveler, not the writer, whose
prose does not suffer from a lack of poetic imagination.

Many of the most frequently cited and easily recognized passages of
the entire *Italienische Reise* can be found in Goethe's descriptions of his
early weeks in Rome, in which the German poet recounts his sometimes dreamlike state. Not until after his actual arrival is Goethe able to
state that Rome was his ultimate goal; he refers to his "Geheimnis" and
his "unterirdische Reise" (*IR*, 134, 1 November 1786). Consequently,
the tone minimizes the significance of the two months of travel toward
Rome; his nearly life-long yearning for the South was very specifically
associated with Rome, or rather, Rome stood in his mind as the embodiment of that desire. His first impressions are again closely related
to the Roman experiences of his father:

Über das Tyroler Gebirg bin ich gleichsam weggeflogen. Verona, Vi-
cenz, Padua, Venedig habe ich gut, Ferrara, Cento, Bologna flüchtig
und Florenz kaum gesehen. Die Begierde nach Rom zu kommen war
so groß, wuchs so sehr mit jedem Augenblicke, daß kein Bleibens mehr
war, und ich mich nur drei Stunden in Florenz aufheilt. Nun bin ich
hier und ruhig und wie es scheint auf mein ganzes Leben beruhigt.
Denn es geht, man darf wohl sagen, ein neues Leben an, wenn man das
Ganze mit Augen sieht, das man teilweise in- und auswendig kennt.
Alle Träume meiner Jugend seh' ich nun lebendig, die ersten Kupfer-
bilder deren ich mich erinnere, (mein Vater hatte die Prospekte von
Rom auf einem Vorsale aufgehängt) seh' ich nun in Wahrheit, und alles
was ich in Gemälden und Zeichnungen, Kupfern und Holzschnitten, in
Gyps und Kork schon lange gekannt, steht nun beisammen vor mir,
wohin ich gehe finde ich eine Bekanntschaft in einer neuen Welt, es ist
alles wie ich mir's dachte und alles neu. Eben so kann ich von meinen
Beobachtungen, von meinen Ideen sagen. Ich habe keinen ganz neuen
Gedanken gehabt, nichts ganz fremd gefunden, aber die alten sind so
bestimmt, so lebendig, so zusammenhängend geworden, daß sie für
neu gelten können. (*IR*, 135, 1 November 1786)[11]

The reality of Rome can never live up to Goethe's own expectations or even replace his imagination; nevertheless, he expresses little disappointment or regret. Just as his words will later influence and even intimidate other traveling writers, his father's imposed impressions and expectations left an indelible mark on the younger Goethe. Was it not inevitable that someone raised in such an atmosphere would either entirely embrace or reject Italy? Both distant and recent pasts influence Goethe's observations and actions. Through his letters the poet simultaneously justifies his actions and choices to those in Weimar. Duty ensured that he would share the sights of Italy with them, if only through his prose. A bit of guilt occasionally surfaces, for example, when Goethe expresses great relief to learn that his correspondents bear him no ill will regarding his sudden disappearance (*IR*, 158–59, 13 December 1786). A great fear of being misunderstood repeatedly motivates the writing traveler, yet early on he alludes to the possible necessity of a long absence from Weimar:

> Ich erhole mich nun hier nach und nach von meinem salto mortale, und studiere mehr als daß ich genieße. Rom ist eine Welt, und man braucht Jahre um sich nur erst drinne gewahr zu werden. Wie glücklich find' ich die Reisenden die sehen und gehn. (*IR*, 159, 13 December 1786)

Again Goethe distinguishes himself from many of his fellow travelers; he implies that as a serious traveler, he either lacks the capacity to truly enjoy himself, or is unwilling to risk it. This is further evidence of the strong pull between duty and pleasure, a feeling that will resurface during his stay in Naples. It is perhaps these same pervasive discrepancies, which his correspondents perceive:

> Beim Aufräumen fallen mir einige Eurer lieben Briefe in die Hand, und da treffe ich, beim Durchlesen, auf den Vorwurf, daß ich mir in meinen Briefen widerspreche. Das kann ich zwar nicht merken, denn was ich geschrieben habe schicke ich gleich fort, es ist mir aber selbst sehr wahrscheinlich, denn ich werde von ungeheuern Mächten hin und wider geworfen, und da ist es wohl natürlich daß ich nicht immer weiß wo ich stehe. (*IR*, 188, 21 February 1787)

Goethe clearly acknowledges the extreme emotions and attractions bidding for his attention.

Goethe's first stay in Rome, nearly four months in duration, is thus characterized by a sense of the overwhelming power of the city. He fervently takes in the main sights and attractions, including the ruins and works of art, and begins practical artistic training. He invests a great deal of time cultivating new friendships within the German circle of

Rome, including Tischbein, Moritz, Reiffenstein, and others. These early weeks also mark the foundation of his friendship with the painter, Angelika Kauffmann, with whom Goethe will spend much time during his second stay in Rome. In the midst of all this, he also manages to transform *Iphigenie* from prose to verse, finishing it by the turn of the year. Despite this flurry of activity, the author's depiction of the initial months in Rome is not distinguished by great pressure to meet conflicting demands. Goethe gradually assimilates to the pace and tone of life, and a hopeful contentment takes the place of the earlier overwhelming sensations. The first months lack the structured approach of formal study prevalent during his second stay. In these early months, Goethe tastes the possibilities and perhaps more silently contemplates the purpose of his stay.

Italienische Reise II: Naples and Sicily

In the literature of the Grand Tour, Naples enjoys the reputation of a diversion, a side trip from Rome, an afterthought. The southern city, endowed with exotic natural beauty and a diverse population, becomes the locus of sensuality, pleasure, and sexuality. Literary critics tend to underestimate the importance of Goethe's stay in Naples and his trip to Sicily, I believe, largely because of the poet's own presentation of this three-month period: this southern sojourn is situated chronologically after Goethe's triumphant arrival in Rome and immediately precedes the *Zweiter Römischer Aufenthalt,* that part of the *Italienische Reise* most privileged by the author in style, tone, and organization. As a result, the poet's nearly seven-week visit to the city of Naples is often dismissed as a vacation-like interlude between the two extended Roman stays; however, Goethe's Neapolitan prose vividly illustrates his deeply felt conflict between duty and pleasure. The focus of the traveling writer's activities and attention shifts while away from Rome and, in a significant way, predetermines the course of his second year in Italy. The fact that Goethe accompanies Tischbein to Naples only accentuates the leading role that the visual arts will play.

Naples, in and of itself, had a decidedly different atmosphere than Rome: in 1787 the renowned city on the bay was the third largest city in Europe, after London and Paris, far larger than Rome, and certainly the largest city Goethe would ever visit.[12] Equally portentous, Johann Caspar Goethe had traveled as far south as the city of Naples in 1740, but did not venture further than Pompeii and Herculaneum. By extending his journey south to Paestum and eventually to Sicily, Goethe literally and symbolically surpassed the boundaries defined by his father and most travelers of the previous generation. The trip to Sicily required, of course, a sea voyage, another novelty to many Germans of Goethe's generation. The trip to Naples can be seen as the first practical application of many of the ideas developed by the poet during his initial months in Rome, especially aesthetic ones. An additional challenge to the reader and the critic surfaces with this portion of the text: this is the first section of the *Italienische Reise* for which the original correspondence no longer exists, as Goethe destroyed it shortly after preparation of the text for publication. In the organization of the final, complete text of the *Italienische Reise,* Goethe situates this portion of his Italian journey as a separate part, a fact too often overlooked.

The city's dramatic geographic situation on the breathtaking gulf, in view of Mount Vesuvius and the rocky islands of Capri, Ischia, and Procida, was well known to northern Europeans and embodied a visible link to the ancient past. Thus, the city and region appealed to the amateur geologist and natural scientist. The pleasant climate and rich vegetation must have seemed even more miraculous to the traveling German, who visited his most southern destinations during what at home would have been the harsh, bleak winter. His observations on the situation of Naples are awe-inspired. In his discussions of Naples and Sicily, Goethe yields to the temptation of extremes, vacillating between disdain and praise, both of which often come across as hyperbole. He feels both an attraction to and a repulsion from the pleasure-seeking Neapolitans, describing the city as a "paradise."

> Jedermann lebt in einer Art von trunkner Selbstvergessenheit. Mir geht es eben so, ich erkenne mich kaum, ich scheine mir ein ganz anderer Mensch. Gestern dacht' ich: entweder du warst sonst toll, oder du bist es jetzt. (*IR*, 224, 16 March 1787)

After an evening in the home of the British Envoy to the Kingdom of the Two Sicilies, Sir William Hamilton, during which Goethe witnessed the famed beauty Emma Hart perform her legendary *tableaux vivant,* Goethe contrasts his initial responses to Rome and Naples: Rome remains the site of serious study and Naples the place simply to experience life (*IR*, 225, 16 March 1787). Goethe expressly excludes himself from the city's pleasure-seekers. Hamilton, a long-time resident of Naples, has become in the eyes of Goethe, a Neapolitan. Goethe is interested in the contrasts now manifested in himself, which he finds reflected in the natural world as well as the effect of Naples and its environs on the outsiders: at what point does one fall irrevocably under the spell of Naples? To what extent does he identify with the pleasure-seekers, and when does he distance himself from them? Throughout his sojourn, Goethe is attracted to the Neapolitan way of life, yet perceives his German nature to be the inhibiting factor:

> Triebe mich nicht die deutsche Sinnesart und das Verlangen mehr zu lernen und zu tun als zu genießen, so sollte ich in dieser Schule des leichten und lustigen Lebens noch einige Zeit verweilen und mehr zu profitieren suchen. Es ist hier gar vergnüglich sein, wenn man sich nur ein klein wenig einrichten könnte. Die Lage der Stadt, die Milde des Klimas kann nie genug gerühmt werden, aber darauf ist auch der Fremde fast allein angewiesen. (*IR*, 233, 22 March 1787)

The search for reconciliation between Germans and Italians, and Germany and Italy pervades the entire journey, and is further intensified in the bifurcation of Italy into the opposite poles of Rome and Naples.

The impact of the strong first impressions of Goethe's Roman experience replays itself in his descriptions of Naples: he stresses the unique nature of a journey such as his and the impossibility of repeating it, like the initial and fleeting reading of a great book (*IR*, 203, 1 March 1787, Abends). The recollection far exceeds the actual experience in stature: thus, the written representation of memory assumes its high price. The Neapolitan descriptions are significantly more awe-struck than those from Rome, where there was a much deeper sense of memory and fulfillment; here Goethe is quite simply overwhelmed, genuinely unprepared for what awaits him (*IR*, 226, 17 March 1787).

The repression evident in the Roman commentary is occasionally threatened in Naples by an almost frightened sense of loss of control amidst the animation of Mount Vesuvius and the bustling citizenry of Naples. During his stay Goethe will attempt to ascend to the crater of Mount Vesuvius three times. His exegesis on his third venture onto the mountain on 20 March 1787 best reflects the stark contrasts of Naples; the extreme beauty of the geographical situation of Naples is predicated on the harsh reality of the ever-looming volcano:

> Das Schreckliche zum Schönen, das Schöne zum Schrecklichen, beides hebt einander auf und bringt eine gleichgültige Empfindung hervor. Gewiß wäre der Neapolitaner ein anderer Mensch, wenn er sich nicht zwischen Gott und Satan eingeklemmt fühlte. (*IR*, 233)

Because his first climb was cut short by the thick smoke and steam, Goethe returned four days later to Vesuvius, this time with a reluctant Tischbein. The volcano's activity again inhibited a clear view of the crater; however, it did afford Goethe a once-in-a-lifetime opportunity for firsthand observation. Tischbein, onto whom Goethe projects fear and discomfort, eventually stays behind as the poet convinces one of their guides to lead him ever closer to the crater between eruptions. Goethe's self-portrayal is more fascinated than fearful. The inherent danger of the situation attracts a different side of Goethe as he moves closer to the crater, holding on to the belt of his young guide. Unfortunately, the view of the crater is not completely clear due to the quickly moving clouds of smoke and steam. Goethe's careful calculation of the time between eruptions, however, proves false, and the poet and guide are caught off-guard by an explosion while standing close to the edge of the crater. They barely escape with their lives, at least as Goethe tells it (*IR*, 209, 6 March 1787). Goethe is again denied a good, clear look at the crater on his miraculous third attempt on 20 March, during which he came closest to a fresh lava flow despite the implicit danger. At the last minute his guide pulls him away to safety.

Goethe's experiences on Vesuvius challenge his own philosophy of science in which he otherwise continually sought unity and harmony. The amateur geologist's fascination with the active volcano is not surprising; however, his ongoing and ill-advised attempt to ascend Mount Vesuvius in the face of continual danger contradicts Goethe's much more controlled scientific and natural observations, including those made in Italy.[13] Goethe's greatest regret upon leaving Naples will be to have foregone another inspection of the mountain in light of a new and apparently more accessible lava flow (*IR*, 367–68, 1 and 2 June 1787). The poet's daredevil episodes on Vesuvius recall both earlier and later experiences, when Goethe entertained risk, flirted with danger, as if to overcome an otherwise paralytic fear. As a student in Strasbourg, Goethe studied the Gothic Münster and repeatedly climbed the stairs of the tower, despite its dizzying heights. Four years after his return from Italy, Goethe accompanied the duke's regiment to France. At Valmy, on 20 September 1792, he raced voluntarily close to the action, confessing to the desire to experience canon fever. His description of the events in the *Campagne in Frankreich* (Campaign in France, 1822) indeed echoes his undeterred obsession with Vesuvius while in Naples.

The excavations at Pompeii seem to have left Goethe somewhat cold and disappointed, especially in light of his enthusiasm for the volcano. Pompeii and Herculaneum, along with the artifacts uncovered there and displayed in the museum at Portici, had quickly established themselves as the main attractions in and around Naples. On 11 March, Goethe made the short trip to Pompeii with Tischbein:

Pompeji setzt jedermann wegen seiner Enge und Kleinheit in Verwunderung. . . . Und so deutet der jetzige ganz wüste Zustand einer erst durch Stein- und Aschenregen bedeckten, dann aber durch die Aufgrabenden geplünderten Stadt auf eine Kunst- und Bilderlust eines ganzen Volkes, von der jetzo der eifrigste Liebhaber weder Begriff, noch Gefühl, noch Bedürfnis hat. . . . Den wunderlichen, halb unangenehmen Eindruck dieser mumisierten Stadt, wuschen wir wieder aus den Gemütern. . . . (*IR*, 214–15)

One imagines though that the ruins of this ancient city destroyed in AD 79 would have held more than lukewarm appeal for the German poet. In a letter penned two days later, his description of the visit, although more positive, modulates in a curt and bland tone:

Sonntag waren wir in Pompeji. — Es ist viel Unheil in der Welt geschehen, aber wenig das den Nachkommen so viel Freude gemacht hätte. Ich weiß nicht leicht etwas Interessanteres. (*IR*, 220)

This is not a speechless reaction of wonderment. When confronted with actual evidence of life in ancient Roman civilization displayed through destruction, the traveler's enthusiasm wanes. This dampening of spirits stems, at least in part, from the omnipresence of death, something to which the poet suffered a lifelong aversion.

The ruins of Paestum, a Greek city south of Salerno, evoke a similar ambivalence from Goethe.[14] Again, his expected awe of the substantial ruins of three Greek temples is subdued, and at first even dubious:

. . . der erste Eindruck konnte nur Erstaunen erregen. Ich befand mich in einer völlig fremden Welt. Denn wie die Jahrhunderte sich aus dem Ernsten in das Gefällige bilden, so bilden sie den Menschen mit, ja sie erzeugen ihn so. Nun sind unsere Augen und durch sie unser ganzes inneres Wesen an schlankere Baukunst hinangetrieben und entschieden bestimmt, so daß uns diese stumpfen, kegelförmigen, enggedrängten Säulenmassen lästig ja furchtbar erscheinen. Doch nahm ich mich bald zusammen, erinnerte mich der Kunstgeschichte, gedachte der Zeit deren Geist solche Bauart gemäß fand, vergegenwärtigte mir den strengen Styl der Plastik und in weniger als einer Stunde fühlte ich mich befreundet, ja ich pries den Genius daß er mich diese so wohl erhaltenen Reste mit Augen sehen ließ, da sich von ihnen durch Abbildung kein Begriff geben läßt. (*IR*, 236–37, 23 March 1787)

The ever-rational Goethe corrects his initial discomfort, by placing the ruins in their historical context. Striking as such negative statements are, they do express a certain candor and honesty, often censored by autobiographers, and offer continuing evidence of Goethe's modernization of the Classical, as in *Iphigenie*. Similarly, in her reading of *Faust*,

Part II, Jane Brown argues persuasively that the ultimate gesture of the play is the destruction of all things classical, embodied in the fall of Euphorion (act 3) and the destruction of Baucis and Philemon (act 5). She reads this as the end of the modern recovery of the Classical as mediated by Goethe through the Renaissance.[15] Surely this is an outcome thinkable only after the poet's own experiences on Italian soil, only after witnessing with some discomfort what did remain of that past in Paestum, Pompeii, and Herculaneum. The idealization of the Classical renders itself unattainable or at least transitory, and Goethe's strategy of modernizing the Classical is one method of avoiding that ultimate renunciation.

Nicholas Boyle offers a fascinating hypothesis regarding Goethe's reaction to Paestum. In a letter to Herder after Goethe's return to Naples from Sicily, Goethe refers to a second trip to Paestum, around 17 May, in which he calls the ruins, "die letzte und fast möchte ich sagen herrlichste Idee, die ich nun nordwärts vollständig mitnehme" (*IR,* 345). In an exhaustive investigation of the accuracy of the dates of the two trips as reported by Goethe in the text as well as other extant notes, and surprisingly, a surviving original letter from the time and contemporary weather reports too complicated to recount here, Boyle concludes the high probability that Goethe visited Paestum only once, before the visit to Sicily, because he wanted "to conceal that even after spending six weeks in Sicily he could still find pure Doric architecture completely strange."[16] During the editorial process from 1814 to 1817, Goethe's primary concern was in countering the Romantic tendencies in art. When his own firsthand experiences of the classical world did not fit his program, Goethe rewrote the reality into fiction and "assigned his one hour of alienation and his insight of genius, to a preliminary stage in his acquaintance with the ancient world," so that his reaction "could appear to be the summary of two months' intensive classical education, which actually never took place" (30).

Goethe definitely exhibits more of a traveler's attitude while in Naples and Sicily and even counts himself among the travelers a number of times, for example, when confessing his desire to buy some of the highly priced artifacts prized by travelers (*IR,* 213, 9 March 1787). He clearly sees himself as a guest in Naples; however, in these instances, he uses the term "traveler" in a positive sense: "Das ist das Angenehmste auf Reisen, daß auch das Gewöhnliche, durch Neuheit und Überraschung, das Ansehen eines Abenteuers gewinnt" (*IR,* 213). This statement echoes the early months in Rome where he is comforted by the unexpected familiarity of his surroundings.

Removed from the scrutiny of the large, established circle of German artists in Rome, Goethe's interest in the visual arts intensifies, moving toward more practical study. His closest contact with the court of Naples comes through his repeated meetings with the German painter Philipp Hackert, King Ferdinand's official court painter. In the context of their friendship, the feasibility of a serious commitment to drawing and painting grows in Goethe's mind. During one extended visit, Hackert informs Goethe that eighteen months of intense study with the painter would nurture his talent to produce good works of art (*IR*, 223). His preoccupation with the visual arts, far from flirtatious, will continue to be a source of indecision and conflict.

This period is also riddled with indecision about the next leg of his journey. Should he or should he not go on to Sicily, and when should he return to Rome? Goethe eventually decides in favor of the opportunity to see the Greek ruins in Sicily, and because Tischbein is unable to join him, he enlists the young German painter Christoph Heinrich Kniep to accompany him as friend and illustrator. Once again the decision to travel is a healing one (*IR*, 239, 26 March 1787). Anxiety and discomfort resurface when the Duke of Waldeck surprises the poet with an invitation to Greece and Dalmatia upon his return from Sicily. Of the invitation Goethe remains silent; he seems never to consider it seriously (*IR*, 241, 28 March 1787).[17]

The seasickness that Goethe experienced on both legs of his six-week Sicilian adventure lends his description of the trip an almost uncanny tone. Rough seas in both directions confined Goethe to his cabin for much of the two trips, where Goethe contemplates *Torquato Tasso* (1790) for the first time in the ten years since setting this work aside. Additional contradictions within his text emerge in an entry posted shortly after arriving on the island:

> Ich habe nie eine Reise so ruhig angetreten als diese, habe nie eine ruhigere Zeit gehabt als auf der durch beständigen Gegenwind sehr verlängerten Fahrt, selbst auf dem Bette im engen Kämmerchen wo ich mich die ersten Tage halten mußte weil mich die Seekrankheit stark angriff. Nun denke ich ruhig zu Euch hinüber, denn wenn irgend etwas für mich entscheidend war so ist es diese Reise. (*IR*, 248, 3 April 1787)

The sea journey was decisive, in that it brought the poet back to *Tasso*, however the crossing itself was anything but calm. Again these remarks resonate with those made during the first weeks in Italy and his initial weeks in Rome, so much so that one wonders whether this declaration was made retrospectively in the editorial process. Although his visit to

Sicily lacks any déjà-vu-like quality and does not fulfill a long-adhered to fantasy, there is again a sense that a reason exists for having endured the journey, whether it be found in the initial return to *Tasso,* or in the eventual main focus of the island sojourn, the search for the *Urpflanze.* Such sentiments are echoed in: "Italien ohne Sicilien macht gar kein Bild in der Seele: hier ist erst der Schlüssel zu Allem" (*IR,* 271, 13 April 1787). Similar remarks concerning Rome or Italy in general seem more genuine than those regarding Sicily; perhaps their greatest power lies in the reminder that Goethe went where few had been. In the constant quest for self-development, opportunities abound for fresh starts while traveling abroad. The lack of imposing models or intimidating shadows frees him unexpectedly during this station of travel.

It is in Sicily, more than any other time during his two-year stay in Italy, that Goethe counts himself among the travelers. He moves from place to place, staying no longer than a few days in any one location. Perhaps not surprising in light of his responses to Paestum and Pompeii, Goethe's accounts of the ruins of Segesta and Agrigento are purely factual and far from awe-inspired, or poetic. In Sicily, however, his descriptions of the fruitful earth are most vivid, even in what at first appears to be a lengthy catalogue of the fruits, vegetables and animal life of the area (*IR,* 297–300, 26 April 1787). Schütze reads Goethe's focus on the *Urpflanze* as a defensive strategy to subdue the overwhelming force of the Sicilian natural environment (*GR,* 21). The climate, geography, and flora make the greatest impact. The traveling poet's insensibility to the ruins of the classical past clashes with his heightened awareness of the bounty of the natural world throughout the entire *Italienische Reise.* It both surprised and challenged his predeparture expectations and is illustrative of the ongoing conflicts and demands felt by Goethe: the struggle between duty and relaxation, restraint and passion, improvement and pleasure, imitation and authenticity. The poet had likely expected a more affirmative response to the ruins and, although he had already sung the praises of the lush Italian landscape in Mignon's song, his preconceptions of the natural world underestimated the depth of its actual splendor. On 7 May 1878, Goethe recounts where and how he sat contemplating a drama based on the story of Nausicäa from Homer's *Odyssey:*

> In einem schlechten, verwahrlosten Bauergarten habe ich mich auf Orangen-Äste gesetzt und mich in Grillen vertieft. Orangen-Äste worauf der Reisende sitzt, klingt etwas wunderbar, wird aber ganz natürlich, wenn man weiß daß der Orangenbaum, seiner Natur überlassen,

sich bald über der Wurzel in Zweige trennt, die mit der Zeit zu ent-
schiedenen Ästen werden. (*IR,* 319)

A naturally occurring orange tree replaces the image of an artificially
cultivated one in the northerner's mind, tames the wilderness, and corrects the confused imagination of the armchair traveler at home.

The visit is also comprised of a number of strange, if not disorienting, incidents, which are often brushed over in discussions of the *Italienische Reise,* remembered by most critics as an overwhelmingly
positive portrayal of Italy. These aberrant occurrences account, in part,
for the unusual tone of much of Goethe's Sicilian prose. On 9 April
1787 Goethe and Kniep visited the famous Villa Pallagonia, a popular
destination, renowned not for its architectural beauty, but rather for
the outlandish, grotesque sculptures added to the garden and villa by
the grandson of the original builder. It seems that Goethe had read or
heard descriptions of the statuary by other travelers of Goethe's generation equally offended by the bad taste of the Pallagonia family, but
nonetheless felt compelled to see it himself. Bolstering his own dissatisfaction, he concludes by mentioning the distaste experienced by his
artist, thus qualified, companion Kniep. The same statuary so objected
to by late eighteenth-century sensibilities is today seen in light of the
artistic style of the late Baroque period.[18]

In Palermo Goethe believes to have discovered the family of the
famed Cagliostro, actually Joseph Balsamo. Pretending to be an English acquaintance of Cagliostro, who had long since deserted his Sicilian
family, Goethe, partaking in some Cagliostro-like deception of his own,
promises to take a letter from them to their now infamous son and sib-
ling. Goethe himself later sends them the money they solicited from
their son in the letter (13 and 14 April 1787).

Ironically, it is in Sicily, disappointed with the ruins he has seen and
far removed from the classical associations of Rome, that in my eyes the
German poet is most closely linked to the classical heritage of the
Greek and Roman empires. This stance results from the physical distance from Rome, which, in turn reflects a further separation from expectations, preconceptions, and the influence of the father. Instead
Goethe associates much of Sicily with the figure of Odysseus and, to a
certain extent, even identifies with him as a fellow traveler; Goethe toys
with the possibility of writing a tragedy about the figure of Nausicäa. In
retrospect he is able to dismiss the dangers and the inconveniences of
travel, especially in the Sicilian period:

Weshalb ich denn auch von allen Unbequemlichkeiten wenig emp-
fand, da ich mich auf dem überklassischen Boden in einer poetischen
Stimmung fühlte, in der ich das, was ich erfuhr, was ich sah, was ich
bemerkte, was mir entgegen kam, alles auffassen und in einem erfreu-
lichen Gefäß bewahren konnte. (*IR*, 321, Aus der Erinnerung)

His conceit of identification with Odysseus, albeit presumptuous, was
surely not uncommon among eighteenth-century travelers and reveals
the sense of, if not impending danger, at least temptation or threat potentially injurious to the traveler.

The unique sense of heightened freedom, primitivity, and expression evident throughout Goethe's account of Sicily lends that period a
unique, almost isolated status within the whole of the *Italienische Reise*.
The insular geographic situation of Sicily and the complicated travel to
and from the island escalate this impression further. Indeed, the sea
voyage back to Naples was even more unpleasant than its predecessor.
His immediate response to the Sicilian side trip is one of overwhelming
disappointment, although Goethe fights the dismissive impulse:

In dieser Lage wollte mir unsere ganze sicilianische Reise in keinem an-
genehmen Lichte erscheinen. Wir hatten doch eigentlich nichts gesehen,
als durchaus eitle Bemühungen des Menschengeschlechts sich gegen die
Gewaltsamkeit der Natur, gegen die hämische Tücke der Zeit und gegen den Groll ihrer eigenen feindseligen Spaltungen zu erhalten. Die
Karthager, Griechen und Römer und so viele nachfolgende Völkerschaf-
ten haben gebaut und zerstört. Selinunt liegt methodisch umgeworfen,
die Tempel von Girgent niederzulegen waren zwei Jahrtausende nicht
hinreichend, Catania und Messina zu verderben wenige Stunden, wo
nicht gar Augenblicke. Diese wahrhaft seekranken Betrachtungen eines
auf der Woge des Lebens hin- und wider Geschaukelten, ließ ich nicht
Herrschaft gewinnen. (*IR*, 336, 12 May 1787)

The seasick passenger may have been able to fight back these negative
associations; however, their mere appearance within the pages of his
edited diary underscores the depth of the unpleasantness. Goethe arrives back in Naples, but not before he endures a harrowing and life-
threatening situation near the rocks of Capri. The older Goethe may
well have enjoyed embellishing these remarks in a display of bravery,
especially with an eye toward negating the less mimetic texts of the
Romantics. This final description contradicts his earlier pronouncement
of the import of this sea journey.

Upon his return from Sicily, Goethe spends another three weeks in
Naples before returning to Rome: he devotes much of his time to observing the daily habits and routines of the inhabitants of Naples. In his

respected guidebook, Volkmann claimed that there are 30,000 to 40,000 idlers in the city, a well-established presumption, which Goethe sets out to challenge. In perhaps his keenest observations focused on a specific group of Italians anywhere in his *Italienische Reise*, Goethe disproves such stereotypes. He details the various strata of Neapolitan society and offers evidence that although appearing needy, nearly all Neapolitans are employed or occupied in some fashion; lazy Neapolitans are hard to find. The very atmosphere and climate of the region keeps the city moving. The good nature with which so many Neapolitans approach their responsibilities is misunderstood by many foreign visitors, who mistake pleasure and enjoyment at work by day as frivolous irresponsibility (*IR*, 355–62, 28 May 1787). With the exception of *Das Römische Carneval* (The Roman Carnival, 1789), Goethe's representations of his final days in Naples contain his most vivid descriptions of a region's inhabitants and daily life and exhibit a deeply felt understanding of their lives. But once again Goethe contradicts himself a few pages later. On 1 June 1787, he describes his need to get back to Rome, because "[hier] wird man immer untätiger" (*IR*, 366). Apparently, unlike the hard-working, but happy Neapolitans, the foreign visitor becomes ever more relaxed. On 3 June 1787, as a fresh stream of lava flows down Mount Vesuvius, Goethe departs from Naples, as if just in the nick of time.

On the return trip to Rome, Goethe travels alone, having left Tischbein behind, reviews his notes, and contemplates his journey. He questions the feasibility of capturing the journey with the written word and articulates the challenge of representing his journey in a way resonant with his reader:

> Und doch tritt gar oft das Lückenhafte der Bemerkungen hervor und wenn die Reise dem der sie vollbracht hat in einem Flusse vorüber zu ziehen scheint und in der Einbildungskraft als eine stetige Folge hervortritt, so fühlt man doch daß eine eigentliche Mitteilung unmöglich sei. Der Erzählende muß alles einzeln hinstellen, wie soll daraus in der Seele des dritten ein Ganzes gebildet werden. . . . Überhaupt, wenn jeder Mensch nur als ein Supplement aller übrigen zu betrachten ist, und am nützlichsten und liebenswürdigsten erscheint wenn er sich als einen solchen gibt; so muß dieses vorzüglich von Reiseberichten und Reisenden gültig sein. (*IR*, 371–72, 4, 5, and 6 June 1787)

These are fitting last words immediately to precede the *Zweiter Römischer Aufenthalt*, a text in which a report written forty years after the fact supplements a selection of each month's correspondence. Goethe recognizes the economy of the genre, the interdependency of its most exemplary texts, and the power of cultural memory; his priority will remain, if not always the individuality of experience, then at least the innovation of his application and exploitation of the experience.

Zweiter Römischer Aufenthalt

The two-fold change in form and tone signals the reader of the *Zweiter Römischer Aufenthalt* to be wary of the authenticity, veracity, and objectivity of the elderly voice. As mentioned earlier, no original textual basis is extant for this large and final installment of the *Italienische Reise*, which was first published in the twenty-ninth volume of the *Ausgabe letzter Hand* in 1829 twelve years after the second volume of his Italian travel report and forty-one years after his return from Rome to Weimar. In the *Bericht* sections of various months, Goethe also inserts previously freestanding texts. I read the disparate structure of this portion of the text as a reflection of the ongoing conflicts within Goethe's own situation, despite the apparent new-found harmony situated in the prose of the highly revised *Zweiter Römischer Aufenthalt*.

The poet's preoccupation with the natural world, experienced so intensely in Naples and Sicily, is replaced in Rome with an extensive study of the visual arts and, even more precisely, with a deep contemplation of the shift from observing to seeing, which, in turn, predicates a deeper sense of commitment and involvement. Upon arriving in Rome, Goethe's enthusiasm for the natural spectacle of Vesuvius shifts to the great works of the visual arts housed in Rome (*IR*, 375, 8 June 1787). Both the sublimation of his joy in reaching Italy earlier in the trip and the battle between duty and pleasure are displaced, at least for a time by a comfortable ease:

> Es ist nur Ein Rom in der Welt, und ich befinde mich hier wie der Fisch im Wasser und schwimme oben wie eine Stückkugel im Quecksilber, die in jedem andern Fluido untergeht. (*IR*, 379–80, *Ende Juni* 1787)

His diligence in finding purpose in all activities and even the dreamlike status of his experiences take on a decidedly different, eventually more subdued tenor:

> Mein jetziges Leben sieht einem Jugendtraume völlig ähnlich, wir wollen sehen, ob ich bestimmt bin ihn zu genießen, oder zu erfahren, daß auch dieses, wie so vieles andre, nur eitel ist. (*IR*, 391, 5 July 1787)

As portrayed by Goethe, the major thematic conflict of his lengthier stay in Rome is between his roles as visual artist and writer. However, a deeper and related struggle ensues within the pages of the *Zweiter Rö-*

mischer Aufenthalt: the inevitable return to Weimar and its terms. How long can the poet extend his Roman sabbatical? Upon his return from Naples, Goethe's earlier impatience for Rome is replaced by the need to let things somehow follow their natural course; the prevalent conflicts of the earlier months of his trip are ameliorated, as he confesses to his correspondents that a longer stay will be necessary (*IR*, 377, 20 June 1787). He is in constant negotiation with Carl August about financial terms and the eventual length of his absence as well as the terms of his position in Weimar upon his return.[19] Goethe's status as traveler is minimized in the *Zweiter Römischer Aufenthalt* as much as possible; he will remain in Rome for more than ten months, but always with an eye toward the return to Weimar. He distills the earlier more scattered interests in an attempt to lend the final Italian act a cohesive shape and purpose. His focus settles on the poetic and artistic fruits of his visit as well as the ultimate value of his Italian sojourn after his return to Germany:

> Dann zieht mich alles nach dem Vaterlande zurück. Und wenn ich auch ein isoliert, privat Leben führen sollte, habe ich soviel nachzuholen und zu vereinigen, daß ich für zehn Jahre keine Ruhe sehe. (*IR*, 416, 28 August 1787)

The return to Weimar looms uninvited and threatens to be anticlimactic. Additionally, a number of his Weimar correspondents begin to noise their own intentions to follow Goethe to Italy. In his report of October 1787, Goethe relishes the role of the first of the circle to have paved the way south for the dowager duchess, Dalberg, and Herder (*IR*, 459–60). Impending visits from German friends unleash an insecurity and increased unrest concerning his own departure. Goethe sees himself as having set in action a line of falling dominoes and delineates the strong impact of his journey on his contemporaries even before his return. The thought of Weimar jeopardizes Roman contentment — two, at the moment still, incompatible worlds. Goethe describes forty years later the impossibility of remaining in Rome to receive close friends like Herder:

> Ergriffen von diesen Gefühlen und Ahnungen fühlte ich mich ganz entschieden, die Ankunft der Freunde in Italien nicht abzuwarten. Denn daß meine Art die Dinge zu sehen nicht sogleich die ihrige sein würde, konnte ich um so deutlicher wissen, als ich mich selbst seit einem Jahre jenen kimmerischen Vorstellungen und Denkweisen des Nordens zu entziehen gesucht, und unter einem himmelblauen Gewölbe mich freier umzuschauen und zu atmen gewöhnt hatte. In der mittlern Zeit waren

mir aus Deutschland kommende Reisende immerfort höchst beschwer-
lich; sie suchten das auf was sie vergessen sollten, und konnten das was
sie schon lange gewünscht hatten nicht erkennen, wenn es ihnen vor
Augen lag. Ich selbst fand es noch immer mühsam genug, durch Den-
ken und Tun mich auf dem Wege zu erhalten, den ich als den rechten
anzuerkennen mich entschieden hatte. Fremde Deutsche konnt' ich
vermeiden, so nah verbundene, verehrte, geliebte Personen aber hätten
mich durch eignes Irren und Halbgewahrwerden, ja selbst durch Ein-
gehen in meine Denkweise gestört und gehindert. Der nordische Reisende glaubt, er komme nach Rom, um ein Supplement seines Daseins
zu finden, auszufüllen was ihm fehlt; allein er wird erst nach und nach
mit großer Unbehaglichkeit gewahr, daß er ganz den Sinn ändern und
von vorn anfangen müsse. (*IR*, 460–61, October 1787 *Bericht*)

In retrospect, Goethe is able to see the process of development he
went through as a traveler forty years earlier. The traveler extraordinaire
lacks confidence in the average German visitor's ability to adhere to his
prescribed manner of travel as promoted in the *Italienische Reise*. Any
lack of insight from reading his letters would clearly not be a fault of
their author; his tone is one of superiority. He fancies himself so
changed that perhaps he fears the disapproval of his old friends. Nor
does he relish the obligatory role of tour guide. Pretending to be a
guide might be a fun game, but never in reality would Goethe wish to
be a *cicerone*. In his report of December 1787, Goethe tells of a game
he played with his circle of German friends during a spell of unpleasant
weather; to pass the time, they fancied themselves tourists:

> Man sagte nämlich: stellen wir uns vor, wir kämen so eben in Rom an,
> und müßten als eilige Fremde geschwind von den vorzüglichsten Ge-
> genständen uns unterrichten. Beginnen wir einen Umgang in diesem
> Sinne, damit das schon Bekannte möchte in Geist und Sinn wieder neu
> werden. (*IR*, 480)

Goethe describes a process that reverses the early Italian sensation of
experiencing things for the first time, while sensing their familiarity. In
a letter of Christmas 1787, Goethe describes his success in having
found a number of similarly minded Germans in Italy. He has learned
the importance of separating authentic travelers from the impostors and
describes the discrepancy between travelers and tourists before the latter word was coined and its more negative connotation developed:

> Denn ich bin unbarmherzig, unduldsam gegen alle die auf ihrem Wege
> schlendern oder irren und doch für Boten und Reisende gehalten wer-
> den wollen. Mit Scherz und Spott treib' ich's so lang, bis sie ihr Leben
> ändern oder sich von mir scheiden. Hier versteht sich, ist nur von gu-

ten, graden Menschen die Rede, halb- und Schiefköpfe werden gleich ohne Umstände mit der Wanne gesondert. (*IR*, 480)

Goethe puts his friends from home off with the advice to wait until after the upcoming winter to journey to Italy. It is also certain that the duke would have looked forward to the return of Goethe in the absence of the others departing for Italy.

By 4 April 1788 he is ready to leave. The decision, once made, seems to transport his mind home ahead of his body (*IR*, 582, 10 April 1788). The three letters included from April 1788 describe the need to tie up loose ends as well as the inability to finish various projects. Conflict between desire and duty, wish and obligation, return.

It is fitting that Goethe should end his *Zweiter Römischer Aufenthalt*, and with that, the entire *Italienische Reise* with the exiled Ovid's elegy of leaving Rome by moonlight. The elderly Goethe still identifies with Ovid's sense of "Rückerinnerung" (*IR*, 596, April 1788 Bericht), and harkens back to the poetic model chosen for a further, but admittedly fictional representation of his Italian, and more specifically Roman, sojourn in the *Römische Elegien*. Whereas Ovid relates his banishment from Rome as he heads toward exile, Goethe leaves Rome to return home, while simultaneously departing from his voluntary pleasurable, utopian exile, soon to be the locus of his memories. Zapperi calls attention to an earlier textual variant that was composed in 1817 as a final gesture for the as yet unwritten *Zweiter Römischer Aufenthalt*, which also contains the Ovid citation.[20] In it, Goethe also refers to Tasso, who, unlike Ovid's forced exile, left Ferrara voluntarily, if not willingly, for Rome. Zapperi postulates that Goethe deletes this direct reference to an exile in the final version as well as any mention of why he must leave Rome (to return to the court of Weimar at the request of the duke), so not to offend the memory of his patron, Duke Carl August, who had died in 1828 (*Z*, 262).

In the report for August 1787, Goethe discusses Moritz's trip to Italy in light of his earlier visit to England and the resulting journalistic treatment of that journey, *Reisen eines Deutschen in England* (Journeys of a German in England) of 1783. At first glance the reader might find that Goethe judges Moritz's original intentions harshly; however, it seems that forty years after befriending Moritz in Rome and more than thirty years after Moritz's death, Goethe is actually passing judgment on the earlier portions of his *Italienische Reise*:[21]

Er war nach Rom gekommen, um nach früherer Art durch eine Reisebeschreibung sich die Mittel einer Reise zu verschaffen. Ein Buchhändler hatte ihm Vorschuß geleistet; aber bei seinem Aufenthalt in Rom wurde er bald gewahr, daß ein leichtes loses Tagebuch nicht ungestraft verfaßt werden könne. Durch tagtägliche Gespräche, durch Anschauen so vieler wichtiger Kunstwerke regte sich in ihm der Gedanke, eine Götterlehre der Alten in rein menschlichem Sinne zu schreiben, und solche mit belehrenden Umrissen nach geschnittenen Steine künftig herauszugeben. Er arbeitete fleißig daran, und unser Verein ermangelte nicht, sich mit demselben einwirkend darüber zu unterhalten. (*IR*, 419)

Goethe delights in the role of mentor, far superior to that of guide, and reports on having altered the course of at least three persons' lives.[22] The role of teacher enters the Italian equation, in addition to Goethe's own education in Rome, and informs the model status he intends for his autobiographical writings.

Forty years later the insertion of monthly reports seemed to the elderly Goethe a way to justify the decisions he had made in Italy. It also provided him with a format for additions and elucidations as he felt necessary. Although Goethe's expressed dialogue with his father is reduced to a minimum in the *Zweiter Römischer Aufenthalt,* probably due to that lengthy span of time, Rome continues to be strongly and positively identified with the father (*IR*, 429, 28 September 1787). As the editorial process proves, that which Rome symbolizes is still possessed by his deceased father in the same way that it can be summoned up in memory or textual representation. A year after the publication of the *Zweiter Römischer Aufenthalt,* Rome became the site of the poet's son August's death. It is tempting to speculate about the impact that event might have had on Goethe's images and final account of Italy. For three generations of the Goethe family, the obligatory trip to Italy had decidedly different outcomes.[23]

The *Zweiter Römischer Aufenthalt* also exhibits a changing composition throughout. By the representation of 1788, the amount of correspondence reprinted in the text is markedly decreased, and in the four final months of the book, most of the embedded texts appear. There are a number of possible explanations for this change. Fewer letters may have been extant from this period, as it seems likely that Goethe corresponded less during the final months. Or possibly, the author cum editor deemed it necessary, in retrospect, to omit more of the correspondence from that period.

Events of another nature may account for the limited number of original letters included by Goethe. Speculation has long centered on Goethe's sexual experiences while in Italy. Such an inquiry is spurred by a reading of the *Römische Elegien,* in which the fictional narrator, himself a German traveler to Rome, details his affair with a young Roman woman named Faustina. Although Goethe, of course, recounts no such story in the *Italienische Reise,* some extant letters to Duke Carl August, published posthumously, allude to such a relationship. Kurt Eissler offers a Freudian interpretation of the speculated events and suggests that Goethe's much delayed sexual initiation occurred in Italy.[24] Nicholas Boyle recounts Goethe's meeting a young widow, probably during January 1788, and speculates that their relationship continued throughout the carnival season (*BI,* 506). In a letter of 16 February 1788 to the duke, Goethe offers the only evidence of any Italian sexual encounters:

> Sie schreiben so überzeugend, daß man ein cervello tosto sein müßte, um nicht in den süßen Blumen Garten gelockt zu werden. Es scheint daß Ihre gute Gedancken unterm 22. Jan. unmittelbar nach Rom gewürckt haben, denn ich könnte schon von einigen anmutigen Spaziergängen erzählen. So viel ist gewiß und haben Sie, als ein Doktor longe experientissimus, vollkommen recht, daß eine dergleichen mäßige Bewegung, das Gemüth erfrischt und den Körper in ein köstliches Gleichgewicht bringt.[25]

That such a relationship should coincide with Goethe's last months in Rome would only compound his sadness in departing for Weimar. He describes the final weeks as the most satisfying of his life, a thermometer against which he will measure the rest of his life (*IR,* 566, 14 March 1788). His ambiguous words could well refer to a consummated relationship, but the conclusion of the same letter is perhaps his only, albeit veiled, reference to such an affair:

> Mein Abschied von hier betrübt drei Personen innigst. Sie werden nie wieder finden, was sie an mir gehabt haben, ich verlasse sie mit Schmerzen. In Rom hab' ich mich selbst zuerst gefunden, ich bin zuerst übereinstimmend mit mir selbst glücklich und vernünftig geworden, und als einen solchen haben mich diese dreie in verschiedenem Sinne und Grade gekannt, besessen und genossen. (*IR,* 568)

It is generally held that he refers here to Moritz, Kaufmann, and his mistress.

Goethe also found himself preoccupied with the woman who has come to be known as the *schöne Mailänderin:* in October 1787 he was introduced to a young Milanese, Maddalena Riggi. Later that month he learns that she is engaged to be married and comments on how he painfully retreated:

> Es wäre wunderbar genug, rief ich aus, wenn ein wertherähnliches Schicksal dich in Rom aufgesucht hätte, um dir so bedeutende bisher wohlbewahrte Zustände zu verderben. (IR, 457, October 1787 Bericht)

In this rare use of the second person, Goethe, the writer, appears to be conversing with himself, the experiencing self. Oswald emphasizes the fictionality of the entire account of the *schöne Mailänderin* as it remains completely within the confines of the report sections of various months (*O*, 102). Certainly her inclusion within the pages of the *Italienische Reise* attests to the innocent nature of their relationship.[26]

Das Römische Carneval

> Nun ist der Narrheit ein Ende. Die unzähligen Lichter, gestern Abend, waren noch ein tolles Spektakel. Das Carnaval in Rom muß man gesehen haben, um den Wunsch völlig los zu werden, es je wieder zu sehen. Zu schreiben ist davon gar nichts, bei einer mündlichen Darstellung möchte es allenfalls unterhaltend sein. (*IR*, 187, 20 February 1787)[27]

Goethe wrote these words on Ash Wednesday 1787 as he prepared to depart for Naples with Tischbein. At the time he had little interest in the traditional Roman carnival and seems to have given it no further thought until preparations for the following year's festivities began. Despite his disavowal of the subject, Goethe did indeed venture, a year later, to put on paper a description of the events based on the carnival of 1788. Earlier that year he had commissioned a series of illustrations of the requisite masks and costumes and sent word of his intention to write an accompanying article to Charlotte von Stein. He asked his servant Seidel, at home in Weimar, to inform the publisher of the "Journal des Luxus und der Moden" (Journal of Luxury and Styles) of his plans.[28] The resulting essay, embedded forty-one years later in the *Zweiter Römischer Aufenthalt,* is one of the few examples of Goethe's work regarding Italy that belongs in the most conventional sense to the traditional genre of nonfiction travel reportage.

When Goethe does attempt a report on the Roman carnival, his initial words echo the sentiment expressed a year earlier, fearing that the celebrated events are beyond description. He warns his reader that what follows may not necessarily meet expectation (*IR*, 518). Thus, his second visit to the carnival ensures him maximum credibility. Goethe's emphasis stresses his role as observer and reporter, not participant. He was close to the action as the festivities were held in the Corso, the street in which he lived while in Rome.

In both structure and tone, the approximately thirty-five page long *Römische Carneval* seems out of place within the *Italienische Reise*. After a short introduction, the author divides his report into twenty-eight generally brief sections, each describing a particular aspect of the carnival. These include, among others, *Spazierfahrt im Corso; Klima; Geistliche Kleidungen; Wache; Masken; Kutschen; Gedränge; Pulcinellen-König; Nacht; Tanz;* and *Letzter Tag* (Ride along the Corso; Climate; Clerical Clothing; Guards; Masks; Carriages; Crowds; Pulcinella King; Night, Dance, Last Day). In opting for the first-person plural form of *wir,* Goethe establishes a much more distanced and less personal relationship to the text than in the *ich* form of his travel diaries, the implication being that the author's experiences are representative of a larger group of observers. Also striking is Goethe's disengagement from the action and activities around him; he clearly perceives himself to be an outside observer and, above all, a foreigner. Tradition permits only Romans to participate in the carnival. The traditional masks and costumes of the participants also accentuate the exclusivity of the events. Indeed the Roman participants even make fun of the many foreigners in their city during the carnival, adopting the northerner's typical clothing as a costume, especially that of a foreign landscape or architectural painter (*IR,* 529).

Goethe's own dismay and sometimes discomfort, certainly subdued within the pages of the article, centers on the precariousness of the dense crowds of people in the streets. During the last week of the carnival, each evening's events culminate in a wild, riderless horse race down the Corso with hordes of spectators lining the streets. Goethe recounts both equine and human injuries as well as casualties that have occurred throughout recent history.

Goethe is hard pressed to find the positive aspect of such crowds as he speculates that the costumes are not intended to attract attention since there are far too many masked participants to be singled out and noticed. Instead, he surmises: "Vielmehr geht ein jeder nur aus, sich zu vergnügen, seine Tollheit auszulassen und der Freiheit dieser Tage auf das beste zu genießen"(*IR,* 527). These words, as well as the close of *Das Römische Carneval,* echo the perception often contemplated by Goethe in Naples in which he recognizes an inherently German inhibition to pleasure and relaxation:

> [Wir] wünschen, daß jeder mit uns, da das Leben im Ganzen, wie das Römische Carneval, unübersehlich, ungenießbar, ja bedenklich bleibt, durch diese unbekümmerte Maskengesellschaft an die Wichtigkeit jedes

augenblicklichen, oft geringscheinenden Lebensgenusses erinnert werden möge. (*IR*, 522)

Significantly, with the exception of *Das Römische Carneval,* Goethe
offers little account of the daily life of the Romans: Naples served
Goethe as the more suitable place for the observation of modern Italian
life, a place, like the carnival, charged with pleasure and fear, amuse-
ment and danger.

Italienische Reise: Conclusions

Because of the critical embrace of Goethe's Italian experiences as the
apogee of his biography, it is hardly a simple task to consider the ultimate significance of this period and the importance of the resulting
text, the *Italienische Reise*. Critics nearly unanimously agree that without his absence from Weimar spent in Italy, Goethe would never have
produced the literary work of the subsequent classical period. Although
this is undoubtedly the case, as his journey afforded him the distance
necessary to reorient himself on his literary activities, the label classical
or neoclassical obscures the often ambiguous relationship Goethe ne-
gotiated with ancient Rome while in Italy.

The journey did much to rouse Goethe from his nearly decade-long
poetic silence. In Italy, Goethe first turned to *Iphigenie,* rewriting the
prose version into blank verse. In 1788 during his second stay in Rome,
he completed the drama *Egmont.* He spent much time thinking about
the unfinished *Torquato Tasso* and *Faust* (1808) for which, while in
Rome, Goethe composed both the *Hexenküche* (Witch's Kitchen) scene
and the monologue for *Wald und Höhle* (Forest and Cave). On his trip
to Sicily, he contemplated a drama based on the story of Nausicäa,
which would remain unwritten except for a brief fragment. Only two
poems definitely composed while on Italian soil are extant: "Cupido,
der lose eigensinnige Knabe" (Cupid, the Free Willful Boy, 1788) and
"Amor ein Landschaftsmaler" (Amor, a Landscape Painter, 1788). The
Römische Elegien were first completed after Goethe's return to Weimar.

The recognized allegiance to the Classical, accepted so prevalently
in the criticism, is highly questionable. The more negative, by which I
mean aversion to the Classical, found sprinkled throughout the *Italienische Reise* has been left unattended, unexpressed, or overlooked
because it is out of place within the programmatic prevalence in scholarship. So much tangible evidence of the ancient Rome and Greece that
Goethe saw in Italy left him with an ambivalence often bordering on
the negative. The ruins of Pompeii, Paestum, and Sicily particularly dis-

appointed Goethe. In some essential way, they did not live up to long-held expectations. Somehow though, his own image of the classical world from which these artifacts stemmed remained intact. He was able to find an alternative footing in the ancient world. The label "Arcadia" is projected only retrospectively on to Italy in 1816 in light of the immense changes throughout Europe as a result of the French Revolution. During the Napoleonic Wars and the early Restoration, the proponents of the Romantic movement and their opponents introduced multiple versions of Italy, which Goethe felt compelled to challenge.

In their final judgment, Grimm, Breymayer, and Erhard overlook the importance of Germany in defining Goethe's image of Italy and neglect any negative connotation that might have existed in the South for the German poet. In its poeticized form the journey leads to an "immerwährende Antike."[29] Marianelli rightly sees that it is actually Italy, or perhaps better stated, the image of Italy, and not the author himself that is reborn in Goethe's text.[30] Boyle, as a biographer, is interested in the actual experiences of Goethe, the German traveler to Italy, and Goethe, the German poet. He comments little on the problematic status of the text, but rather concentrates upon the events recounted in that text and other extant documents of the era while ignoring the lag between journey and texts. Significantly, he undervalues the greater purpose of the poet's second stay in Rome, stating that "Goethe was mentally fully prepared for his return to Germany when he set out from Naples . . . with the two great 'images' within him of Paestum and Sicily" (*B1*, 490). Boyle draws this conclusion despite his own insight elsewhere into Goethe's likely manipulation of the true nature of his visit(s) to Paestum. I have argued that, on the other hand, both Paestum and Sicily left Goethe with an anticlimactic and uncomfortable sensation. Contrary to Boyle's interpretation, Goethe returned to Rome with a sense that there was still much more to accomplish while in Italy. Boyle searches for the purpose behind the second year in Rome and locates its significance within the poet's redefinition in relation to his future in Germany. Rome, in the end, was an *Ersatz* Germany (*B1*, 491–92). Boyle successfully posits Goethe's Rome of 1787 and 1788 as an ideal Weimar: there he lived as he wished to live in Weimar, free of external responsibilities. Ironically though, Duke Carl August's financial support made Goethe's idealized existence possible. This German artistic and intellectual colony in Rome seemed, in many ways, an embodiment of the life Goethe had dreamt of in the pre-Weimar years in Frankfurt (*B1*, 493). Yet Boyle's ultimate conclusions only diminish the stature of the journey:

> For all the superficial appearance of new worlds and new starts,
> Goethe's time in Italy was, at its profoundest level, "a recapitulation,"
> like the Swiss journey of 1779, but more successful. It was an attempt
> to make sense of his life so far, to integrate the man he had been, and
> the art he had practiced in Frankfurt, with what he had been and had
> done for twelve years in Weimar, to accommodate his Storm and
> Stress origin to the reality of a courtly existence rather than be re-
> duced to a sterile silence by their incompatibility. (*B1*, 514–15)

Boyle does express the sense conveyed in Goethe's representation of his
journey as the return to a long-held dream or place visited years before.
The term "recapitulation" though seems to obliterate the sense of personal growth Goethe found in experience. It was essential that this
transformation take place not in Weimar, but in Italy — the Italy of
Goethe's mind perhaps, not necessarily the one he actually set foot in.
Boyle's judgment ignores the necessity and ultimate impact of presence
in the face of twenty-five years of cultural, political, and societal revolution:

> Goethe did not spend the years from 1786 to 1788 in Italy, as he
> much later admitted when searching for a title-motto for what is now
> known as *The Italian Journey;* he spent them in Arcadia, in a creation
> of his mind and heart, his needs and longings into which as much of
> the real Italy was mixed as was necessary to convince him that the ob-
> ject of his desires had a place and habitation on this earth. (*B1*, 653)

The ancient model for Arcadia left the German poet cold, largely due
to his unattainable expectations; however, in light of the strong stance
of the Romantics, a retrospective alternative is highly preferable.

Jochen Schütze makes the bold claim that Goethe was never really
away from home despite the approximately 40,000 kilometers he covered during this lifetime. He argues that the displacement of travel presupposes a displacement of the self, something that, in Schütze's eyes,
Goethe did not experience. Instead, the poet felt at home wherever he
was (*GR*, 15). Schütze cites the numerous instances of familiarity
Goethe felt during his Italian excursions, as well as the poet's avoidance
of danger, with the exception of his Vesuvian encounters. The critic's
impulse to challenge the deeply entrenched status quo of the *Italienische Reise* is correct despite the lack of adequate consideration of the
convoluted *Entstehungsgeschichte* of the text. In addition, Schütze
paints an erroneous image of Goethe who did not enjoy himself while
underway.

In disregarding the tumultuous interruption between journey and
representation, he places the text within a sterile vacuum:

Die große Italienische Reise, dieser Inbegriff einer Bildungsreise, war einerseits Goethes Weltreise, andererseits ein fast zweijähriger bezahlter Urlaub. Um der Erfahrung willen hätte er sie nicht auf sich nehmen müssen, auf die ganze Empirie konnte er verzichten. (*GR,* 102)

As I will argue in the following chapters, the *Italienische Reise* should be read more as a rebuttal of the Romantic and post-Napoleonic *Welt-anschaaung* than as a mimetic representation of personal experience.

Just as Goethe projected the concept of Arcadia back onto his Italian experiences years after his journey, so will he create a poetic Arcadia in his *Römische Elegien* shortly after his return to Weimar. This is only possible in a fictional realm, where the images of ancient and contemporary Rome can intersect and coexist. If much of the enduring Italy of Goethe's expectations proved to be fictional, how does it compare to the fictional Italy depicted in the *Römische Elegien?*

3: *Römische Elegien*

THE MOST PROMINENT examples of Goethe's fictional works directly influenced by his Italian experiences are the *Römische Elegien* and the *Venezianische Epigramme*. With their decidedly more defined narrative structure, the *Elegien* offer a clearer portrait of the German traveler than do the epigrams. In light of the great span of twenty-one years between their publication dates, the compatibility of the resulting Italian images put forth in the *Römische Elegien* and the *Italienische Reise* comes into question. The contemporary audience response to the poetic cycle surely played a role in the propagation of Goethe's "Italy" years prior to the *Italienische Reise's* publication as well as in Goethe's editing of the text. Begun shortly after the poet's return to Weimar, the *Elegien* constitute his most immediate response to the Italian experience. A complicated portrait of the northern traveler emerges against both ancient and modern backdrops.

The most direct textual connection to the *Römische Elegien* remains Goethe's final entry in the *Italienische Reise*, a direct citation from Ovid's *Tristia*.[1] More than four decades after his journey, Goethe associates his departure from Rome, and ultimately from Italy, with Ovid's banishment from Rome. Goethe's last gesture is, therefore, his most classical of allusions, a surprise in light of the ambiguity of his relationship to the classical heritage of Italy. Goethe's emulation of Ovid in his first great poetic endeavor after his return to Germany heralds the advent of Weimar Classicism with its adaptation of the meter of classical Greek elegy, the elegiac distich, and the Latin tradition of the erotic love elegy as perfected by Ovid, Catallus, and Propertius. Although the *Elegien* were not the first work published by Goethe to be associated with his long absence from Weimar, they were certainly the most personal.[2]

The explicit sexual nature of the *Römische Elegien* precipitated a much-discussed scandal: the first publication of the cycle in Schiller's *Die Horen* in 1795. Erotic poetry was nothing new in the 1790s, but what most shocked Goethe's contemporaries, not excluding his closest friends, was the infusion of what was perceived to be personal experience into the poems. The public could not easily excuse the middle-aged confession as they did the vaguely fictionalized work of the young and unknown author of *Werther*. The individualistic tone of the cycle aroused the most suspicion and sparked the most controversy as the audience projected the newfound, self-confident, and fiercely independent attitude of the narrator onto Goethe. Karl Eibl locates the source of the public's discomfort on the part of Goethe's audience in the poet's use of the first person. In addition, Goethe's elegies lacked the moralistic or humorous conclusion typical of their classical models. Eibl reiterates that the social and moral standards of the day did not grant Goethe the same dispensation reserved by readers for the Latin elegists.[3] The critical taboo on the *Elegien* persisted for nearly two centuries. A candid discussion of the cycle's publication history, as well as the four elegies Goethe self-censored, did not begin until the 1970s when H. G. Haile focused attention to all twenty-four elegies. Citing the *Elegien* as the first incidence of large-scale censorship of Goethe's work, he traces both Schiller's and Goethe's roles in the process:

> The two men seem to have agreed, however, that the public was not yet ready for truly classical poetry, in the sense of poetry uninhibited by modern conventions. . . . We are at one of the truly ironical junctures in intellectual history. Goethe and Schiller, in the annals of poetry and philosophy the most powerful champions of the morality of beauty, and self-appointed arbiters of "das Gute Wahre Schöne" . . . conspire to bowdlerize Goethe's charming and dignified lyrics.[4]

The most respected of critics continued Goethe's gesture of silence.

Hans Rudolf Vaget's reading includes all twenty-four elegies and situates the four so-called Priapean elegies as a frame around the others that make up the more familiar narrative. He adroitly describes Goethe's strategy in presenting an erotic subject:

> The *Roman Elegies* are founded on the realization that in modern times erotic poetry depended on classical form for its very survival. The elegiac distich that Goethe chose to adopt for this purpose proved, on the whole, effective enough in achieving the subtle distancing that was essential to the success of the undertaking.[5]

I consider only the originally published set of twenty elegies in my reading because the inclusion of the other four does not alter their inherent image of Italy. Also, the other writers considered here, most specifically Platen, knew the cycle only in its grouping of twenty. Their presence does, however, reinforce the fictional narrative status and the ironic self-consciousness of the cycle.

The critical discussion of the *Römische Elegien* centers largely on Goethe's appropriation and renewal of both the genre and meter of

classical elegies, and mythology. In addition many scholars have
searched for an underlying structure upon which the cycle is built.
Many hundreds of pages have been devoted to the biographical situations supposedly informing the poems. Less than a month after his return to Germany, Goethe made the acquaintance of Christiane Vulpius.
This fact, along with the plenitude of speculation on Goethe's own
sexual activities while in Rome, has influenced too strongly many of the
critical readings of the *Römische Elegien*. Notwithstanding the illumi-
nating biographical details of the genesis of the cycle, the reader must
acknowledge the fictional status decisively established by Goethe in the
poetry. The elegies are without question both direct and indirect responses to experience; however, I am most interested in a perception of
travel portrayed in the cycle, which is reminiscent of that which
emerges throughout the *Italienische Reise*. Further examination reveals
that the tension between Weimar and Rome, so often palpable in the
pages of the travel report, strongly permeates Goethe's *Römische Elegi-
en* as well. The situation in Germany, not only during the traveler's absence, but also after his return home, is constantly set up in opposition
to the Roman present.

Goethe began his *Römische Elegien* in the autumn of 1788 and
completed the cycle by the spring of 1790. Originally referred to as
Erotica Romana, this title was then replaced by *Elegien, Rom 1788*, a
choice that both intensifies the merely Roman atmosphere of the original title and eliminates any titular indication of erotic themes. The inclusion of a date also establishes the juxtaposition of the ancient genre
with the modern and alludes to a biographical component. The third
and final version of the title established in 1806 upholds the suppression of the erotic in the title, although by this time the reputation of
the work certainly preceded the poems themselves.[6] It also introduces
the ambiguous duality of the Roman theme borne out in the cycle: the
historical and literary pasts of Ancient Rome are intermingled with references to the present-day city. Goethe's protagonist is a northern European traveler to Italy who alternately assumes the roles of distanced,
observing poet and active visitor to Rome.

The Italy of the *Römische Elegien* is a mythologized realm referred to
in the most abstract as *das Süden* and in the most specific instance as
Rom. As underscored by the title, Rome as a representative of Italy is the
poet's focus: the classical Rome of the great Latin poets, the modern-
day Rome visited by the northern traveler, and the contemporary Rome
of the average Italian resident of the city. The traveling, first-person
poet privileges the oldest version of Rome; the greatest amount of de-

scription is assigned to its golden age, made most specific through many references to Latin mythology, history, and poetry. In contrast, late eighteenth-century Rome remains, with few exceptions, non-specific and abstract. Goethe describes few of the frequently visited attractions in detail; instead he mentions a select and limited number of locations and works of art, almost exclusively in reference to earlier Roman history. The image of late eighteenth-century Rome in the *Elegien* focuses solely on the personal and private; for example, in the well-known fifteenth elegy, the northerner visits a popular Italian wine tavern, or *Osterie,* in the hopes of seeing his Roman lover.

The *Römische Elegien* are first and foremost love poems that detail a two-fold love affair between a traveling poet from northern Europe and a young Roman woman, and are paralleled by his affection for ancient Roman culture. Rome binds these two poetic narratives together, as the narrator frequently addresses the city and that which it represents. The best-known elegy of the cycle, the fifth, begins:

> Froh empfind' ich mich nun auf klassischem Boden begeistert,
>   Lauter und reizender spricht Vorwelt und Mitwelt zu mir. (1–2)[7]

This enthusiastic image of the classical ground was soon absorbed into the public's own image of Goethe in Italy. Within the pages of the *Italienische Reise,* Goethe often imagines life in ancient Roman times, but when the remnants of that civilization disappoint, he envisions a sanitized classical scene in his mind. The traveling poet of the elegies instead locates the true meaning of the classical past of Rome in the present, and it is in this fifth elegy that the greatest harmony of self exists for the narrator.

Chloe Chard reads the women encountered in Italy, both in eighteenth-century fiction and first-person travel narrative as sights, much like ruins and antiquities. Although Goethe erases nearly all evidence of the personally sensual from his *Italienische Reise,* her argument applies particularly well to the narrative component of the *Römische Elegien.* She explains the interactions of the foreign traveler with the Italian female as an "attempt at assimilation and appropriation."[8] The potentially positive experience she describes, informs the *Römische Elegien* and may have biographical basis, but is absent from the *Italienische Reise:*

> Women who evoke the antique . . . are presented not only as inviting the traveler to convert the historical into the personal, but also, by virtue of their own identity as youthful, living beings, as actively reanimating a past that seems devoid of life. (104)

The coexistence of historical periods though, along with the pressures of the conflict between home and abroad, manifests itself throughout the cycle of the *Römische Elegien*. The personal, private, and public spheres continuously intersect: it is only through the fictional status of the cycle that a fabricated harmony can exist.

Sander Gilman posits a male lover in his reappraisal of the *Römische Elegien*. He reads the sketches of the male form, prevalent in Goethe's Italian sketchbooks, as "the product of Goethe's seeing the Other during his Italian journey. He sees the male as sexual object (in his art) and describes (in his poetry) the female as the representation of touch."[9] The priority of experience in Weimar elided with the expectations of his audience created an immediate response to the sensuality of Italy, evidence enough against Gilman's claims. Karl Hugo Pruys's recent contribution to the growing list of pseudo-sensationalist books on Goethe, aimed at the layperson, calls into question the primacy of the much-loved topic of the women in the poet's life and posits Goethe's sexual orientation to be bisexual, if not homosexual, despite his lack of any real substantial proof. He considers neither the priority of the male form in classicism nor the cult of male friendship prevalent during Goethe's lifetime.[10]

As Goethe describes himself in varying capacities throughout the *Italienische Reise*, the northerner in the elegies constantly negotiates his role as traveler, poet, and lover within the larger context of the cycle, ever mindful of the example of the Grand Tourists before him. Any constraints sensed by the traveler are imposed not by the Italians, but rather by foreigners: the influence of the Germans who traveled before him and those left behind at home. Even in their absence they exercise control over the traveler. The first elegy immediately introduces the central conflict:

> Ahnd' ich die Wege noch nicht, durch die ich immer und immer,
> Zu ihr und von ihr zu gehn, opfre die köstliche Zeit.
> Noch betracht' ich Palast und Kirchen, Ruinen und Säulen,
> Wie ein bedächtiger Mann sich auf der Reise beträgt? (7–10)

Entering the narrative *in medias res*, the reader encounters the northerner already established in Rome: his journey to and through northern Italy is not recounted. The speaker is mildly torn between the original intent of his travels and his newfound clandestine activities in Rome; but the neglected sight-seeing is regretted far less than time spent away from his lover. A list of generic tourist sights passed along the route to his lover serves to rationalize his choices. Images cultivated throughout the *Römische Elegien* echo those of the later *Italienische Reise,* although the attitude with which the first elegy concludes imposes conditions on the privileged status of Rome. In contrast, the subject of Goethe's frequent enthusiastic outbursts in his travel report exists without qualification:

> Eine Welt zwar bist du, o Rom, doch ohne die Liebe
> Wäre die Welt nicht die Welt, wäre denn Rom auch
>   nicht Rom. (I: 13–14)

Only the experience of sexual love elevates Rome in the eyes of the elegiac narrator, already an adherent to the long-standing cult of Rome upon arrival.

Rome receives much praise throughout the *Italienische Reise:* it is the "Hauptstadt der Welt" (*IR,* 134) and the fulfillment of his childhood dreams (*IR,* 135). During his second stay in Rome, Goethe declares that in Rome he begins "wie neu erzogen zu sein" (*IR,* 478). The city becomes both parent and educator. In the first elegy the experience and expression of love constitute the uniqueness of Rome, precisely encapsulated in the anagram of Roma, Amor.[11] Thus, Goethe subscribes to a much older tradition, evident in his choice of the elegiac form.

More than any of the other nineteen published elegies, the second addresses the plight of the late eighteenth-century traveler most explicitly:

> Ehret wen ihr auch wollt! Nun bin ich endlich geborgen!
>   Schöne Damen und ihr Herren der feineren Welt;
> Fraget nach Oheim und Vettern und alten Muhmen und
>   Tanten;
>   Und dem gebundnen Gespräch folge das traurige Spiel.
> Auch ihr übrigen fahret mir wohl in großen und kleinen
>   Zirkeln, die ihr mich oft nah der Verzweiflung
>   gebracht.
> Wiederholet, politisch und zwecklos jegliche Meinung,
>   Die den Wandrer mit Wut über Europa verfolgt.
> So verfolgte das Liedchen *Malbrough* den reisenden Briten
>   Einst von Paris nach Livorn, dann von Livorno nach
>   Rom,
> Weiter nach Napel hinunter und wär' er nach Smyrna
>   gesegelt;
>   Malbrough! empfing ihn auch dort, Malbrough! im
>   Hafen das Lied.

> Und so mußt' ich bis jetzt, auf allen Tritten und Schritten
>   Schelten hören das Volk, schelten der Könige Rat.
> Nun entdeckt ihr mich nicht so bald in meinem Asyle,
>   Das mir Amor der Fürst königlich schützend, verlieh.
> Hier bedecket er mich mit seinem Fittig. Die Liebste
>   Fürchtet, römisch gesinnt, wütende Gallier nicht,
> Sie erkundigt sich nie nach neuer Märe, sie spähet
>   Sorglich den Wünschen des Manns, dem sie sich
>   eignete, nach,
> Sie erfreut sich an ihm, dem freien, rüstigen Fremden,
>   Der von Bergen und Schnee, hölzernen Häusern
>   erzählt,
> Teilt die Flammen, die sie in seinem Brust entzündet,
>   Freut sich, daß er das Gold nicht wie der Römer
>   bedenkt.
> Besser ist ihr Tisch nun bestellt; es fehlet an Kleidern,
>   Fehlet am Wagen ihr nicht, der nach der Oper sie
>   bringt.
> Mutter und Tochter erfreun sich ihres nordischen Gastes
>   Und der Barbare beherrscht römischen Busen und Leib.
>
> (1–28)

Again the words resonate with many of the early concerns of the *Italienische Reise*. The word *geborgen* (1) recalls phonetically the rebirth Goethe strongly attaches to his experience in Italy in its similarity to the word *geboren*. In addition, *geborgen*, meaning hidden, recalls the incognito that Goethe held so dear in the early months of his trip. As the narrator continues, it becomes clear that Rome, and especially the hiding place with his Roman lover, serve as his shelter, asylum, and protection from the opinions of others, here most likely referring to the recent French Revolution. Analogous to this predicament is the prevalence of the sixteenth-century satirical English song "Marlborough" to which every British tourist is continuously subjected.[12] The narrator, apparently an advisor or minister to his king, not unlike Goethe's service to Carl August, must listen repeatedly to political opinions and complaints, a situation Goethe ably avoided under cover of his early incognito. In the *Römische Elegien* the sanctuary of the hiding place assumes the protective role of the incognito. There the German traveler is not obliged to play the role of either famous German writer or traveling political dignitary. Amor replaces the king as *Fürst*, offering the protagonist the shelter the king cannot provide for him abroad. It is telling that this, the only description of the mundane practicalities of travel and transportation in the entire cycle, recounts the route of the British rather than German traveler.

The second elegy also establishes the familiar dichotomy of north and south, which prevails throughout the entire cycle and indeed throughout the majority of German writing on Italy: contrasts of landscape, geography, climate, architecture, physiognomy, character, and morality. "[Der] frei [e], rüstig [e] Fremde"(21) describes the snowy mountains and wooden structures of his homeland.[13] The first-person narrator is replaced temporarily by the third, and the elegy closes, having firmly established the image of the "nordischer Gast," from whose presence both mother and daughter benefit. The conflation of the visiting northerner with the conquering Barbarian establishes the poetic traveler in an unbroken line of German rulers in Rome, going back to the reign of the Frederick II as Holy Roman Emperor. This modern emperor forsakes the traditional weapons of his predecessors, instead offering the young Roman woman and her mother material pleasures not afforded them by their own social status. This also confirms the prevalent view held in the eighteenth and nineteenth centuries that, compared to the Italians, the northern European travelers were much more liberal in their cash expenditures.

The genesis of the second elegy underscores the importance of Goethe's own strategy of distancing, or at the least disguising, biography from fiction in the *Römische Elegien*. The fourth elegy of the manuscript of 1788 is an earlier version of the second elegy published in Schiller's *Die Horen,* as cited above. The first half of the earlier version unequivocally establishes Goethe as the traveler in the *Römische Elegien:*

> Fraget nun wen ihr auch wollt mich werdet ihr
> > nimmer erreichen
> > Schöne Damen und ihr Herren der feineren Welt!
> Ob denn auch Werther gelebt? ob denn auch alles fein
> > wahr sei?
> > Welche Stadt sich mit Recht Lottens der Einzigen
> > rühmt?
> Ach wie hab ich so oft die törigten Blätter verwünscht,
> > Die mein jugendlich Leid unter die Menschen gebracht.
> Wäre Werther mein Bruder gewesen, ich hätte ihn
> > erschlagen,
> > Kaum verfolgte mich so rächend sein trauriger Geist.
> So verfolgte das Liedchen Malbrough den reisenden Briten

> Erst von Paris nach Livorn, dann von Livorno nach Rom
> Weiter nach Napel hinunter und wär er nach Madras
> > gesegelt,
> Malbrough empfing ihn auch dort Malbrough im Hafen
> > das Lied.
> Glücklich bin ich entflohn sie kennet Werthern und Lotten
> Kennet den Namen des Manns der sie sich eignete
> > kaum.
> Sie erkennet in ihm, den freien rüstigen Fremden
> Der in Bergen und Schnee hölzerne Häuser bewohnt.
> > $(1-16)^{14}$

Here the reader encounters a much more personal and impassioned argument for the flight and anonymity of the poet than in the definitive, published version. Ironically, these lines concerning the uncomfortable and often even intolerable association the poet feels when the public sphere invades deeply into his personal and private life definitively identify Goethe as the first-person narrator and protagonist of this earlier draft. In the edited version of the elegy, written sometime after 1789, the French Revolution and its political implications present Goethe with the perfect material to displace the personal. It is unclear when Goethe first edited this so-called *Werther-Fassung*, but it has been speculated that it could have been as late as 1794.[15] The very points of contention here are echoed in the *Italienische Reise* as Goethe reports that his reputation as the creator of *Werther* continually precedes him.

The strict division of north and south continues throughout the cycle strongly defining, among others, the seventh elegy:

> O wie fühl ich in Rom mich so froh! Gedenk ich der Zeiten,
> > Da mich ein graulicher Tag hinten im Norden umfing,
> Trübe der Himmel und schwer auf meinen Scheitel sich
> > neigte,
> > Farb' und gestaltlos die Welt um den Ermatteten lag,
> Und ich über mein Ich, des unbefriedigten Geistes
> > Düstre Wege zu spähn, still in Betrachtung versank.
> Nun umleuchtet der Glanz des hellen Äthers die Stirne,
> > Phöbus rufet, der Gott, Formen und Farben hervor.
> Sternenhelle glänzet die Nacht, sie klingt von Gesängen
> > Und mir leuchtet der Mond heller als ehmals der Tag.
> > $(1-10)$

The words and images again anticipate the *Italienische Reise*. Mythological references abound, and such figures serve as guides to the traveler now referred to as the *Wandrer* (16). Instead of the popular Volkmann guidebook, or a paid private guide called a *cicerone*, the poetic narrator relies on a legion of Roman gods and figures to lead him through the city on a tour of the classical sites, including "der Capitolinische Berg" (24) and "Cestius Denkmal" (26).

As the narrative unfolds, the traveler assumes a number of roles in addition to that of the *Wandrer*, striking a chord reminiscent of the many and frequent conflicting duties described by Goethe in his travel report. The foreigner, as traveler and guest, is temporarily replaced in the eleventh elegy with the image of the poet and artist. The narrator speaks now of a "Dichter" (1) and a "Künstler" (3). The sculptor works in his studio on freshly cut marble and describes the statues, including the Apollo Belvedere. This poem also refers back to the infamous fifth elegy in which the poet counts out the hexameter on his lover's back, claiming only now to understand truly the marble sculpture he has seen while in Italy. The plastic arts were a major occupation of Goethe during his two stays in Rome, and he himself collected a number of plasters for study. However, where the work of the poet is analogous to that of the sculptor in the *Römische Elegien*, Goethe, the traveler, describes with great passion the depth of the inner conflict between the plastic and literary arts. The theme of sculpture carries over into the following elegy, but here the sculptors are presented more as artisans than fine artists. The contemporary carvers, somehow not the equal of their classical predecessors, have finished their work in Rome and retreat from the city. As they return to their faraway homes, the traveler and his mistress hear their presence in the street. The narrator does not share the carver's desire to return to a distant home.

Shortly thereafter, his latest guide, Amor himself, reminds the peaceful protagonist of the ultimately temporary status of guest and tourist:

> Siehe, dir bin ich nun gar nach Rom gefolget; ich möchte
> Dir im fremden Gebiet gern was gefälliges tun.
> Jeder Reisende klagt, er finde schlechte Bewirtung;
> Welchen Amor empfiehlt, köstlich bewirtet ist er.
>
> (XIII: 5–8)

Amor did not lead this traveler to Italy, but willingly assists him in Rome. This elegy exploits the semantic connection in German between *führen* and *verführen*, blurring the line between leading and leading

astray, guidance and seduction. Finally, in the fifteenth elegy, the protagonist's nationality is specifically identified as he sits at a table with
the other Germans in the local, Roman wine tavern (9). The incompatibility of north and south is most severely rendered as the narrator's
disdain for the North reaches its high point:

> Cäsern wär ich wohl nie zu den Britannen gefolget,
>   Florus hätte mich leicht in die Popine geschleppt!
> Denn mir bleiben weit mehr die Nebel des traurigen
>   Nordens
> Als ein geschäftiges Volk südlicher Flöhe verhaßt. (1–4)

Travelers had long complained about the mosquitoes of Rome, yet this
is a minor inconvenience to bear in comparison to the burdens of the
North.[16] In this much cited elegy, the German narrator sees his beloved
in the Roman wine tavern, but is unable to acknowledge her in the
presence of his German friends. She cleverly writes the appointed hour
of their upcoming and clandestine rendezvous in spilled wine on the
tabletop. He recalls:

> Aber die köstliche *Vier* blieb mir ins Auge geprägt
>   Stumm war ich sitzen geblieben und biß die glühende
>   Lippe
> Halb aus Schalkheit und Lust, halb aus Begierde mir wund.
>   Noch so lange bis Nacht! dann noch vier Stunden zu
>   warten! (22–25)

The burden of the secrecy becomes increasingly difficult to bear.

The four concluding elegies deal with the disintegration of the frag-
ile harmony established within the secrecy of the narrator's Roman love
affair. The concerns of home and reputation threaten to impinge upon
the much longed for peace of the earlier elegies. A scarecrow in the
vineyard scares the German away; he does not pursue his lover that
evening, having mistaken the scarecrow for her uncle. She explains:

> Nun! sein Wunsch ist erfüllt, er hat den losesten Vogel
>   Heute verscheucht, der ihm Gärtchen und Nichte
>   bestiehlt. (XVI: 9–10)

Other realities of life interfere with the classical fantasy: the eighteenth
elegy mirrors some of Goethe's more private letters to Carl August
from Italy. Ironically, it is during this personal confession of his fear of

the dangers of love, for example venereal diseases, that the speaker singularly names his beloved Faustina:

> Gar verdrießlich ist mir einsam das Lager zu Nacht.
> Aber ganz abscheulich ists auf dem Wege der Liebe
>   Schlangen zu fürchten und Gift unter den Rosen der
>   Lust;
> Wenn im schönsten Moment der hin sich gebenden Freude
>   Deinem sinkenden Haupt lispelnde Sorge sich naht.
> Darum macht mich Faustine so glücklich, sie teilet das
>   Lager
> Gerne mit mir und bewahrt Treue dem Treuen genau.
>   (XVIII: 4–10)[17]

The poetic facade is further jeopardized as Goethe rewrites mythology, causing the contemporary to interrupt the (modernized) Classical; the constraints imposed upon the idyllic exile by the contemporary realities intensify. Here the narrator speaks of a feud between Amor and Fama for which there is no classical basis. Fama, representing fame and reputation, has only disdain for the lovers. The fictional traveler fears the revelation of his Roman love affair at home, despite his own confession of his lover's existence and identity in the previous elegy:

> Und so geht es auch mir, schon leid ich ein wenig; die
>   Göttin
> Eifersüchtig sie forscht meinem Geheimnisse nach.
> Doch es ist ein altes Gesetz, ich schweig und verehre,
>   Denn der Könige Zwist büßten die Griechen, wie ich.
>   (XIX: 67–70)

In the twentieth and final elegy of the published cycle, Amor is blamed for the poet's confession. The narrator realizes now that his Roman affair must remain a secret; even friends entrusted with this knowledge could endanger his existence at home. Gradually the German in Rome clearly redirects his focus and considers life back home after the conclusion of the idyllic Roman interlude. Here the poet can confide the reason for his happiness only to the hexameter and pentameter of the elegy:

> Dir Hexameter, dir Pentameter sei es vertrauet
>   Wie sie des Tags mich erfreut, wie sie des Nachts mich
>   beglückt. (21–22)

The lover may elude suspicion and discovery, but her clever actions are in vain; it is the visiting northerner who will ultimately betray her confidence. Like the mythical king Midas, whose donkey's ears betrayed his secret, so too will the elegiac distich cause readers to speculate about the author. Circumstances ensure the elision of fact and fiction in the minds of the late eighteenth-century audience. The *Elegien* close with the following self-referential lines, which reveal the secret lovers to the *Quiriten*, the citizens of Rome:

> Und ihr, wachset und blüht, geliebte Lieder, und wieget
> Euch im leisesten Hauch lauer und liebender Luft,
> Und entdeckt den Quiriten, wie jene Rohre geschwätzig,
> Eines glücklichen Paars schönes Geheimnis zuletzt. (29–32)

Goethe tactically underscores the fictional status of the elegies and their ironic tone; the public nature of the literary work shatters the private sphere privileged within, both literally and biographically.

Although they have little in common with the *Italienische Reise*, the *Römische Elegien* are clearly predicated upon his long journey. Within the bounds of this classical literary reference and his adaptation of its form and genre to his own style and to the German tradition, Goethe creates an Italy not found within the pages of his *Italienische Reise* twenty-five to thirty-five years later: an Italy his acquaintances and audience would come to expect as an immediate response to the Italian sojourn. Boyle concludes that the *Elegien*, "with their classical metres and allusions and deliberate stylizations, are art, not nature, a literary game, not confessional poetry, and yet they serve in the end a confessional purpose" (*B1*, 640). I read the *Römische Elegien* as the poet's confession that the Italian adventure somehow facilitated a new way of life in Weimar, including a relationship with Christiane Vulpius, one most likely impossible without the Italian experience. Within the *Elegien* Goethe projects a poetic and classical harmony onto his Italian memories, a harmony out of place in the *Italienische Reise*. By no means minimizing the innovation of the *Italienische Reise*, Goethe carefully and deliberately regulates the degree to which the most private and personal experiences will inform the ultimate public form of his travel narrative.

Goethe's Second Italian Journey

Because of its omission from Goethe's own autobiographical writing, many readers do not even realize that Goethe ventured a second time to Italy. Within two years of returning to Weimar, the poet made another trip south; a journey portrayed in complete contrast to his representation of its famed predecessor. Motivation for the trip made all the difference: in 1790 Goethe traveled, not of his own volition, but rather in an official capacity, on behalf of Duke Carl August, in order to meet the dowager duchess on her way back from an extended tour of Italy to Weimar. Goethe's newly established domestic situation made his existence in Weimar completely unlike the life he had left behind in 1786, and Italy no longer beckoned as the unattainable goal. Just as the actual first journey could not always meet Goethe's unrealistic expectations, a return trip would hardly be able to exceed the first in ambition and scope. Goethe reluctantly left Weimar on 10 March 1790 and arrived in Venice on 31 March, where he was to wait for Anna Amalia. Because her return from Rome was postponed, Goethe waited in Venice until 6 May. They would finally reach Weimar on 20 June, two years and two days after his first homecoming from the South.

While in Venice Goethe devoted himself to scientific and natural studies as well as the Venetian school of painting. As the city struggled to recover from severe flooding, Goethe found mud and stench, a far cry from his first encounter, so closely linked to paternal memory. Restless and anxious to return to Weimar, he began what would later become his *Venezianische Epigramme* modeled on the style of the Latin writer Martial. This cycle, far less a cohesive narrative than the *Elegien,* consists of just over one hundred epigrams and treats a diversity of subjects, from the city of Venice and the Venetians to a young acrobat named Bettina; from the prostitutes of Venice, referred to as lizards, to Newton's color theory and the French Revolution. It also expresses a strongly anti-Christian sentiment. Twenty-four epigrams were published anonymously in two 1791 issues of the *Deutsche Monatsschrift;* 103 epigrams appeared in Schiller's *Musenalmanach für das Jahr 1796.*[18]

Although for a time Goethe saw the negative tone of the *Epigramme* as supplanting the much more positive portrayal of Italy in his earlier *Elegien,* this view did not take hold in his contemporary readers, who, like many today, were baffled by the *Venezianische Epigramme.* Despite such pointedly anti-Italian references as those in the fourth elegy, the epigrams seem barely to have attracted the attention of his readers who adhered to the singularly positive association of Goethe with Italy:

> Noch ist Italien, wie ichs verließ, noch stäuben die Wege,
> Noch ist der Fremde geprellt, stell er sich wie er auch
>   will;

> Deutsche Rechtlichkeit suchst du in allen Winkeln
> vergebens,
> Leben und Weben ist hier, aber nicht Ordnung und
> Zucht;
> Jeder sorgt nur für sich, ist eitel, mißtrauet dem andern,
> Und die Meister des Staats sorgen nur wieder für sich.
> Schön ist das Land, doch ach! Faustinen find ich nicht
> wieder,
> Das ist Italien nicht mehr, das ich mit Schmerzen
> verließ. (1–8)[19]

Goethe's Weimar correspondents of the first trip most certainly could not reconcile his previous exuberant enthusiasm for Italy with his utterly negative attitude vis-à-vis the second trip. Much of this response resulted from Venice's special status almost outside of or separate from the rest of Italy. Because there is little connection to ancient Rome in Venice, an aversion to Venice is not synonymous with a rejection of the Classical. Indeed Goethe's strongest statement during the second visit to Italy was his steadfast refusal to travel further to southern Italy to visit many of his friends still in Rome, including Angelika Kaufmann. Aspects of the present, such as the French Revolution and the presence of a wife and son in Weimar, cancel the earlier priority of historical memory, the pull of the North now greater than the pull of the South.

Goethe himself is solely responsible for the ultimately positive status of Italy within his biography. The editorial process he employed thirty and forty years after his journey could easily have included reference to the second visit to Venice, but incompatibility of the tone of the second trip with Goethe's overall conception of the *Italienische Reise* and his overriding need to counter more recent representations of Italy precluded its admittance. The exploitation of foreign tourists and the backward, dirty conditions, only briefly mentioned in the *Italienische Reise,* enter the foreground as the poet relegates the previously positive to a distant memory. On 3 April 1790 Goethe wrote to the duke from Venice what is certainly his most personal anti-Italian sentiment:

> Übrigens muß ich im Vertrauen gestehen, daß meiner Liebe für Italien durch diese Reise ein tödlicher Stoß versetzt wird. Nicht daß mirs in irgendeinem Sinn übel gegangen wäre, wie sollte es auch? aber die erste Blüte der Neigung und Neugierde ist abgefallen. . . . Ich fürchte meine Elegien haben ihre höchste Summe erreicht und das Büchlein möchte geschlossen sein. Dagegen bring ich einen Libellum Epigrammatum mit zurück, der sich Ihres Beifalls, hoff ich, erfreuen soll. In manchen

Augenblicken wünsch ich Sie mit mir zu sehen, nur damit Sie Sich in Deutschland besser freuten. (*ISR*, 523)

Now even Germany appears in a more attractive light when compared to Italy; however, this negation of the idyllic South of the *Römische Elegien* is only temporary; by 1816 Goethe will boldly declare that he too was in Arcadia. The battle for aesthetic predominance will by then overshadow any mimetic urge as the aging poet challenges the young Romantics.[20]

Figure 2. Italia und Germania *(Italy and Germany, 1811–1828) by Friedrich Overbeck. Reproduced with the permission of the Bayerische Staatsgemäldesammlungen, Neue Pinakothek, Munich.*

4: Eichendorff and the Romantic Return to Italy

THE TIMING OF GOETHE'S JOURNEY on the eve of the French Revolution lent both the immediate memory of his trip and its evolving myth a heightened import as the consequences of 1789 changed the face of European travel. The ensuing Napoleonic Wars, which dominated the first fifteen years of the nineteenth century, along with their wartime obligations for young men and the generally unstable political climate, prohibited many travelers from pursuing lengthy journeys in the fashion of Goethe. Focused, goal-oriented travel on the scale of a Grand Tour lost value only to be challenged by the familiar trope of *Wandern,* which exemplified the spirit of aimless Romantic travel.[1] Consequently, the genre of travel reportage is underrepresented in the first two decades of the nineteenth century. The Romantics, not usually associated with nonfiction genres, preferred lyric poetry and shorter prose forms like the novella and fairy tale. Not only did historical and political events conspire to interfere with the actual movement of these authors around Europe, but their Romantic *Weltanschauung* privileged earlier times and places, accessed primarily through their fantasy and art. Mimetic realism is subordinated as these writers send their fictional protagonists to journey far in their stead, often to Italy. Its classical connotations, still strong in the minds of the reading public, face an oppositional interpretation as the early Romantics refocus attention on Italy as the seat of the Roman Catholic Church and pre-Renaissance art, especially that of Raphael and his predecessors. During the early nineteenth century, the image of Italy is most strongly bifurcated in the perceptions of German writers and travelers.

During the years between Goethe's return to Weimar and his preparation of the text of the *Italienische Reise* for publication, strongly divergent refigurations of Italy began to pervade German letters, along with a decidedly ambiguous relationship to the concept of travel itself. In contrast to the methodical itinerary of a Grand Tourist, who utilizes his journey as a means of self-improvement and documents his progress along the way, the travel depicted in German Romantic literature is far less organized, often approaching the chaotic. Commonly represented travelers include the wandering journeyman artist and the courtly poet.

In its most basic sense, travel indicates the process of movement from one place to another; the more refined definition, which informs this study, assumes that one of these places is the familiar home, and that the other is represented in the foreign destination. As I have argued in the case of the *Italienische Reise,* Goethe clearly saw his travels as crucial in defining the life he would lead upon his return to Weimar; although abroad, he constantly oriented himself on Germany, as evidenced in the letters sent to an audience at home, a format he maintained in the later editorial process. Although Italy and Weimar at times appear incompatible, Goethe continually strives for a harmonious balance. The Romantics exhibit a far more tenuous relationship between home and abroad, the familiar and the unfamiliar. Their writings, far less grounded in reality, often depict mythical geographies, which in extreme cases confound the visitors. Most attempts to follow the Romantic figure on the map will fail. Travel becomes a frightening test to be endured. The early nineteenth-century spectrum of travel includes a vast range from voluntary, privileged nomadism, on the one hand, to spontaneous, elected journey turned obligatory exile on the other. The aesthetic debates of the first two decades of the nineteenth century form the backdrop against which these antagonistic classical and Romantic representations of Italy developed simultaneously and in continual response to one another. The visual arts strongly inform Eichendorff's prose texts and are inextricably woven with his conceptions of Italy.

The centrality of the figure of the artist in the Romantic period has long been acknowledged in literary criticism. Coupled with the greatly increased emphasis on Christianity, specifically on the pre-Reformation Church, the artist is endowed with religious significance: the artist, whether painter or poet, becomes quasi-priest, preserver of art and religion. Nowhere are such ideas so well exemplified as in the prose of Tieck and Wackenroder and the art of the Nazarene painters in Rome. The collaborative work of two early Romantic writers and theorists did much to cement the Romantic image of Italy even before the dawn of the nineteenth century. In 1797 an anonymous work of mixed genre appeared, a loose narrative synthesis of theoretical and art historical writings: Wilhelm Heinrich Wackenroder and Ludwig Tieck's *Herzensergießungen eines kunstliebenden Klosterbruders* (Confessions from the Heart of an Art-Loving Friar). Although Wackenroder, universally acknowledged to have been the more adept art historian of the pair, wrote the majority of its components, two of Tieck's selections manifestly illustrate their impressions of Italy.[2] Crucially, both of these short pieces were written nearly a decade before Tieck himself would travel to

Italy. Wackenroder, who met an early death in 1798, never saw the land of his fantasy. The origins of Wackenroder and Tieck's fascination with Italian art and culture most likely lie with their time in Göttingen as university students in 1793 and 1794, where two professors, Forkel and Fiorillo, influenced their thinking.[3] The musician, Johann Nikolaus Forkel, is of less interest here; however, Johann Domenik Fiorillo, a professor of art, was also the curator of the university's collection of engravings. Born in Germany, Fiorillo had spent many years in Rome and Bologna, and offered private drawing lessons in addition to his university lectures in Göttingen. It is evident that he also imparted his students with an appreciation for Dürer.

In the brief "Sehnsucht nach Italien" (Longing for Italy), Tieck assumes the voice of an older retrospective narrator, recalling his youthful yearning for the South:

> Durch einen seltsamen Zufall hat sich folgendes kleine Blatt bis jetzt bei mir aufbewahrt, das ich schon in meiner frühen Jugend niederschrieb, als ich vor dem Wunsche, endlich einmal Italien, das gelobte Land der Kunst, zu sehen, keine Ruhe finden konnte.[4]

It remains a mystery whether the narrator's pain slowly subsided throughout many unfulfilled years or was relieved by an actual visit to the "land of art." Personal experience is subordinated to deep-seated and long-nurtured desire. The subsequent lines, supposedly on a page preserved since his youth, could hardly be said to describe the "praised land," but instead remain abstract and unspecified, a quality that applies to nearly all Romantic narratives on Italy:

> Bey Tage und in der Nacht denkt meine Seele nur an die schönen, hellen Gegenden, die mir in allen Träumen erscheinen, und mich rufen. Wird mein Wunsch, meine Sehnsucht immer vergebens seyn? So mancher reist hin und kömmt zurück und weiß dann nicht wo er gewesen ist und was er gesehen hat, denn keiner liebt so innig das Land mit seiner einheimischen Kunst. (*TW*, 59)

In their underlying tone, Tieck's remarks strongly anticipate those of Goethe by twenty years. Both narrators, one autobiographical and one fictional, intimate a mandate for a certain inner capacity or natural receptivity for truly appreciating Italy. Tieck concludes his short text with a poetic reiteration of his longing, in which his emotions replace even the most abstract description of Italy; Italy as a geographic destination is subsumed under the label "Kunstheimat." Art takes its place far above any geographic specificity: the longing for art becomes synonymous with the longing for home, a home long since unattainable.[5]

In the second of Tieck's relevant excerpts from *Herzensergießungen,* "Brief eines jungen deutschen Malers in Rom an seinen Freund in Nürnberg" (Letter of a young German painter in Rome to his friend in Nuremberg), a young journeyman artist writes home from Italy to his friend Sebastian, who stayed behind in the studio of Albrecht Dürer in Nuremberg. Art, religion, and love are conflated into one integrated Italian experience. Again, Italy as a historical reality receives little attention; in fact, the author stresses the impossibility of capturing this either in words or on canvas:

> Soll ich Dir weitläufig schreiben, wie das gelobte Land Italia beschaffen sey, und mich in unzusammenhängende Bewunderungen ergießen? Es finden da keine Worte ihren rechten Platz, denn wie mag ich, der Sprache so ganz unkundig, Dir den hellen Himmel, die weiten paradiesischen Aussichten, durch die die erquickende Luft spielend ziehet, würdig darstellen? Weiß ich doch kaum in meinem eigenthümlichen Handwerke Farben und Striche aufzufinden, um das, was ich innerlich sehe und fasse, auf die Leinwand hinzuzeichnen? (*TW,* 113)

Again, these sentiments presage similar ones of Goethe by twenty years. For Tieck's narrator, the Italian experience is internalized, divorced from its outside surroundings, yet at the same time, Italian characteristics and characters replace those of Germany. For example, Raphael is now preferred to Dürer,[6] and Roman Catholicism is acknowledged to be the only true religion of art. The experience culminates in the young artist's love for an Italian woman, aptly named Maria, and his ultimate religious conversion. In the irresistible force of a spiritually infused art, Tieck anticipates the much stronger opposition between Germany and Italy of the later Romantics, such as Eichendorff, in which the *Kunstheimat* will be revealed to be illusory; the protagonists will be truly at home only in an idealized, albeit medieval Germany.

The journal *Propyläen* (Propylaea), published by Goethe with the help of Schiller, Heinrich Meyer, and Friedrich August Wolf from 1798 to 1800, should certainly be read as a reaction to the changing currents as represented by *Herzensergießungen.* In his introductory essay for the first volume (1798), Goethe, not unlike Wackenroder and Tieck in the *Herzensergießungen,* campaigns for the artistic harmony of prerevolutionary Europe; however, he longs for a more recent past than the Middle Ages, expressing grave concern for the multitude of works of art claimed by the French troops in Italy. The poet presents Italy as a giant museum in jeopardy and questions the country's survival as a school for artists. So much of what defined the Italian experience for the Grand Tourists was now on its way to Paris.[7] The Classical is defended in the face of Napoleon's pillaging of Italy. Thus, ten years after his return to Weimar and nine years after the French Revolution, Goethe expresses a nostalgia for an inaccessible, and ultimately, nonexistent Italy. In a decidedly different gesture, members of the younger generation would attempt to establish a long-since vanished Germany within contemporary Italy.

The school of German Romantic painters now known as the Nazarenes remains a prime example of life imitating art: they strove to live the life and attain the ideals put forth by Tieck and Wackenroder in *Herzensergießungen* and in *Phantasien über die Kunst* (Fantasies on Art), which was published in 1799 by Tieck after Wackenroder's death.[8] The original members of the group met while studying at the Academy of Fine Arts in Vienna, a bastion of Winckelmannian Classicism, and in 1808 formed the *Lukasbund* as a reaction to the strict concept of art propagated by the academy. This post-revolution generation questioned their predecessors, and in an anti-revolutionary tack, instead searched for a new national German art modeled on the distant past. This new ideal would soon be situated in a variety of loci, including medieval poetry, a new interest of German linguists; *Volkspoesie,* such as that advocated by Herder; old legends and fairy tales like those collected by the Grimms; and the medieval visual arts, mainly religious in theme and of both German and Italian origin. They upheld Dürer as their symbolic German mentor and went to Italy largely because of their interest in Raphael and his predecessors, namely Giotto, Fra Angelico, Perugino, and Pinturicchio, who privileged the harmonious union of form and content. Their interest in establishing a national German art while in a foreign land is not surprising in light of the many historical examples of German cultural movements orienting themselves on foreign models and the comparatively late development of the German language into a full-fledged literary language.

In May 1810 four members, Friedrich Overbeck (1789–1869), Franz Pforr (1788–1812), Ludwig Vogel (1788–1879), and Johann Konrad Hottinger (1788–1828), moved to Rome and took up residence in the abandoned cloister of San Isidoro. As a result these German artists were soon dubbed "the Brothers of San Isidoro."[9] Beginning in 1811, a second wave of German artists with similar views joined the earlier arrivals, including Peter Cornelius, Wilhelm Schadow, and Philipp Veit, the son of Dorothea Schlegel and friend of Eichendorff.

Upon closer look, the work of the Nazarenes is surprisingly varied in theme. Their religious works generally depicted Old and New Testament scenes, portraits of Maria, and lives of the saints. Their secular themes included famous events in medieval history; legends recounted by Romantic writers such as Wackenroder, Tieck, Brentano, and the Grimms; and portraits of all kinds, including self-portraits, double portraits, and group portraits. Of special interest here is the genre of so-called friendship paintings in which the artist depicted pairs or groups of friends, sometimes including himself in the composition. The prime example of such a work, and undoubtedly the most well-known and widely recognized work by any of the Nazarenes, remains Friedrich Overbeck's *Italia und Germania* (Italy and Germany), painted between 1811 and 1828 (see figure 2).

An important visual document in the cultural history of the German predilection for Italy, Overbeck's painting is very much the *Sinnbild* of the Nazarene movement. Italia and Germania, personified as two young women, sit side-by-side clasping hands, their respective landscapes represented minimalistically behind each. The Italian landscape consists of a Romanesque church and some nondescript ruins in the distance. Behind Germany rises a burgeoning medieval town. The distant sky shines brighter above the northern portion of the landscape. The two women are situated at an imaginary geographic midpoint, a place where Dürer's Germany borders metaphorically on Raphael's Italy. On the spectator's left side of the canvas, a quiet, contemplative Italia looks downward; Overbeck assigns her a stature and pose reminiscent of many depictions of the Madonna. In contrast, Germania proffers an attentive, longing gaze past the allegorized Italia toward something beyond the Italian landscape, full of serious expectation. Italia is dressed in a simple gown of rich red and gold, a black shawl draped around her lap, while her German neighbor is clad in the simple, northern earth tones of green, brown, and orange, the style decidedly medieval. She wears her blond hair long, adorned with a garland of greens and simple wildflowers. Overbeck's Italia wears her dark hair atop her head, under a wreath of the more sophisticated laurel. The artist's contemporary audience was certainly aware of the laurel's association with sublime achievement in poetry and the arts; thus, Italy has long since attained her preeminent status and serves now as a model for fledgling Germany. Germania looks to the South, to the past, in order to renew her future.

The art historian Herbert Schindler offers a straightforward reading of the painting:

Hier werden nicht die gegensätzlichen Elemente von Nord und Süd, sondern die gleichgestimmten, sich ergänzenden Wesenheiten dargestellt, was letztlich eine Überwindung der Gegensätze durch die Kunst allegorisiert.[10]

I would suggest that the supposed harmony achieved by Overbeck is perhaps more questionable than at first glance. The current Italian landscape is barren and dark, but Italia does not long for an identity to be found outside of her own borders. She accepts Germania's admiration and validation of her monumental achievements, but does not appear to offer the same in return to her northern neighbor for the renewal of that past. Germania has failed to capture the attention of the introspective and withdrawn Italia; as a result, the northerner appears ready to jump up and head south. In a similar fashion, the Nazarene painters failed to engage the interest of the Italian public. They did not aim for assimilation within contemporary Italy, but instead strove programmatically for the recognition of their fellow Germans.

The Nazarene movement became the focus of much discussion within cultural circles back in Germany; perhaps due to the vast geographic distance between Rome and Germany, the group was often invoked by its vocal opponents as the representative example of all that was wrong with the Romantic visual arts. Goethe, as self-editor, interjected into his *Italienische Reise* negative sentiments concerning these painters, who first ventured to Rome twenty-three years after his return to Weimar. His opinions are closely linked to those of his friend Johann Heinrich Meyer, a Swiss painter Goethe befriended in Rome, who eventually became the director of the Weimar Academy of Art. Meyer's role evolved from that of painter to art historian and aesthetic theorist, and he collaborated with Goethe on a number of projects, including the *Propyläen* from 1788 to 1790 and *Über Kunst und Altertum* (On Art and Antiquity) from 1816 to 1832. The latter series contained Meyer's essay "Neudeutsche religios-patriotische Kunst" (New German Religious Patriotic Art) in the volume of 1817; it remains the most scathing attack on the Nazarene school as a representative of Romantic tendencies, but, importantly, not a personal attack on the individual artists themselves. Although written by Meyer, it clearly represents the alliance in opinion between Meyer and Goethe; the abbreviation "W. K. F.," standing for *Weimarische Kunstfreunde* (Weimar Friends of Art), served as a signature to the essay. Goethe himself edited Meyer's text and prepared the manuscript for publication. As early as 1814, Goethe contemplated a programmatic repudiation of the ideals upheld by the Nazarenes; however, he and Meyer did not begin their intensive

discussion and study of the matter until the summer of 1816. This period coincides exactly with the poet's composition of his own *Italienische Reise* in which a similar, although more subtle, polemic is at work.

Meyer begins by tracing the strong trends of contemporary German
art back to the 1780s, the decade in which he first made Goethe's acquaintance in Italy. Various factors in the years immediately after
Goethe's departure from Rome conspired to secure the way for a return
to an older, pre-Renaissance model for art: the influential artist
Friedrich Bury advocated a closer study of the Florentine school of
painters, thus shifting the focus away from Rome and, most importantly, in 1797 Tieck and Wackenroder's *Herzensergießungen eines
kunstliebenden Klosterbruders* appeared. Meyer mentions the fact that
many attributed this anonymous tract to Goethe, a gesture that served
to validate its ideas.[11] Surely the irony of that particular situation did
not escape the *Weimarische Kunstfreunde*. The movement afoot was
also supported by the writings of the Schlegel brothers as a decidedly
more patriotic, nationalistic way of thought was soon wed to the Romantic idealization of medieval Catholicism. Meyer places Philipp Otto
Runge and Caspar David Friedrich in the lineage leading to the Nazarenes, and then offers a brief introduction to the work of Cornelius,
Overbeck, and Schadow. The author goes out of his way to praise the
talents of these various artists in this essay, which is anything but a personal attack; instead he faults their misled intentions, a result of the
times. The ultimate blame lies with the political climate of the first decade of the nineteenth century.[12] The artists would do better to follow
the superior model of the ancient Greeks; for when one follows an infe-
rior example such as the old German and Italian masters, then the resulting work can only be mediocre. To its audience Meyer's essay came
across as a desperate plea against the younger generation.

A number of references to Goethe's contemporaneous correspondence deftly illustrate the vehemence and desperation with which
Goethe viewed the subject. In March 1817, he wrote to Knebel:

> Mein zweites Rhein-und-Main Heft wird ehstens aufwarten und wird
> als eine Bombe in den Kreis der Nazarenischen Künstler hinein plumpen;
> es ist gerade jetzt die rechte Zeit, ein zwanzigjähriges Unwesen anzu-
> greifen, mit Kraft anzufallen, und in seinen Wurzeln zu erschüttern.[13]

On 29 May 1817, Goethe wrote to Zelter:

> Die darin [im zweiten Heft] enthaltene[n] Kriegs- und Friedenserklä-
> rungen werden unausgesetzt verfolgt werden. Ich habe nicht viel Zeit
> mehr aufrichtig zu sein, wir wollen sie benutzen: der Anblick ist nur gar

zu närrisch, wenn man von unserm Standpunkte aus deutlich schaut, was für unglaubliche Vorzüge und Vorteile das Jahrhundert hat, was für treffliche Individuen darin wirken, und wie doch alles durch einander-geht, eine Würkung die andere aufhebt, so daß mir alle Menschen, die ich einzeln spreche, vernünftig und, wie ich sie in Bezug betrachte, ver-rückt erscheinen. Das geht so weit, daß ich mir manchmal selbst zwei-schürig vorkomme und mich erst wieder von solchem Zweifel erhole wenn ich mit Menschen spreche, die theoretisch und praktisch in ihrem Fach zu Hause sind. (*ZWJ*, 106)

Goethe and Meyer were among the last to experience Italy and the process of travel to Italy in the tradition of the Grand Tour. It is hardly surprising that their exigent warnings went unheeded and that few came to their defense in the ensuing debates. Because the events of the early part of the nineteenth century so shook the foundations of Euro-pean culture and society, a return to the apparently harmonious stabil-ity proposed by Goethe and Meyer was not a feasible alternative.[14]

A full two years after Goethe and Meyer's attempt to damage the reputation of the Nazarenes, Friedrich Schlegel came to the painters' defense. In 1819 he championed their work and defended their choice of subject matter and art historical models in an essay titled "Über die deutsche Kunstausstellung zu Rom, im Frühjahr 1819, und über den gegenwärtigen Stand der deutschen Kunst in Rom" (On the German Art Exhibit in Rome in Spring 1819 and on the Current Status of German Art in Rome). A large exhibit of the work of German artists re-siding in Rome was organized in conjunction with the visit of the Aus-trian Emperor Franz to Italy. Unfortunately, the emperor's own response to the exhibition was rather cool, and as a result, the sparse coverage of the event in the German-speaking press was largely am-bivalent, if not negative. Friedrich Schlegel, in the service of Metter-nich, also visited Rome in the spring of 1819. He was able to visit his wife, Dorothea, who was on an extended stay in Italy, as well as her sons, Johannes and Philip, both members of the Nazarenes. After his return to Vienna that summer, Dorothea exhorted Schlegel to come to the defense of the German artists in the face of one particularly promi-nent and anonymous review in the *Allgemeine Zeitung* on 23 July 1819.

Although ultimately unsuccessful in resuscitating the reputation of the artists in question, Friedrich Schlegel argued in defense of the art-ists' *altdeutsche Manier* (old German manner), refuting each and every complaint of the *Allgemeine Zeitung* review. The general influence of the great painters of the past was not to be avoided; the Nazarenes rightly privileged the overall *altdeutsch* style, a gesture that Schlegel insisted was not synonymous with imitation.[15] Of course, Schlegel's Catholic bias only served to exacerbate the nepotism some readers surely perceived in his views. Goethe would likely have been pleased that the popularity of the Nazarene school soon waned and remained greatly underappreciated until well into the twentieth century. Recently, art historians have begun to acknowledge the impact of these German painters in Rome on their successors, including the Pre-Raphaelites in Victorian England.

The works of Tieck, Wackenroder, and the Nazarenes assume large roles in the ongoing cultural debate on Italy in the first quarter of the nineteenth century. I have argued that, despite the overwhelming scholarly consensus on Goethe's writing on Italy, an overlooked, underlying ambivalence concerning much of Italy's classical heritage persists in his work. It is precisely such remarks in Goethe's *Italienische Reise* that anticipate much of this Romantic response to Italy. Romanticism and Weimar Classicism developed simultaneously and in response to one another. The Romantics, like the majority of Goethe's critics, seem oblivious to the frequent ambiguity that qualifies a purely neoclassical reading of the older poet. The early and high Romantics, of course, wrote before the publication of even the first volumes of the *Italienische Reise,* a text often placed in the center of the classical program. They instead were cognizant of a more stylized conception of Italy, notably that of the *Römische Elegien.* Eichendorff, as a late Romantic with the advantage of time on his side, is in a position to respond both to Goethe's more immediate and delayed responses to Italy. Eichendorff's depictions of landscape and nature, the Italian people, art, sexuality, and modes of travel will most directly rejoin the myth of Italy so closely associated with Goethe by early nineteenth-century Germans.

Like many of his contemporaries, including Novalis, Brentano, and Hoffmann, Joseph Freiherr von Eichendorff never ventured to Italy. In addition to the unstable political situation in Europe throughout his young adulthood (he participated briefly in the War of Liberation from late 1813 through 1814), Eichendorff's once prominent family's precarious financial situation precluded any extended foreign journeys beyond a visit to Paris in 1808. His studies brought him from his Silesian home as far as Heidelberg and Vienna. Consensus states that Eichendorff's poetry, when viewed across the spectrum of his long career, is strikingly uniform in style, theme, and structure. Throughout his prose oeuvre as well, Eichendorff tends repeatedly toward familiar themes, albeit in different ways. Often referred to as the last Romantic, Eichendorff offers some of the most extreme examples of the movement's tendencies. His work is thus informed by many of his predecessors, so much so that Paul Requadt comments that "ohne Novalis, Tieck und Arnim wäre Eichendorffs Italien nicht entstanden, er verwertet Elemente aus ihrer Bilderwelt; er scheint sie fast zu plagiieren."[16] Eichendorff's poetry on Italy lacks the darker, more critical side of his prose treatment of the subject, although it does reflect his usual juxtaposition of Germany and Italy.

Intercalated in his final novel, *Dichter und ihre Gesellen* (Poets and Their Companions), published in 1834, we find some of Eichendorff's most celebrated lyric, much of which, not coincidentally, is about Italy. These poems serve to reiterate the various prose figures' relationships to their homeland and to Italy.[17] In "Rückkehr" (Return), which originally appeared in the twenty-fourth chapter of the novel, the Baron Fortunato has just returned to Germany from Italy. By singing this song, he calls forth Florentine, who interrupts. After her welcome disruption, Fortunato continues:

> Ich komme aus Italien fern
> Und will Euch alles berichten,
> Vom Berg Vesuv und Roma's Stern
> Die alten Wundergeschichten.
>
> Da singt eine Fei auf blauem Meer,
> Die Myrten trunken lauschen —
> Mir aber gefällt doch nichts so sehr,
> Als das deutsche Waldesrauschen![18]

Ultimately, the poet's actual presence in Italy is irrelevant; for he plans to rely on "die alten Wundergeschichten." The discourse on Italian travel is, by 1834, already reduced to the terms of modern mass tourism and sightseeing; one can easily speak of Vesuvius and Rome outside the realm of personal experience. Artists and travelers had long since catalogued, sketched, described, and praised such geographic loci in their works; this compartmentalizing gesture divorces reality from representation, a result not unlike that of the Romantic movement as a whole. To a far greater extreme, mimesis played but a minor role in the literary project. The predominant association of Italy is now distilled to the blue sea and the eternally green myrtle, images vague yet universal enough to be transmitted via legend, painting, and poetry. Even such positive attributes cannot surpass the poet's love for the *Waldesrauschen* of Germany. In Italy the fairy spirits possess the power to intoxicate through song, whereas the German forest itself is endowed with such powers. This north-south juxtaposition is still a harmonious one, although the poet's preference for home is clear. Ricarda Huch commented on the similarity of Eichendorff's various portrayals of Germany and Italy both with "rauschende Gärten, Wasserkünste, verfallene Paläste, verliebte Mädchen." The divergence is found instead in their moods.[19]

"Sehnsucht" (Longing), one of Eichendorff's most famous poems, deliberately recalls Goethe's "Kennst du das Land." Here Italy and Germany, together with their respective reductive landscapes, are set in opposition. This poem, alternately referred to by its first line "Es schienen so golden die Sterne," appears shortly after "Rückkehr" within *Dichter und ihre Gesellen.* Interestingly, it is Fiametta who produces this song: upon hearing the call of the post horn, her thoughts turn immediately to her homeland, a point-of-view analogous to Goethe's poem as sung by Mignon.[20] Whereas Mignon recalls her home with the longing of a long-since departed *Wanderer,* imploring Wilhelm first as her *Geliebter,* then as her *Beschützer,* and finally as her *Vater* to return there with her, Fiametta presents her Italian perspective indirectly through the eyes and words of two young German journeymen. While traveling through the northern landscape, described by Fiametta with such attributes as *Bergeshang, Felsenschlüften, Wälder,* and *Klüften* (*DG,* 334), the men sing of their destination. The powerful, indeed threatening, landscape here is the German one, for it is their dreamlike incantation of Italy that will lead them seemingly fearlessly through the *Waldesnacht.* In sharp contrast, the Italian landscape is man-made and architectural, an artificial landscape of statues, gardens, stones, palaces, and fountains (*DG,* 325). Italy, which so often poses a threat to the German visitors of Eichendorff's prose, is a comfort to the approaching Germans and the displaced Fiametta. "Sehnsucht" thus reflects the mirror image of "Rückkehr": an Italian (woman) longing for Italy while in Germany versus a German (man) just returned from Italy recalling the homesickness he felt while in Italy. Eichendorff twice repaints Overbeck's *Italia und Germania.*

Eichendorff's deliberate choice of names for his characters in his prose fiction reflects his vast reading as well as his intention to situate his own work within a larger, international tradition. Boccaccio's work is the privileged source for much of Eichendorff's Italian references. Fiametta, spelled by Eichendorff with one "m," of *Dichter und ihre Gesellen,* recalls the most favored female figure in Boccaccio's oeuvre. Fiammetta, spelled with two "m's" in Italian, is the central storyteller in his *Filocolo* (1336–1338?), the narrator of the *Elegia di madonna*

Fiammetta (*Elegy of the Madonna Fiammetta*, 1343–1344?), and again the privileged female storyteller in the *Decameron* (1348–1352). Although no proof exists, much attempt has been made to situate Fiammetta within Boccaccio's own biography.[21] In the *Filocolo* Fiammetta tells the romance of Florio and Biancifiore, a story that Boccaccio derived from the French medieval tale of Floire and Blanchefleur. In turn, these international figures will inform those of Florio and Bianka in *Das Marmorbild* (The Marble Statue, 1819).

Although many of Eichendorff's works, including *Dichter und ihre Gesellen,* deal at least in part with Italy, two of his shorter prose pieces are most exemplary of his extreme appropriations and interpretations of Italy: *Das Marmorbild* and *Aus dem Leben eines Taugenichts* (From the Life of a Good-for-Nothing, 1826). Because my own reading ascribes greater importance to his *Taugenichts* as a response to Goethe's *Italienische Reise,* a brief discussion of *Das Marmorbild* will serve as an introduction.

Friedrich de la Motte Fouqué commissioned *Das Marmorbild* in 1814. Completed in 1817, the novella appeared in Fouqué's *Frauentaschenbuch für das Jahr 1819* (*Women's Pocketbook for the Year 1819*). When published in book form in 1826, along with the premiere of *Aus dem Leben eines Taugenichts,* it suffered in critical comparison to the nearly unanimously praised *Taugenichts. Das Marmorbild* draws on a number of sources and a lengthy tradition of stories of animated statues and the *Venusberg.* Eichendorff identified for Fouqué his chief source as Eberhard G. Happel's *Grösseste Denkwürdigkeiten der Welt oder so genandte Relationes Curiosae* (The Greatest Memorable Occurences of the World or the so-called Relationes Curiosae). He culled material on Venus from two stories in this volume of 1687: "Die Teuffelsche Jungfrau" (The Devilish Virgin) and "Die seltzahme Lucenser-Gespenst" (The Strange Spirit of Lucena).[22] Eichendorff was not alone in his treatment of the goddess Venus, but rather situated himself in a succession of writers, including Tieck, Brentano, Arnim, and Hoffmann, which would later encompass Fouqué, Alexis, Heine, and Wagner. In 1853 Eichendorff himself would return to the subject in *Julian,* an epic poem employing a variety of verse forms and based on the life of Emperor Julianus Apostata.

Part of the Romantic rejection of classicism involved the redefinition of mythological figures, imbuing them with negative or even evil attributes. By the turn of the nineteenth century, the *Venusberg* has been relocated to the gates before Rome and becomes the seat of demonic seduction.[23] *Das Marmorbild* straddles the concerns of the coexisting literary programs of the first quarter of the nineteenth century, simultaneously idealizing and demonizing Italy.

Adhering to the Romantic tendency toward the fantastic and the disdain of reality, Eichendorff's Lucca, dictated as the setting by the source material, remains nondescript. The only other Italian geographic location mentioned in *Das Marmorbild,* albeit briefly, is Milan. Indeed, without these two references, the geographic location of the narrative would not be fixed, and because neither is as invested a concept as Rome or Venice, the setting is reduced to the most minor of narrative roles. The overall medieval atmosphere conjures up a much stronger association than the tag "Lucca." In spite of its lack of mimetic reference, it is precisely the courtly milieu that constitutes the Italian nature of the piece: Italy as a two-sided coin, where the idyllic is constantly threatened by a demonic aberration of classical Rome. In this strongly bifurcated setting, the darker forces of Roman mythology battle against a courtly Christian poet, an opposition emblematic of the clash between the classical and the Romantic. Thus, the unity of religious conviction and art avowed by Wackenroder and Tieck in the wandering journeyman is ascribed instead to the wandering poet.

Eichendorff's narrative describes the experiences of a young traveler named Florio, who meets the *Minnesänger,* Fortunato, and the beautiful, young Bianka. His encounters with these two figures are frequently interrupted and obscured by a striking Venus-like figure, who in Florio's view is sometimes woman, sometimes cold statue. Her hold on Florio increases until his escape as she and her palace dissolve into ruins. Upon fleeing Lucca, Florio is reunited with Fortunato, Pietro, and Bianka. It is only then, near the narrative's conclusion that the appellation Italy appears. The narrator describes their intentions: "Alle drei hatten sich vorgenommen, mit einander das schöne Italien zu durchschweifen, und luden Florio freudig ein, mit ihnen zu reisen" (*MB,* 422). Only after having survived and defeated the darker Italy does the option of visiting the safer, benevolent, more historically accurate Italy present itself. As the travelers ride past the ruins of Venus's castle, Fortunato offers the song, referred to by Eichendorff in his collected poetry of 1837 as "Gotterdämmerung" (Twilight of the Gods), Part II. He sings of Italy as the tomb of the classical, mythological gods upon which a new garden is sown, a new empire is constructed:

> Von kühnen Wunderbildern
> Ein großer Trümmerhauf,
> In reizendem Verwildern

Ein blüh'nder Garten drauf.

Versunknes Reich zu Füßen,
Vom Himmel fern und nah
Aus anderm Reich ein Grüßen —
Das ist Italia! (*MB*, 423)

From this sunken empire Venus rises; permanently turned to stone, she is rendered harmless. The Madonna replaces the pagan goddess as the most sublime representation of woman as Christianity completely erodes the classical tradition. The disguised Bianka reveals her true identity to enter into a Christian union with Florio. Any earlier sadness is now banished from the newfound, idyllic, natural paradise, which is again surprisingly generic in description: "Und so zogen die Glücklichen fröhlich durch die überglänzten Auen in das blühende Mailand hinunter" (*MB*, 428).[24] National origin and destination remain nearly superfluous: Germany is not an explicit issue in the text, most likely because the text remains derivative of many sources.

Eichendorff's conception of travel within *Das Marmorbild* is decidedly medieval, reserved for poets, knights, and the aristocracy. In addition, this activity will be endowed with a pedagogical element for Florio. The protagonist's mysterious encounters with Venus in Lucca are in large part an initiation, or coming-of-age trial, much like the eighteenth-century Grand Tour. The privilege of leisure travel will be earned only through the successful completion of the challenges found at Lucca. Eichendorff's narrative does not recount Florio's journey to Lucca, but the protagonist describes his own decision to take up traveling after his initial unsuccessful attempts at poetry. In the end Florio returns voluntarily through travel to the role of poet:

> Ich habe jetzt . . . das Reisen erwählt, und befinde mich wie aus einem Gefängnis erlöst, alle alten Wünsche und Freuden sind nun auf einmal in Freiheit gesetzt. Auf dem Lande in der Stille aufgewachsen, wie lange habe ich da die fernen blauen Berge sehnsüchtig betrachtet, wenn der Frühling wie ein zauberischer Spielmann durch unsern Garten ging und von der wunderschönen Ferne verlockend sang und von großer, unermeßlicher Lust. (*MB*, 385–86)

The process of getting from one place to another was not highly valued during Eichendorff's lifetime: both political and practical circumstances undermined leisure touring. But in Eichendorff's Romantic view, with little room for reality, the traveler moves unimpeded through flower-filled meadows and over blue mountains in a nearly trance-like state.

Florio is a prime exponent of Romantic yearning for a lost time or place, his poetry of desire reminiscent of Goethe's self-described, long-incubated longing for Italy. Unlike Goethe's virtually unattainable expectations confined in a specific space, Florio's desire is more general, the thirst for another place, any place other than the familiar, other than home.

During his final encounter with the figure of Venus in her palace, Florio reiterates the dreamlike quality of his present experiences, recalling childhood afternoons looking at pictures of Lucca and other destinations his father collected while traveling:

> da dachte ich nicht, daß das alles einmal lebendig werden würde um mich herum. Mein Vater trat dabei oft zu mir und erzählte mir manch lustiges Abenteuer, das ihm auf seinen jugendlichen Heeresfahrten in der und jener von den abgemalten Städten begegnet. (*MB*, 418)

For a short time he equates his own adventures with those of his father. In contrast to Goethe, who knew from a young age that an Italian journey based on the model of his father's own was expected of him, Eichendorff's protagonist feels astonished to find himself abroad, living out childhood fantasies. Yet Florio's remarks recall passages in Goethe's *Dichtung und Wahrheit* and the *Italienische Reise*. Eichendorff composed the first draft of *Das Marmorbild* between June 1816 and March 1817: by then three volumes of Goethe's autobiography as well as the first volume of his travel report had appeared. Eichendorff's most transparent reference to Goethe though is Florio's imitation of Werther: in contrast to his peripatetic father, Florio throws himself down in to the grass and look for hours at the clouds (*MB*, 418–19). Eichendorff respects Goethe's achievement in *Die Leiden des jungen Werthers,* although, not surprisingly, he sees the figure of Werther as the prime example of what will happen when one is not guided by a deep Christian faith. In *Der deutsche Roman des achtzehnten Jahrhunderts in seinem Verhältnis zum Christentum* (The German Novel of the Eighteenth Century in its Relationship to Christianity," 1851) Eichendorff judges Werther to be "ein moderner Narziß."[25] Despite Eichendorff's strong attachment to the religious principles of the Romantic program, his work, like that of many of his contemporaries, is surprisingly devoid of institutionalized religion. The churches and priests of Italy and Germany are absent; Christianity is instead present solely in the defeat of paganism. The tendency of Eichendorff's figures to marry at the end of their Italian adventures, upon their return home, can be seen as a moralistic correction of the eroticism often associated with Italy that informs Goethe's *Römische Elegien*.

Paul Requadt summarizes the plight of Eichendorff's protagonists in Italy in the question of how Italy can serve a pedagogical function if it represents such a threat to the individual.[26] Such Romantic texts convincingly exemplify the etymological root of the word "unheimlich," usually translated as uncanny, which first took on the meaning of an almost alienating emotional discomfort and fear in the late eighteenth century.[27] Such a sense of displacement is characteristic of Eichendorff's protagonists, who long for their home. In *Aus dem Leben eines Taugenichts*, Eichendorff swings to the opposite extreme of the *Unheimlichkeit* prevalent in *Das Marmorbild:* the uncanny borders on the absurd as Eichendorff mocks the tradition of Germans in Italy.

In May 1826 the Vereinsbuchhandlung of Berlin published in one volume *Aus dem Leben eines Taugenichts und Das Marmorbild. Zwei Novellen, nebst einem Anhange von Liedern und Romanzen von Joseph Freiherrn von Eichendorff.* The *Taugenichts* garnered nearly unanimous critical acclaim, and the text itself went through at least five editions before Eichendorff's death in 1857. In the century and a half since, the novella has continued to find acclaim with every generation of readers. It remains Eichendorff's only prose work to enjoy international success today.

The work has confounded critical attempts at classification within traditional genre boundaries. The significance of this text lies in the ways the author plays with the apparently superficial simplicity of the narrative, an aspect that is ironic given the status of the protagonist as a simpleton and the text's references to the picaresque, baroque figure of Simplicissimus. The text satisfies the length restrictions of a novella as Eichendorff himself called it; however, this label hardly goes far enough in describing the many forces at work within the narrative. Because of the lack of informed self-development, the text can also be read as an anti-*Bildungsroman* in much the same way as the earlier *Ahnung und Gegenwart* (Presentiment and the Present, 1815). In *Aus dem Leben eines Taugenichts*, Eichendorff also contorts the familiar Romantic form of the fairy tale; supplementing the more traditional components of coincidence, an outside, omnipotent force, and an anonymous protagonist, Eichendorff confounds the tradition through his use of a first-person, therefore autobiographical, narrator. Eichendorff's final choice of title emphasizes his apparent orientation on the model of Goethe's large, autobiographical project, although he deletes the first-person possessive pronoun. The narrative stance thus surprises the unsuspecting reader.

Central to my own reading is Eichendorff's reaction to the form of the adventure and travel report throughout the *Taugenichts*. A reader familiar with Goethe's own conception of autobiography and travel report is continually struck throughout Eichendorff's text at the depth at which the *Italienische Reise* is at play in the author's mind. While most commentators fleetingly mention the genre of German-language travel narrative concerning Eichendorff, few have investigated the intertextual relationship of Goethe's and Eichendorff's texts. By parodying such traditional Grand Tour journeys and the immediately canonical narratives of such adventures, Eichendorff not only calls into question both of these traditions, but also the modern infeasibility of such experience and self-representation. In this way, the Italian reflections in *Taugenichts* are immensely more significant and engaging than those evident in Eichendorff's other works. His *Marmorbild* and its bifurcated image of Italy are derivative of many sources and models, but lack the ironic perspective evident in *Taugenichts*. At the end of a long line of Romantic writers and on the threshold of the Biedermeier era, it is through his *Taugenichts* that Eichendorff will distinguish himself from his predecessors. The critical and public reception of that work to this day bears out this fact.

A closer look at the genesis of the *Taugenichts* narrative illuminates the priority of Eichendorff's text within the corpus of German literary images of Italy. Scholars have dated the work on the *Taugenichts* project from 1817 based on the existence of brief notes regarding the second chapter, apparently drafted while Eichendorff lived and worked in Breslau. The double page of notes is no longer extant, but early twentieth-century literary historians reported its contents in addition to certifying its authenticity (*ALT,* 789). These notes refer to the Taugenichts's decision to flee from Vienna for an unspecified destination. The earliest extant manuscript for the novella is titled *Der neue Troubadour* (The New Troubadour), also of 1817. Beyond a few historical facts included in Eichendorff's narrative, for example, a reference to the death of E. T. A. Hoffmann in 1822, there is no evidence to document the process of completion. Sometime between 1821 and 1824 Eichendorff returned to the project in question. The public's first glimpse of the *Taugenichts* occurred in 1823 in Breslau with the publication of the first two chapters in *Deutsche Blätter für Poesie, Literatur, Kunst und Theater* under the title of *Ein Kapitel aus dem Leben eines Taugenichts* (A Chapter From the Life of a Good-for-Nothing). The text of this journalistic publication is nearly identical to the manuscript of *Der neue Troubadour*. Both these incomplete versions break off suddenly with the

Taugenichts poised in his treetop perch watching his beloved countess on the balcony with the unidentified young man.

Although it is unclear when Eichendorff completed the second chapter and wrote the final eight, the eponymous hero rashly decides to flee to Italy, significantly within the final few pages of the second chapter included only in the final version. The early notes and versions of the narrative lack any reference to Italy, but it is likely that this was in Eichendorff's mind at the earliest stages of the text's development. The first two portions of the *Italienische Reise*, the more traditional portions of it at that, appeared respectively in 1816 and 1817; these works clearly informed Eichendorff's own conception of Italy.[28] As Eichendorff's thoughts turned back to his *Taugenichts*, Goethe's travel report was reaching a wide audience of readers and offering them a decidedly non-Romantic conception of Italy. Having never traveled to Italy himself, Eichendorff equated Goethe's presentation with the supposed reality the Romantic movement endeavored to eradicate. Thus, the dominoes continue to fall: a late Romantic writer responded to what he saw as a classical view, which itself was published largely to negate the earlier Romantic conceptions of Italy.

The years during which Eichendorff worked sporadically on the *Taugenichts* correspond biographically with the most tumultuous period of his life. Within six years he moved from Breslau to Danzig to Königsberg, assuming various government posts after completing the necessary exams; his first three children were also born during this period. Most painful was his family's loss of his childhood home at Lubowitz, which was finally auctioned in 1822. As Hartwig Schultz has pointed out, these circumstances, coupled with the growing pressures of his employment, left Eichendorff little time for writing, and contrast sharply with the life he ascribes to his Taugenichts.[29]

As in *Das Marmorbild,* the Taugenichts's Italy is strikingly generic and lacks fine definition. The only geographic reference point Eichendorff offers, beyond the vague reference to the town of "B.," is that of Rome, and in this instance he challenges Goethe's orientation on this ancient city. Goethe composed his autobiography to illustrate his development as a poet, and his account of his trip in large part culminates in the arrival at, and the two stays in, Rome. For the Taugenichts, all roads will also lead to Rome, but without intent; instead he is led by apparent coincidence. The Taugenichts travels haphazardly, without preparation, and usually sets out because of crisis.

His journey begins as his father banishes him from his home; the father, of course, chides his lazy son, while wearing his own night cap during the daylight hours. As the first-person narrator describes it, he is only too happy to go out into the world to seek his own good fortune; in fact, he claims to have had the same idea just a few days earlier. The father sets the wheels in motion that will bring his son to Italy, but it is ultimately the porter in Vienna who plants the seed in the protagonist's head to travel to Italy. The Taugenichts's journey will introduce him to a number of potential father figures. Goethe, on the other hand, had a demanding father with specific plans for his son's education and life; it is he that instilled his son with a desire for Italy, which eventually arises as a flight from restraint, responsibility, and the duke. Goethe's avoidance of Italy for many years served as a silent rebellion against his father. In contrast to the masterly choreographed adventures of Goethe, it is pure coincidence that will lead the Taugenichts to Vienna as the passing carriage offers him a ride; for he simply states that he is heading in that direction. In Vienna the Taugenichts will experience an idyllic world unlike any he has ever seen, a place to call home, but only after he has withstood the challenges presented. Because Eichendorff originally referred to the Taugenichts's initial destination (Vienna) as "W," I argue that Wien should be read as a parallel to Weimar.[30] Both the Taugenichts and Goethe leave home and spend an interim period in a courtly situation, be it an undisclosed number of weeks as a gardener and then as a toll collector, or a decade as a ducal minister. The Taugenichts must come back to his second home, Vienna, in order to find his beloved, not a countess, but a commoner. Goethe returns from Italy, not to Frankfurt as his father had imagined years earlier, nor to his relationship with Charlotte von Stein, but within two weeks, to a commoner who works in an artificial-flower workshop.

The Taugenichts moves on to Italy out of heartbreak and his usual motivation, misunderstanding. In his most obvious reference to Goethe's formulation of Italy, Eichendorff's Taugenichts describes Italy *in nuce* to a farmer while asking for directions: "Nach Italien, wo die Pomeranzen wachsen" (*ALT*, 489). The Taugenichts has derived his notion of Italy completely from the porter. Just as his father stands as a questionable model, so does the porter, continually portrayed as the ultimate philistine. After receiving no assistance from the farmer, the Taugenichts recalls the porter's description:

> Der Portier mit der kurfürstlichen Nase, welcher überhaupt viele Kenntnisse von der Weltgeschichte hatte, sagte oft zu mir: "Wertgeschätzter Herr Einnehmer! Italien ist ein schönes Land, da sorgt der liebe Gott für alles, da kann man sich im Sonnenschein auf den Rücken legen, so wachsen einem die Rosinen ins Maul, und wenn einen die Ta-

rantel beißt, so tanzt man mit ungemeiner Gelenkigkeit, wenn man auch sonst nicht tanzen gelernt hat." (*ALT,* 489)

The porter has a dubious, if interesting, knowledge of world history; his formulation of Italy matches neither that of the late eighteenth-century Grand Tourists, nor that of the earlier Romantics, such as Tieck and Wackenroder. He regales the young Taugenichts with a legend that, like other Romantic reflections of the South, lacks any realistic reference. The porter's remarks ultimately serve to confirm the Taugenichts's decision to head for Italy; for how could he return to his village without having seen the world and making something of himself? Seeing the world once meant seeing Italy.

The territory traversed between Vienna and Italy introduces the Taugenichts to the unusual, if not uncomfortable, atmosphere he will discover in Italy. In fact, it seems as though Italy begins immediately as he leaves his toll collector's house behind and encounters one hindrance after another: initial disorientation, an ominous forest, a strange village, and robbers. Italy, once located, has an unexpected effect on our traveler, but perhaps not altogether surprising in light of his predisposition for sleep. Traveling on the box of the postal coach, certainly not a place conducive to sleep, the somnolent Taugenichts cannot keep his eyes open. He explains:

> Ich wollte mir doch Italien recht genau besehen, und riß die Augen alle Viertelstunden weit auf. Aber kaum hatte ich ein Weilchen so vor mich hingesehen, so verschwirrten und verwickelten sich mir die sechszehn Pferdefüße vor mir wie Filet so hin und her und übers Kreuz, daß mir die Augen gleich wieder übergingen, und zuletzt geriet ich in ein solches entsetzliches und unaufhaltsames Schlafen, daß gar kein Rat mehr war. Da mocht' es Tag oder Nacht, Regen oder Sonnenschein, Tyrol oder Italien sein, ich hing bald rechts, bald links, bald rücklings über den Bock herunter. . . . (*ALT,* 502)

This unpleasant sleep contrasts sharply with his peaceful Sunday naps in the palace garden. Italy exercises an hypnotic power over the unskilled traveler; instead of holding his piqued interest, the landscape and air anesthetize him and his senses. At his first stop, the Taugenichts continues to react to and describe Italy solely in terms of his preconceived and derivative ideas: he sees that which will fulfill his limited memory. Sitting in the inn, he orients his reactions to the present on the past, remembering the gypsy-like peddlers he had encountered in Germany (*ALT,* 502). One might expect the alert traveler to revel in the climate, landscape, history, art, or cuisine of Italy, but not in the thought of its peddlers. The Taugenichts's supposed ease is short-lived and ends abruptly with the unexpected arrival of the hunchbacked dwarf. Above all, he is threatened by his increasingly frustrating inability to communicate; he speaks no Italian, only feigns French, and the little man's command of German is worthless:

> Denn mir war in dem fremden Lande nicht anders, als wäre ich mit meiner deutschen Zunge tausend Klafter tief ins Meer versenkt, und allerlei unbekanntes Gewürm ringelte sich und rauschte da in der Einsamkeit um mich her, und glotzte und schnappte nach mir. (*ALT,* 504)

Of course, with the exception of his poetry, the Taugenichts's own native language skills were never stellar; language is reduced, at best, to a questionable medium, which too often results in misunderstandings. (This figure stands in sharp contrast to his multilingual creator.) Keenly aware of his status as foreigner, his first independent experiences as a traveler in Italy are hardly positive.

With the sudden departure of his employers, Guido and Leonardo, the Taugenichts is left alone and finds himself trapped in the tracks of a seemingly predestined journey. He graduates to the role of a supposedly more refined traveler inside the carriage. At the mercy of the postilion, with whom he cannot communicate, intense fear replaces the earlier urge to sleep. The height of his disorientation comes as the coach travels uncontrollably through a suddenly ominous mountainous landscape. Most divergent from the Viennese palace is the many-towered castle atop the mountain peak, certainly a staple of English Gothic novels.[31]

During his highly unusual stay in the strange castle, the Taugenichts will experience, after a short period of acclimation, a sense of contentment. He relishes the relaxation afforded him during his stay in the seemingly enchanted castle, which deviates greatly from the frenetic pace of his earlier uncontrollable journey. The intoxicating effect of the southern climate seems to work its charms further; yet, ironically, this short-lived happiness occurs simultaneously with the most extreme case of misunderstanding and incomprehension in the entire narrative. The domestic staff falsely takes the Taugenichts to be a girl, specifically the young countess Flora, disguised in young man's clothing. He thus becomes the object of their laughter as his behavior and appearance continuously belie their expectations. Language is again a barrier, although the Taugenichts confesses to have learned a few words of Italian. As narrator, he reports various conversations, but it remains unclear as to how the information is exchanged. The traveler no longer seems intimidated by the unexpected nature of his experiences; instead of questioning the inexplicable circumstances, he declares unequivocally that all Italians are crazy (*ALT,* 511). Whereas the mountain often serves metaphorically as the seat of self-enlightenment, the Taugenichts ascends only to greater self-delusion.

The increasing comfort offered him in the castle refuge acts to fulfill the porter's prophecy (*ALT,* 514). Eventually though, the Taugenichts tires of his new-found Italian existence:

> So verging ein Tag nach dem andern, bis ich am Ende anfing, von dem guten Essen und Trinken ganz melankolisch zu werden. Die Glieder gingen mir von dem ewigen Nichtstun ordentlich aus allen Gelenken, und es war mir, als würde ich von Faulheit noch ganz auseinander fallen. (*ALT,* 515)

This rare moment of insight stands as an anomaly within the Taugenichts's biography, where idleness is the rule rather than the exception. He forgets that his more industrious moments have been mere aberrations, such as his role as toll collector, where hardly a soul passed by. During such an exceptional moment of self-introspection, the Taugenichts expresses his initial sentiments of homesickness by singing the song that a journeyman taught him years before, which ends with the salutation: "Grüß Dich Deutschland aus Herzensgrund" (*ALT,* 516). Like an incantation, this song will evoke the interruption that brings to an end his palatial existence: the letter from Vienna. But alas, this document too will be misinterpreted, and aside from jolting the Taugenichts out of his immobility, does not lead to clarification.

Although the two settings are vastly different and their similarities are at first glance easy to overlook, for me the Taugenichts's description of the mountaintop castle, its garden, and its strange inhabitants indeed recalls Goethe's own narrative on the palace of Palagonia[32] with its grotesquely exaggerated baroque figures. Although not situated on a mountaintop like its fictitious counterpart, "das viereckte Schloß steigt über alles empor" (*IR,* 261). Goethe's visit to the famous Sicilian palace surely represents the most extreme example of artistic discomfort he experienced while in Italy. When presented with this artistic and architectural aberration, his education and exposure left him ill-prepared for both the whimsy and extreme humor of the Sicilian Baroque; the arbitrariness of the decoration most offends Goethe's artistic sensibilities (*IR,* 264). Analogously, the Taugenichts's mountaintop adventure represents the height of his confusion. Both travelers find themselves completely out of their usual elements.

The pair of old caretakers in Eichendorff's fictitious castle exhibits the sharp features of grotesque sculpture. The old woman especially disgusts the Taugenichts as she grinds her toothless jaw, thus appearing as if she were chewing on the end of her long, pointy nose. In contrast, Goethe meets no inhabitants in the palace near Palermo, but rather ascribes to the multitude of misshapen statues along the road to the palace the role of occupants. It is precisely their many deformities that make them unfit residents. The German traveler's inventory of statues includes hunchbacks and dwarfs, reminiscent of the little spy in the *Taugenichts*, among other strange creatures such as animals crossed with humans and figures with swapped heads.

The disfigured sculptural forms exhibited in both works are not created out of the classic material, marble, but rather out of substandard, less durable media. The Taugenichts shudders at the sight of the neglected boxwood topiary in the decrepit castle garden. The son of a poor miller, now experienced as a court gardener, is astonished to find laundry hanging among pieces of broken statuary on a dried-up fountain:

> Die Gänge waren alle mit hohem Grase bewachsen, die künstlichen Figuren von Buchsbaum waren nicht beschnitten und streckten, wie Gespenster, lange Nasen oder ellenhohe spitzige Mützen in die Luft hinaus, daß man sich in der Dämmerung ordentlich davor hätte fürchten mögen. (*ALT,* 512)

In a similar fashion, Goethe disdains the statues carved from shell tufa:

> Denke man sich nun dergleichen Figuren schockweise verfertigt und ganz ohne Sinn und Verstand entsprungen, auch ohne Wahl und Absicht zusammengestellt, denke man sich diesen Sockel, diese Piedestale und Unformen in einer unabsehbaren Reihe, so wird man das unangenehme Gefühl mit empfinden das einen jeden überfallen muß, wenn er durch diese Spitzruten des Wahnsinns durchgejagt wird. (*IR,* 263)

Goethe's remarks clearly inform the *Taugenichts.* Perhaps Eichendorff intentionally pokes fun at Goethe's typically neoclassical rejection of the palace of Palagonia. Lacking the necessary artistic education and vocabulary to critique the castle in an erudite fashion, the Taugenichts relies solely on his instinct and gut feeling. Upon arrival his initial reaction is one of discomfort: "es war mir eigentlich recht unheimlich zu Mute" (*ALT,* 509). His underlying malaise, although at times off set by the excessive pampering, prevails, culminating finally in his dramatic escape. The Taugenichts concludes from his experiences in the strange castle: "ich glaube die Leute in Italien sind alle verrückt" (*ALT,* 511), whereas Goethe presents the creator of the palace near Palermo as an exception, an aberration, a non-artist. Although Goethe states that the best and worst examples of art must be comprehended within the larger historical context, he singles out the Prince of Palagonia: "man erzeigt ihm viel zu viel Ehre wenn man ihm nur einen Funken Einbildungskraft zuschreibt" (*IR*, 261). Eichendorff, it seems, chides Goethe for his restrained imagination.

Upon escaping from the bizarre mountaintop castle, the Taugenichts soon learns that he is but a few miles from the city of Rome. He does not seem surprised, as is the reader, that such foreboding mountains are in the vicinity of the major Italian destination of the eighteenth and early nineteenth centuries. The Taugenichts's initial reaction to the news that Rome is near recalls Goethe's own childhood memories of Italian fantasies; Eichendorff once again alludes to Werther lying in the grass:

> Da erschrak ich ordentlich vor Freude. Denn von dem prächtigen Rom hatte ich schon zu Hause als Kind viele wunderbare Geschichten gehört, und wenn ich dann an Sonntags-Nachmittagen vor der Mühle im Grase lag und alles ringsum so stille war, da dachte ich mir Rom wie die ziehenden Wolken über mir, mit wundersamen Bergen und Abgründen am blauen Meer, und goldnen Toren und hohen glänzenden Türmen, von denen Engel in goldenen Gewändern sangen. (*ALT*, 521)

But from whom did the Taugenichts hear these stories? Surely not from his father, the miller. The Taugenichts has heard not only such enchanting legends, but also frightening ones. Approaching Rome he recalls:

> Sie sagen, daß hier eine uralte Stadt und die Frau Venus begraben liegt, und die alten Heiden zuweilen noch aus ihren Gräbern heraufsteigen und bei stiller Nacht über die Heide gehn und die Wanderer verwirren. Aber ich ging immer grade fort und ließ mich nichts anfechten. (*ALT*, 522)

Interestingly, Goethe, too, approaches Rome with some trepidation as the weighty tradition of the classical past itself poses the greatest danger:

> Mit dem was man klassischen Boden nennt, hat es eine andere Bewandnis. Wenn man hier nicht fantastisch verfährt, sondern die Gegend real nimmt, wie sie daliegt, so ist sie doch immer der entscheidene Schauplatz, der die größten Taten bedingt, und so habe ich immer bisher den geologischen und landschaftlichen Blick benutzt, um Einbildungskraft und Empfindung zu unterdrücken, und mir ein freies klares Anschauen der Lokalität zu erhalten. Da schließt sich denn auf eine wundersame Weise die Geschichte lebendig an, und man begreift nicht

wie einem geschieht, und ich fühle die größte Sehnsucht den Tacitus in Rom zu lesen. (*IR*, 130–31)

Here the poet represses the imposing power of the imagination, the same fantasy that the Romantics privileged above all else. Goethe and the Taugenichts will meet vastly different fates in Rome. Although coincidence dictates the majority of the Taugenichts's decisions, Eichendorff's authorial motivations are of course deliberate. In this way it is striking that the Taugenichts's Roman adventures primarily concern the visual arts.[33] Shortly upon entering the city, he encounters two contrasting influences, the white-clad figure and the young German painter. The protagonist will continually search for and ultimately misunderstand the elusive *weiße Gestalt*, and the German painter living in Rome assumes the role of mentor and guide.

This nameless painter parallels in part Tischbein's role in Goethe's Italian stay. It is Tischbein who protects Goethe's incognito and offers him a place to stay. In addition, Tischbein accompanies Goethe to Naples and is responsible for introducing him to the many prominent German artists in Rome. Most importantly, the painter created the most recognized visual depiction of Goethe; Eichendorff's young German painter adds the Taugenichts to a religious canvas, specifically to immortalize him:

> "Siehst du," sagte der Maler, "dem einen Hirtenknaben da will ich deinen Kopf aufsetzen, so kommt dein Gesicht doch auch etwas unter die Leute, und will's Gott, sollen sie sich daran noch erfreuen, wenn wir beide schon lange begraben sind und selbst so still und fröhlich vor der heiligen Mutter und ihrem Sohn knien, wie die glücklichen Jungen hier." (*ALT*, 527)

Of course, the Taugenichts will outdo the painter by ensuring his own legacy in his autobiography. Eichendorff further parodies Goethe's own involvement with the German painters and serious contemplations of the arts in Rome as he describes the Taugenichts's great impatience in sitting for his portrait. Unable to take his role seriously, he makes faces in the mirror to fight his boredom. Ultimately, the Taugenichts is dispensable; nothing would prevent the portraitist from replacing his likeness with another. Knut Rybka reads Eichendorff's description of the Madonna as a direct response to Goethe's description of Tischbein's portrait of him in the Campagna. As the painting was not on public display until the mid-nineteenth century, Eichendorff knew of it only indirectly, specifically through Goethe's own account of it of 29 December 1786 in the *Italienische Reise*. Rybka draws a number of interesting parallels, both credible and dubious:

> An die Stelle Goethes als der Hauptfigur in der Mitte einer Landschaft mit den Spuren antiker Großbauten träte Taugenichts als Nebenfigur am Rande einer Hütte mit der heiligen Mutter und ihrem Kind; aus der präsentablen Leinwand wird notdürftiges Papier; Goethe und Tischbein leben im Rome ganz komfortabel, sie haben aber eine ästhetische Beziehung zu den Ruinen der Vergangenheit, während für Taugenichts und den römischen Maler Ruin und Ruinertes reale Gegenwart sind: und so lagert denn Goethe im Bild auf einem umgestürzten Obelisken, während Taugenichts vor dem Bild auf einem zerbrochenen Stuhl sitzt . . .; für Tischbein ist es ehrenvoll gewesen, den berühmten Goethe zu malen, während es für Taugenichts ehrenvoll ist, von einem richtigen Maler gemalt zu werden. . . . Und muß es, bei so viel Umkehrung, nicht unvermeidlich, da Goethe von einem gewissen *Tischbein* gemalt wird, die *Stuhllehne* sein, die zerbricht?[34]

Because the painting had not yet assumed its cultural impact at the time of Eichendorff's writing, it is doubtful that he invested it with such conscious and detailed citation.

This Madonna is strikingly reminiscent of the Nazarene style and serves as Eichendorff's contribution to the debate that ensued with Meyer's essay in *Kunst und Altertum*. In addition, the other painting described at the close of the seventh chapter, in which the Taugenichts believes to have discovered his *schöne gnädige Frau,* certainly recalls Overbeck's *Italia und Germania*. Although that painting was not completed until 1828, two years after the publication of *Aus dem Leben eines Taugenichts,* an earlier study was finished as early as 1811. Despite Eichendorff's earlier friendship with Philipp Veit, it is unlikely that he knew of Overbeck's plans. Rather this portion of the text is evidence of the currents afoot within cultural discourse. In fact, the Taugenichts's beloved recalls features of both the figures of Italia and Germania:

> sie stand in einem schwarzen Samt-Kleide im Garten, und hob mit der einen Hand den Schleier vom Gesicht und sah still und freundlich in eine weite prächtige Gegend hinaus. (*ALT,* 528)

The Taugenichts finds only the illusion of his love within the painting and in Italy.

Eichendorff's second veiled excursus on the visual arts within *Aus dem Leben eines Taugenichts* confronts the illusion of artistic representation and deals with the staging of *tableaux vivants,* again reminiscent of Goethe's *Italienische Reise* and the much-enjoyed, contemporary pas-

time. In addition, Eichendorff confounds the contemporary debate on
the visual by establishing a contest between "ut pictura poesis" and "ut
musica poesis." In Eichendorff's case, the constructed *tableau* is nearly
interrupted as the Taugenichts and the painter enter the country garden to find the musical performance of two young women, one singing
and one playing the guitar, under the direction of a man. The reader is
unaware that they are performing a living picture until the *tableau* is
actually interrupted by a squabbling young couple. The ensuing encounter reveals that the musicians were animating a painting by Johann
Erdmann Hummel, titled *Gesellschaft in einer italienischen Locanda
[die Fermata]* (Gathering at an Italian Inn [the Fermata]), which had
been exhibited in Berlin in 1814. The otherwise unremarkable painting
achieved its notoriety through a short story by E. T. A. Hoffmann, in
which it plays a great role: *Die Fermata* of 1816. Eichendorff was among
Hoffmann's audience on 4 February 1815 when the author read aloud
from it for friends,[35] although his lack of firsthand knowledge of the
painting has been documented. Eichendorff's descriptions stem solely
from Hoffmann's own.[36] Eichendorff reverses Hoffmann's use of the
visual arts in that he paints fictitious works into his narratives. Whereas
Goethe's generation saw this form of entertainment as a homage to the
forms of classical art, if not always great art in and of itself, Eichendorff
pokes fun at the artificiality of such *tableaux*. The illusion never attains
complete credibility and is consistently threatened with interruption.
Even the idyllic landscape, removed from the confusion of the city,
cannot protect the staging of the *tableau*. The chambermaid reveals the
greatest surprise: the ultimate disruption of the *tableau* was itself choreographed, staged solely to transmit a message to the Taugenichts. In
this way a previously privileged artistic situation is exploited to accommodate satire.[37]

The remainder of the Taugenichts's Roman experiences entails un-
raveling the mysterious identity of the white figure and the location of
his beloved lady. Rome, in whose prospects the Taugenichts initially so
greatly rejoiced, will prove to be a great disappointment, hardly indis-
tinguishable from the earlier confusions and misunderstandings of his
Italian journey. Upon learning that his countess has long since returned
to Vienna, he unequivocally decides to follow her and reveals that he
has been in Rome only two days: his brief encounters with the arts
contrast sharply to those savored by Goethe over a much longer period.
The Taugenichts declares:

Die Wasserkunst, die mir vorhin im Mondschein so lustig flimmerte, als wenn Englein darin auf und nieder stiegen, rauschte noch fort wie damals, mir aber war unterdes alles Lust und Freude in den Brunn gefallen. — Ich nahm mir nun fest vor, dem falschen Italien mit seinen verrückten Malern, Pomeranzen und Kammerjungfern auf ewig den Rücken zu kehren, und wanderte noch zur selbigen Stunde zum Tore hinaus. (*ALT,* 541)

In the traveler's mind, all things associated with Italy are now contained within the city of Rome, even German painters and the Viennese chambermaids.

In contrast to the striking absence of Goethe's journey home in his narrative, the return trip to Vienna plays an important role in Eichendorff's tale. Along the way he encounters a trio of traveling musicians from Prague as well as a number of other colorful characters. It so happens that everyone has heard of him, and as they speculate over the personal qualities of the future groom, they begin to reveal his destiny. He chooses though to return to Vienna under the wraps of an incognito.

Also significant on his return trip is Eichendorff's rare reference to a historical fact. In order to choose a route north, the traveling musicians refer to an old, torn map of the Old German Empire:

[er] zog endlich unter allerlei Plunder eine alte zerfetzte Landkarte hervor, worauf noch der Kaiser in vollem Ornate zu sehen war, das Zepter in der rechten, den Reichsapfel in der linken Hand. (*ALT,* 543)

The narrator's description of the emperor and his symbols on the map are evidence of the map's antiquity. The apparent medieval facade of the action is called into question as the narrator hints that he is telling the story in a time after the demise of the empire. This political statement, a nostalgia for an earlier, apparently more harmonious time, stands as a singular exception within Eichendorff's narrative. Surprisingly, however, unlike his chaotic and aimless trip south, the Taugenichts's return to Vienna, even with such a dubious map, is relatively uncomplicated: he is guided by others and, more importantly, by the secure knowledge that the countess awaits him there.

Only the palace garden in Vienna can serve as the setting of ultimate clarification; ironically, it is the location in which the confusion originated. Because Italy was not a seriously chosen goal, the process of travel can not lead to self-development: what the Taugenichts lived instead was a long-distance race, overcoming hurdle after hurdle. The final and perhaps greatest irony resides in the Taugenichts's decision to take his bride, not a countess after all, to Italy after their impending nuptials:

> "... gleich nach der Trauung reisen wir fort nach Italien, nach Rom, da gehn die schönen Wasserkünste, und nehmen die Prager Studenten mit und den Portier!" (*ALT,* 561)

For the hero recalls the fountains of Rome, but discounts all unpleasantness experienced in Italy. Analogous to the final gesture of *Das Marmorbild,* the Taugenichts can only now fully appreciate Italy; however, by the 1820s Eichendorff associates Italian travel with such banal sights as the Roman fountains. The age of tourism has begun.

Curiously, Detlev Schumann fails to mention *Aus dem Leben eines Taugenichts* even in passing. Instead he concentrates primarily on the early novel, *Ahnung und Gegenwart,* as a response to *Wilhelm Meisters Lehrjahre* and *Faust, Part I,* in addition to selected remarks concerning Goethe's work culled from Eichendorff's large body of literary-historical writings. He contends that Eichendorff struggled throughout his long career with the omnipresence of Goethe and concludes that this strong influence resulted in a sustained and markedly ambivalent stance vis-à-vis the older poet.[38] *Aus dem Leben eines Taugenichts* is certainly not the product of a writer terribly intimidated by Goethe's presence and stature in German literary circles. Eichendorff's reception of Goethe is perhaps best described as a case of influence without anxiety, no doubt a result of the younger poet's unwavering religious faith. Schumann's study did much to prompt Knut Rybka's book-length investigation of the relationship of *Aus dem Leben eines Taugenichts* to Goethe.[39]

Rybka posits that the implied traveler in Goethe's *Italienische Reise* is Werther, an original, though unconvincing, thesis in the end. Rybka suggests that the publication of a new edition of *Die Leiden des jungen Werthers* in 1824, on the occasion of the novel's fiftieth anniversary, may have prompted Eichendorff to reread and reconsider the work. The gesture of equating Werther with the traveler reconciles for Rybka the conflicting angles of desperate flight and deliberate self-education found within the *Italienische Reise:*

> Goethe sieht sich über mehrere Stationen seiner Reise von Werther verfolgt, und erst nach der sizilianischen Offenbarung vermag er sich umzuwenden und den endlich entmythologisierten Werther an sich heranzulassen.[40]

A number of points disprove Rybka's claims. As Rybka correctly states, there are only four references to Werther within the entire text of the *Italienische Reise,* and in them Goethe does express his frustration at being repeatedly associated with his early novel. It is certainly more a case of being shadowed or haunted by the reputation of Werther than consciously identifying with the figure. In addition, Rybka barely addresses the importance of the three decades between Goethe's journey and his composition of the text. There are a multitude of differences between the actual journey and the poet's representation of it. By 1816 Goethe was certainly recognized as the author of much more than just *Werther*. If one argues that Goethe finally overcame the ghost of Werther in Sicily, then one can argue equally, if not more persuasively, that it is in Sicily that Goethe overcame the often stifling influence of his father and the majority of German travelers to Italy before him who traveled only as far south as Naples. Curiously, Rybka fails to mention the early version of the second *Römische Elegie*, which Goethe later revised for publication. In it, the British traveler, continually haunted by the song of Marlborough wherever he goes, suffers a fate not unlike that of the traveling Goethe, who is identified solely as the author of *Werther*. In the poem Goethe stresses the futility of equating the author with his creation.

Most significantly, Rybka fails to acknowledge the extent to which Goethe himself participated in the tradition of a highly charged German predilection for Italy: he argues that Eichendorff borrowed his Italian cliché, as represented in the ideas of the porter, directly from Goethe. The rather generic components of this cliché, including lemons, oranges, and sunshine, are the prevalent images in Mignon's song, themselves derivative of the long tradition. Certainly, Goethe informs much of Eichendorff's narrative; however Rybka minimizes, if not ignores, the extent to which Goethe codified much of what was already part of a cultural public domain. For his own response to Italy was as much a response to expectations and preconceived notions as it was to the actual sights and sounds around him. It is enough to view these two pivotal texts in the context of the ongoing debate on Romanticism without equating both Eichendorff's and Goethe's travelers as Werther.

A discussion of Eichendorff's use of Italy and its relationship to other German conceptions of Italy, most notably to Goethe's, would not be complete without mentioning Eichendorff's "Auch ich war in Arkadien!" a short, satirical prose piece published posthumously by the author's son Hermann in 1866. Although Eichendorff alludes to Goethe's *Italienische Reise* and to the genre of the *Reisebericht*, it was his son's choice of title for the previously unpublished and untitled piece that nearly overemphasizes the place of Goethe in this short text. The elder Eichendorff's intent in "Auch ich war in Arkadien!" is clearly to parody the liberal political opposition in Germany in the early 1830s as specifically represented by the Hambacher Festival of late May 1832, in which approximately 30,000 participants (among them many so-called southwestern Democrats) called for sovereignty of the people and increased individual freedoms. Eichendorff remained a strict conservative both individually and of course within his service to the Prussian government. Eichendorff closes the satire with the allusion to the Latin "Et in arcadia ego," Goethe's motto for the *Italienische Reise*. Eichendorff's narrator questions what he has just reported, which he claimed earlier to have experienced firsthand:

> Und in der Tat, da ich's jetzt recht betrachte, ich weiß nicht, ob nicht am Ende alles bloß ein Traum war, der mir, wie eine Fata Morgana, die duftigen Küsten jenes volkersehnten Eldorados vorgespiegelt. Dem aber sei nun wie ihm wolle, genug: auch ich war in Arkadien![41]

As editor, Hermann von Eichendorff also omitted the first three paragraphs of his father's manuscript from its first publication. In this brief introduction, the senior Eichendorff immediately announces his intention to write a *Reisebericht*. However, the nature of his journey will call into question that literary form, which, in spite of its rich tradition, had been left virtually untouched by the German Romantics:

> Da säß' ich denn glücklich wieder hinter meinem Pulte, um dir meinen Reisebericht abzustatten. Es ist mir aber auf dieser Reise so viel wunderliches begegnet, daß ich in der Tat nicht recht weiß, wo ich anfangen soll. Am besten, ich hebe, wie die Rosine aus dem Kuchen, ohne weiteres sogleich das Hauptabenteuer für dich aus. (*A*, 85)

The circumstances of his particular journey to a place that remains unnamed throughout the text far exceed the boundaries of such a confining model. In the next paragraph the first-person narrator continues to parody the nonfiction travel report; he had recently lived like a hermit and then prepared to set out on his journey, dressed in Nazarene style, complete with a Dürer hair style and a special traveling suit. He refers to the *Postwagen*, the traditional mode of transportation, as the "fliegende Universität" (*A*, 85). He soon discovers that his entire conception of life and travel is utterly outdated: "ich [könnte] mit eben so viel Erstaunen als Beschämung gewahr werden, wie weit ich in der Kultur zurück war" (*A*, 85). Both the late eighteenth-century tradition and the Romantic rehabilitation of the wandering journeyman are called into question in the face of political turmoil. The editorial gestures of Hermann von Eichendorff deleted these colorful remarks and completely altered the parodic tone of this political text. Eichendorff's opposition to the liberal political movements in Germany clearly defines "Auch ich war in Arkadien!" The satirical gestures aimed at the privileged status of idealized travel reportage occupied a secondary role in his agenda, but nonetheless link his text in both spirit and form to his *Taugenichts*.

One important question remains: why did Eichendorff return in 1834 to the relatively tame and benign portrayals of Italy in the poems "Rückkehr" and "Sehnsucht" eight years after the publication of *Aus dem Leben eines Taugenichts* and fifteen years after the first appearance of *Das Marmorbild*? Eichendorff continually dismissed in his prose, and again in his poetry, the quest for an authentic Italy, a goal that so preoccupied Goethe in the *Italienische Reise*. In his *Römische Elegien* Goethe created the Italy he sensed his audience expected, and only thirty years after his original journey did he begin to discuss the Italy he believed to have discovered. In their poetry both Eichendorff and Goethe emphasize the "alte Wundergeschichten," albeit derived from two different historical periods. In Eichendorff's later poetic gestures, Germany takes center stage as the authentic object of desire. This is possible only after he has cast out the demons from Italy and demythologized the cultural metaphor of Italy.

Goethe presents within his *Italienische Reise* his search for self-identity and awareness after a period of crisis in his life; in contrast, Eichendorff describes in *Aus dem Leben eines Taugenichts* a process of continued self-delusion and confusion: in short, a loss of self through travel. Self-representation itself, for example in the form of an autobiography, is jeopardized, not to mention the possibility of self-awareness. In his parody of autobiography, Eichendorff succeeds in subverting the predominate paradigm of travel and self-creation into a sort of anti-travel: the Taugenichts does not perceive his journey as a vehicle for *Selbstbildung*.

This new concept could perhaps be defined as an early incarnation of tourism. Hans Magnus Enzensberger locates the roots of modern tourism in the European Romantic movement. Derived from the English, the German "Touristen," according to Enzensberger, made its first appearance in dictionaries in the year 1800 and "Tourismus" in 1811. The author stresses the underlying motivation in leisure travel to this day as the sentimental longing for a far-away place:

> Diese Wurzeln lagen in der englischen, französischen und deutschen Romantik. Autoren wie Gray und Wordsworth, Colderidge und Byron, Rousseau und Chateaubriand; Seume und Eichendorff, Tieck und Wackenroder, Chamisso und Pückler haben die Freiheit, die unter der

Wirklichkeit der beginnenden Arbeitswelt und an der politischen Restauration zu ersticken drohte, im Bilde festgehalten. Ihre Einbildungskraft hat die Revolution gleichzeitig verraten und aufbewahrt. Sie
verklärte die Freiheit und entrückte sie in die Ferne die Imagination, bis
sie räumlich zum Bilde der zivilisationsfernen Natur, zeitlich zum Bilde
der vergangenen Geschichte, zu Denkmal und Folklore gerann. Dies,
die unberührte Landschaft und die unberührte Geschichte, sind die
Leitbilder des Tourismus bis heute geblieben. Er ist nichts anderes als
der Versuch, den in die Ferne projizierten Wunschtraum der Romantik
leibhaftig zu verwirklichen. Je mehr sich die bürgerliche Gesellschaft
schloß, desto angestrengter versuchte der Bürger, ihr als Tourist zu
entkommen.[42]

Crucially, Eichendorff, a man who experienced only limited and cur-
tailed journeys, is included among inveterate travelers like Byron. The
distinction between the listed authors as authentic or imaginary travelers is irrelevant to Enzensberger's argument. His association of Eichendorff with Romantic *Sehnsucht* is certainly accurate; however, with this
in mind, a pointed irony resides in the fact that, for Eichendorff's tourists, travel remains a persistent and often dangerous, frightening struggle for identity, the goal of which is simply to return home.

While it is customary to associate Eichendorff with the topos of
Romantic *Sehnsucht,* his ironic tendency is often overlooked. Eichendorff's strategy of rejecting travel as a mode of self-styled education anticipates the publication of the first modern travel guidebooks in the
1830s by John Murray in England and Karl Baedeker in Germany.
Their advent signals the end of the grand, poetic travel report; henceforth, only the most necessary information will be distilled into a single,
pocket-sized volume. If only the Taugenichts had a guidebook; maybe
then he would know in which direction Italy lies.

Figure 3. Il Trionfo di Venezia *(The Triumph of Venice, 1579–1582) by Paolo Veronese. Sala della Consiglio Maggiore, Palazzo Ducale, Venice. Photograph © CAMERAPHOTO-Arte, Venezia.*

5: Platen's *Sonette aus Venedig* and the Post-Romantic Aestheticization of Italy

OF ALL THE ITALIAN DESTINATIONS sought out by foreign travelers, Venice took on an increasingly unique status throughout the course of the nineteenth century. Easily accessible to travelers in the 1820s, but unlike a growing number of other Italian destinations, Venice maintained an exceptionally exotic air. Its long maritime history and earlier links to Byzantium lent the city strong oriental connotations. It gradually became the prevalent symbol of an irretrievable, yet recent European past, one not easily forgotten.[1] In 1797, as part of the Treaty of Campo Formio, Napoleon offered Venice to Austria in exchange for any claim to Belgium; thus came the end of the 1100-year tradition of the Doges' rule.[2] Goethe's generation was the last to witness its republican glory; post-Napoleonic visitors flocked to Venice in search of hints of her former greatness. In place of the Roman ruins of the South, Venice sheltered gems of Byzantine and Renaissance art and architecture, and the still recent memory of a free political system. The republic's demise ensured its longevity as a haven for the imagination.[3] Byron acknowledges the literary transmission of the city's image in *Childe Harold's Pilgrimage,* published in 1818:

> I lov'd her from my boyhood — she to me
> Was as a fairy city of the heart,
> Rising like water-columns from the sea,
> Of joy the sojourn, and of wealth the mart;
> And Otway, Radcliffe, Schiller, Shakespeare's art,
> Had stamp'd her image in me, and even so,
> Although I found her thus, we did not part,
> Perchance even dearer in her day of woe,
> Than when she was a boast, a marvel, and a show.[4]

Byron establishes the dichotomies of past and present; glory and decay; and fantasy and reality, all of which find expression in the European discourse on Venice throughout the ensuing century. This fractured image of the city precedes Platen's *Sonette aus Venedig* by a mere six years. As lengthier travel to Italy resumed, geographic specificity regained its pre-Romantic import. The city's status as a literary object would reach its culmination at the turn of the twentieth century. Much of the German fascination with Venice experienced around 1900 is the direct legacy of Platen.

Simply in terms of the length of time spent in Italy, August Graf von Platen-Hallermünde had a much longer, more permanent and direct relationship with Italy than did Goethe, Eichendorff, or Heine. His Italian experiences are best divided into two distinct periods. His initial encounter with Italy, during the fall of 1824, was that of traveler and aspiring German poet. Less than two years later, Platen returned to Italy where, with the exception of a few brief visits home, he led a peripatetic existence for the final decade of his life. Notwithstanding the poetic product of that first journey to Italy, the *Sonette aus Venedig,* published in 1825, Platen's works are largely forgotten.[5] Instead the poet is more widely known for the dubious distinction of having been Heine's challenger, adversary, and victim in perhaps the most notorious of all German literary scandals.

Platen's *Sonette aus Venedig,* acknowledged to be among the finest in the German language, are particularly relevant to a study of German figurations of Italy: the sonnets and their unified presentation immediately bring to mind Goethe's two Italian poetic cycles. Although Platen's relocation to Italy in 1826 resulted in a large number of poems and other related works, I am most concerned with his more limited Venetian stay of 1824 as a traveler and his response to Goethe. I will refer to his later Italian experiences only marginally.[6]

Platen's life story is both strange and pathetic, at all times full of contradiction. A Protestant of northern German descent, he spent most of his life in the staunchly Roman Catholic kingdom of Bavaria and later in Italy. Although of aristocratic lineage, Platen's branch of the family had long since lost its privileged position. His youth and young adulthood are characterized by indecision and unhappiness. After receiving his early schooling in a military academy, Platen entered the service of the Bavarian court as a page. In 1814 at the age of eighteen he had the choice of continued military service or a university education, either option to be funded by the Bavarian court: Platen choose the first, an unlikely decision in light of Platen's biography.[7] In 1818 Platen received authorized military leave and a scholarship for a three-year course of university study, which he began in Würzburg. In another misguided decision, Platen switched from law to the diplomatic track in 1820. By this time he found himself in Erlangen, and only the continued intervention of such influential people as Schelling assured

Platen of repeated extensions of his military sabbatical. The early 1820s brought his first publications as well as the study of orientalism, which led to his experimentation with the poetic form of the ghazal. Platen's early travels took him to Vienna and Prague; in 1821 he visited Jakob Grimm in Kassel and Goethe in Jena.[8] His adolescence and young adulthood were equally plagued by his own confusion about and denial of his sexual identity. His diaries and correspondence recount an ongoing series of abrupt terminations of close male friendships as well as what emerges to be a pattern of blatant lack of self-knowledge and insight.

Platen's continued devotion to literature and language is much the antithesis of the indecision and repression prevalent in other areas of his life. His lack of financial stability and independence initially precluded full-time devotion to his writing. Interestingly, Platen's poetic career is characterized by a strong attraction to generic forms, structure, and meter; such choices may be reflective of his strict military upbringing, but are clearly consistent with conservative anti-Romantic trends. In addition, Platen has been a difficult figure to situate in the more traditional spectrum of literary history. A self-appointed heir to Goethe's poetic mantle, he found himself out of sync with a generation dominated by the Romantics; Platen's fixation on structural forms lends an air of pedantry and overshadows any imaginative streak. The Romantics favored generally freer and more emotional styles. Goethe and Schiller appropriated even more complicated forms, for example, the elegy, in which they endeavored to assume the spirit, but not always the strict metrical structure of a classical form. In contrast to both extremes, Platen felt most at home within more constrained poetic borders.

Platen's choice of the sonnet form as an expression of his initial Italian experience is interesting in multiple registers. Limited in length, the sonnet is among the strictest of poetic forms, adhering to both a formal rhyme scheme and rigid interior structure. Seventeenth-century German Baroque poets first granted the sonnet a privileged status. After falling into near obscurity in the eighteenth century, the sonnet was reintroduced by the Romantics, most notably August Wilhelm Schlegel. Despite his friendship with Schlegel, Platen's interest in the sonnet was quite different than that of the Romantics:

> [Platens] spätere "Bekehrung' zum Sonett war dennoch alles andere als eine Bekehrung zur Romantik: Sie muß vielmehr im Gegenteil als der Versuch gedeutet werden, den Romantikern diese 'plastische' Form definitiv zu entreißen. . . . Platens eigene Sonette sind denn auch nicht romantisch verklingend, sondern prägnant profiliert, er hat der Romantik das Genre tatsächlich "weggenommen.".[9]

Despite his interest in Shakespeare's sonnets, which he read in the early 1820s, Platen shares the German preference for the Petrarchan model. In fact, all of his sonnets are Petrarchan; even his sonnet on Shakespeare disavows the use of rhymed couplets (*P*, 370–71). When considering Platen's choice of the form for his Venetian renderings, the depth of the German fixation on the Italian Renaissance is evident. His preoccupation with Renaissance Venetian painting achieves a contextual symmetry with the early Renaissance poetic model of Petrarch. In addition, the subject matter of Petrarchism also echoes in Platen's career-long obsession with the theme of unrequited love.

I maintain that Platen also selected the sonnet for his discussion of Venice precisely because it is a model not readily associated with Goethe. Goethe, well-versed in Italian literature and familiar with the sonnet, was hardly inclined to experiment with the form until the publication of A. W. Schlegel's *Gedichte* in 1800. The Goethe-Schlegel correspondence includes much debate on the form and the German language's suitability for it. As a result of this interaction with Schlegel, the Weimar poet did experiment to a limited extent with this poetic form. His 1807 metasonnet, "Das Sonett," ends with the confession:

> Nur weiß ich hier mich nicht bequem zu betten,
> Ich schneide sonst so gern aus ganzem Holze,
> Und müßte nun doch auch mitunter leimen.[10]

Goethe admits he has succumbed to pressure to keep up with new literary fashions, but acknowledges his discomfort with what he perceives to be the narrow bounds of the genre. In fact, he seems rather perturbed to be writing sonnets, implying that they are somehow not as complete or worthy as some other poetic forms.[11]

Platen's rejection of the more prevalent literary conventions of the early nineteenth century led to frequent criticism of the impersonality and restraint of his work. Such ambivalence vis-à-vis Platen's poetry has its roots in the comments of his contemporary critics. Eckermann wrote a review of the *Neue Ghaselen* at Goethe's request in 1823, describing Platen's work as follows:

> Innigen Antheil heischen sie nie; auch das leidenschaftliche Gefühl berührt uns nur leicht, denn der Alles verkühlende und im Gleichen haltende Geist und gute Laune sind immer zu handen.[12]

Jakob Grimm appraised Platen's work in relation to other German work, singling out his rhymes, constructed much less carelessly and freely than some of Schiller's and even Goethe's. He finds Platen's use of language purer than that of his contemporary, Rückert, but concludes in words that would long be associated with Platen: "Dagegen scheint mir Platen hin und wieder an das Kalte und Marmorne zu streifen."[13] The emotionless connotations implicit in the ultimate metaphor of marble overshadow his generally positive review. Grimm's evaluation continued to inform the opinions of readers throughout the nineteenth century. Goethe provided the other now infamous and influential comment concerning Platen's poetry. As Eckermann reports on 25 December 1825:

> Es ist nicht zu leugnen, sagte Goethe, er besitzt manche glänzende Eigenschaften; allein ihm fehlt — *die Liebe.* Er liebt so wenig seine Leser und seine Mit-Poeten als sich selber. . . . Noch in diesen Tagen habe ich Gedichte von * * * gelesen und sein reiches Talent nicht verkennen können. Allein, wie gesagt, die Liebe fehlt ihm, und so wird er auch nie so wirken, als er hätte müssen. Man wird ihn fürchten, und er wird der Gott derer sein, die gern wie er negativ wären, aber nicht wie er das Talent haben.[14]

It is easy to imagine the depth of hurt the insecure Platen must have felt at reading these remarks.

Although Platen did not achieve the kind of fame he had longed for during his lifetime, his work gained admiration as the century progressed and then witnessed a true resurgence at the turn-of-the-century with poets and critics alike. His attention to aesthetic form and the poetry on cities, especially Venice, had a great influence on Rilke among others. Readers found an affinity between such writers as Stefan George and Platen. An active Platen-Gesellschaft flourished from 1925 to 1933, and in 1930 Thomas Mann offered the society his own passionate defense of the poet in a speech ("August von Platen") in which he challenged Goethe's infamous remarks. Mann argues for a passion discernible in Platen's work despite the poet's lack of self-knowledge. He situates Platen in the tradition of unhappy knights with a homosexual affinity, including Tristan and Don Quixote, and concludes that Platen's antipathy is a direct result of the experience of being the object of so much hatred.[15]

Notwithstanding a relatively small number of articles concerning Platen and his work published during the 1960s, postwar interest in the poet did not accelerate until the 1970s. This modern scholarship, at first preoccupied with restorative attempts to situate his poetic oeuvre within the standard categories assigned to the nineteenth century, is now strongly concerned with the implications of his sexual proclivities for an understanding of his work. At times these two currents overlap.

Heinrich Henel views Platen as a representative of the first post-classical generation, whose work is best understood as *Epigonenlyrik*. Platen was influenced neither by his own experience (*Erlebnisdichtung*) nor deep philosophical matters (*Gedankenlyrik*), he lived too early in the nineteenth century to be either a realist or a symbolist.[16] He is concerned not only to situate himself in the tradition of fine German poets, but also to join their most elite ranks. Henel understands Platen as representative of his generation and the poet's dilemma as a direct result of the ongoing dichotomy between Romantic and Classical (261), a struggle, which I have shown to be embodied in the concurrently divergent German representations of Italy, found in the first quarter of the nineteenth century. Although Henel deals at length with Goethe's own contemplations on the subject of influence and imitation, he does not delve into the possible relationship between Platen's *Sonette aus Venedig* and Goethe's works on Italy.[17]

Jürgen Link interprets Platen's pattern of rejection of and experimentation with genre as the poet's ongoing strategy to invest aesthetic forms with meaning as a distraction from or a replacement for his increasingly pessimistic outlook. In contrast to the many critics who view Platen's ongoing preoccupation with form as merely a technical exercise devoid of deeper intellectual insight, Link situates Platen as a forerunner of Baudelaire, Mallarmé, and Valéry.[18]

Friedrich Sengle's chapter on Platen in his three-volume study of the *Biedermeierzeit* remains an invaluable resource. He argues that the key to understanding Platen lies in the era in which he lived: the Restoration. Platen and all the details of his life, including his sexual preference, intense self-loathing, and vacillation between claims of greatness and utter lack of self-confidence, are fathomable only within the context of that historical epoch. Sengle convincingly demonstrates Platen's affinity with the German Baroque poets, who overwhelmingly preferred technique to content, favored conscious imitation of their forerunners, and studied the craft of poetry. The poet's predisposition to the *althumanistische Tradition*, and not to the highly privileged claims of originality, experience, and nature of the *Goethezeit*, is to be understood as a direct response to the environment of post-Napoleonic Europe.[19]

Link's resuscitative gesture is taken up in 1980 by Richard Dove in *The "Individualität" of August von Platen*, in which he sets out to defend Platen against charges of being an epigone interested only in formal structures and lacking imaginative creativity. Platen's desire for fame situates him in the company of Rousseau and Byron.[20] Dove concedes Platen's attention to form, restraint, and aesthetics, but upholds a reading that accommodates the often deeply veiled personal quality of the poems, albeit not in the sense of traditional *Erlebnislyrik* (122). He overlooks the excessive and pathetic musings that are prevalent in Platen's private correspondence and diaries, which also inform much of his literary oeuvre, and excuses the poet's tendency toward exaggeration, labeling it a rhetorical device necessary in his egotistical quest for fame (142). Instead Dove shifts the onus to understand upon Platen's unreceptive, callous audience.

Frank Busch compares Platen's homoerotic tendencies with those of Thomas Mann, stressing that although Platen was aware of his sexual preference, the society and historical epoch in which he lived denied him the vocabulary and freedom to express this directly. Paradoxically the "Gefühlskultur" of the 1820s was remarkably strict and intolerant.[21] Thus, Platen was repeatedly surprised and devastated at the rejection of men he had assumed to be his friends and the harsh reaction of many of his readers, including Heine. In the wake of the harsh reality of Heine's attack, Busch recognizes an evolution in Platen's poetry, away from the more biographically informed early works toward an increased sublimation in the later poems (15).

Further general studies of homosexuality and literature dealing with Germany or with the homosexual artist's attraction to the South almost always refer in some way, however limited, to the situation of August von Platen. Robert Aldrich correctly places Platen in the tradition of Winckelmann, underlining the dual attraction of Italy for a nineteenth-century writer in Platen's situation: the opportunity for the study of aesthetics and the possibility of a much freer homosexual lifestyle. Aldrich, who is not a Germanist, overlooks Platen's lifelong struggle for personal contentment, insinuating that he eventually overcame this in Italy. In a far more blatant misreading, Aldrich does not acknowledge the depth of Platen's own self-denial and lack of insight.[22] Paul Derks offers an extremely comprehensive view of the literary quarrel between Heine and Platen as well as the social, legal, and historical background of homosexuality in Europe (140–73).

Peter Bumm's biography of 1990 is perhaps the most important publication on Platen in recent memory and remains the only modern attempt at a comprehensive evaluation of the poet's life and work. Bumm offers an exhaustive biography that incorporates within its narrative of Platen's life interpretive readings of many of his works.[23] Bumm belongs to the prevalent school of readers who see the homosexual ori-

entation as the decisive factor in understanding Platen; he argues that
the poet's prolonged repression of his sexuality contributed only further to his inability to deal with the reality of everyday life (*PB,* 58).
Platen's work should indeed be read within the context of the South as
a place of exile for northern Europeans, among them a large number of
homosexuals. Remarkably, the secondary literature on Platen's *Sonette
aus Venedig* has, thus far, failed to address what I see as two major
points: Platen's conscious response to Goethe's *Römische Elegien* and
the narrative implications of Platen's own editorial revisions to his cycle
for its overall image of Italy.

Because Platen is no longer read and editions of his work are few, a
brief summary of the complicated and often ignored publication history
of the *Sonette aus Venedig* will be valuable. Most discussions of the
sonnets fail to acknowledge the different stages within the cycle's evolution (see appendix). The original self-published version of the *Sonette
aus Venedig* appeared in 1825 and contained sixteen sonnets. In 1828
Cotta published a cycle of fourteen sonnets as part of the collected *Gedichte.*[24] The same fourteen were selected by Platen for the second expanded edition of his *Gedichte,* published in 1834 by Cotta and
considered the *Ausgabe letzter Hand.* In 1839, four years after Platen's
death, Cotta published a one-volume edition of his collected works,
which remained in print throughout the nineteenth century. It restored
the three omitted sonnets, but tacked them rather haphazardly onto
the end of the grouping of fourteen. In 1910 the historical-critical edition of Platen's complete works in twelve volumes appeared, edited by
Max Koch and Erich Petzet. This edition's presentation of the *Sonette
aus Venedig* also includes all 17 sonnets; the editors returned the three
sonnets Platen omitted from the 1828 and 1834 publications to what
would have been their original positions in the set.[25] Henel's 1968 selection replicates Koch and Petzet's selection and order. The 1982 edition of Platen's poetry, edited by Link and Wölfel, presents the
fourteen sonnets as they appeared in *Gedichte* of 1834; however, the
three omitted sonnets are reprinted in a supplementary grouping of
sonnets later in the volume. These various editorial changes, on the
part of both Platen and his later 'editors, alter the overall impact, the
narrative effect, and the resulting reading of the *Sonette aus Venedig:*
surprisingly, this issue has not been adequately addressed in Platen
scholarship. These variant readings shape Platen's representation of Italy and his response to Goethe's multiple texts.

The 1910 critical edition of Platen's works printed the Venetian
sonnets with parallel excerpts from his diaries and correspondence as

footnotes. This is evidence of the unusual status of these poems within the Platen oeuvre and criticism; despite the fact that readers continually see the poet's eschewal of personal experience (like Goethe's *Erlebnislyrik*) in his work, these poems are repeatedly read as autobiographical. Angelika Corbineau-Hoffmann reads Platen's diary entries for Venice, originally conceived as a travel report for his parents, as the basis for the sonnet cycle:

> In atemloser Aktivität stellt sich ihr Verfasser als Idealfigur eines Bildungstouristen dar, der keine Kirche, kein Gemälde ausläßt, der manches mehrmals besichtigt und, bedingt durch seinen Übereifer, gelegentlich den Eindruck des Karikaturalen erweckt. [D]ieses Tagebuch [ist] kein persönliches Dokument . . . nur die lyrische Projektion des eigenen Gefühlsraumes auf den poetischen Ort Venedig gewinnt via fictionis eine gewisse Authentizität — genauer: erst Venedig ermöglicht diese Projektion; durch sie wird es zu einem poetischem Ort.[26]

Platen, who adhered to the habit of keeping a daily journal, often practiced various foreign languages within the pages of his diary; there are passages in English, French, and Portuguese; however, his entries from his 1824 visit to Venice are exclusively in German.[27]

Platen's own comments regarding the sonnets are enlightening and illuminate the status of personal experience within his program. He wrote in his diary on 10 October 1824:

> Heute habe ich die zwölf Sonette abgeschlossen, die das Leben Venedigs darstellen sollen. Sie können nur für diejenigen Interesse haben, die es gesehen haben. (*PT*, 707)

The poet's initial impulse is to distance himself from his work: in his opinion, the sonnets represent Venetian life, not necessarily the poet's life in Venice. In addition, Platen discounts the visual preference of the finished poems, acknowledging that his is not a detailed version. Instead, his work will interest only those who have already witnessed Venice with their own eyes. Perhaps autobiographical, in this instance, should be read as a sketch of emotional responses. Such a claim is substantiated by the dedication Platen penned for the initial publication of the *Sonette*:

> Dem deutschen Freunde, den die Sterne lenken
> Zu dieser Inselstadt vom Meer beschäumet,
> Sei dieses kleine Buch ein Angedenken,
> Wenn er am Ufer der Lagune säumet,
> Wenn Lieb und Kunst ihm schöne Stunden schenken,

122 ⛊ ITALY IN THE GERMAN LITERARY IMAGINATION

> Wenn er, gestreckt in einer Gondel, träumet;
> Und legt er's weg, so mag er leise sagen:
> Hier hat vor mir ein fühlend Herz geschlagen! (*P*, 861–62)

Platen acknowledges the large company of traveling German writers. His collection of poetic glimpses is proof of what he sees as his deeply emotional response to Venice; however, this is qualified, in both the above excerpt from the diary and this motto, by the insistence that his reader has either been or is in Italy in order to obtain fully the value of his work. The purely personal, although implied, is subordinate to the universal experience.

Platen's insistence upon a specific, predetermined response to a limited set of carefully screened attributes of Venice has done much to fuel the debate on whether the *Sonette aus Venedig* are anything more than a series of snapshots, a sort of lyrical travel guide. Bumm acknowledges this quality of Platen's work, citing the context in which he lived: "Reiseführer gehören zum Biedermeier wie der Weltschmerz und das Parapluie," but sees the *Sonette aus Venedig* as much more (*PB*, 353). Sengle, too, counters Platen's harshest critics with the charge that they are not familiar with even the most important of Biedermeier concepts. Only naive readers could fail to see the deeper meaning behind the many works of art and images associated with Venice; for Sengle, Platen is one of many poets of the time who integrated such aspects into their work (448).

The assumption that only the German traveler to Venice can truly understand the sonnets upholds the poet as a true representative of the Biedermeier age, the era of the early development of modern tourism; however, the literary critics cited fail to investigate this connection at length. Platen anticipates the first Baedeker guides, which will be published in the 1830s; but in sharp contrast to a writer like Eichendorff, who eschews mimetic representation of Italy altogether, Platen, in projecting his ideal reader, upholds the necessity of firsthand knowledge and experience. At a time when the appeal of the foreign had waned and travelers generally sought out the more familiar, Italy was not as exotic as it was at the time of the journey of Goethe's father's nearly one hundred years earlier. The Napoleonic Wars interrupted the flow of travelers around Europe. When the final defeat allowed for normalization, travelers not only encountered new political situations, but the younger generation had to reconcile their preconceived ideas about their destinations, mediated via works of art, travel reports, and the more general cultural environment, with the reality they discovered.

Chloe Chard describes how there was a tendency among early tourists in the nineteenth century to avoid danger: they employed this strategy to limit the shock of interaction with the other. Instead of seeking out volcanoes to scale, as did their eighteenth-century predecessors, these post-Revolution travelers preferred to limit their encounter with the sublime within controlled boundaries such as the visual arts.[28] Despite this change, sight does, however, remain the privileged sense of the traveler; this is especially the case in the modern tourist concepts of sightseeing, photography, and postcards, more aptly referred to as *Ansichtskarten* in German. One travels in order to collect experiences, views, memories, and even sonnets, as Platen's title implies.[29]

Platen departed from Munich for Venice on 21 August 1824 and arrived there on 8 September, where he would stay until 9 November. His late August departure for Italy calls to mind Goethe's own departure for Italy from Karlsbad on 3 September 1786. During the third week of his stay the poet confesses, in a tone remarkably reminiscent of Goethe in Naples:

> Ich befinde mich in einem sonderbaren Zustande, den ich nicht zu definieren weiß. Venedig zieht mich an, ja, es hat mich mein ganzes früheres Leben und Treiben vergessen lassen, so daß ich mich in einer Gegenwart ohne Vergangenheit befinde. (*PT*, 684, 25 September 1824)

As the sonnets reveal, his personal past is supplanted by Venice's. Platen consciously cloaks his fears of unfulfilled expectation with the narcotic effects of the city. These sentiments conform largely to the power invested in a journey to Italy and echo Goethe's own desire to leave difficulty behind in the hope of discovery.

In his diary, Platen followed the practice of detailing his reading habits and reviewing the works he read; his comments on the first volume of Goethe's *Italienische Reise* are revealing. Platen prefers this later installment to the earlier volumes of *Dichtung und Wahrheit:*

> Der Stil, über alle Beschreibung liebenswürdig und hinreißend, erinnert durch seine größere Einfachheit an die älteren und schöneren Zeiten des Dichters, da er noch nicht die Spuren der Ueberkunstelung trug. Man muß Goethen durchaus schätzen und liebgewinnen, wenn man das Buch liest, welche Empfindungen die früheren Teile nicht in mir rege machten. Man bemerkt, welchen Vorzug die allmähliche Selbstbiographie eines Tagebuchs vor einer in späteren Jahren aus kalten Erinnerungen hat. Das Buch ist keine Reisebeschreibung, vielmehr eine Beschreibung von den Eindrücken der Dinge auf den Verfasser. (*PT*, 699, 1 December 1816)

This analysis could easily describe Platen's own later purpose in the *So-nette aus Venedig*, although verse will replace prose. Oddly, he does not mention his own curiosity for Italy at this time.

Goethe introduces his epistolary entries on Venice with a prefatory passage that expresses his ecstatic enthusiasm upon arriving in Venice. This jubilation, I would argue, has as much to do with Italy in general as with Venice in specific. Venice is the first city of Italy he will visit; it is the first well-known, historically endowed destination reached, and the name Venice enjoyed the standing of near mythology in his father's reminiscences of the South. Consequently, the effect of his arrival in Venice is even grander than the description of his approach to Rome:

> So stand es denn im Buche des Schicksals auf meinem Blatte geschrieben, daß ich 1786 den acht und zwanzigsten September, Abends, nach unserer Uhr um fünfe, Venedig zum erstenmal, aus der Brenta in die Lagunen einfahrend, erblicken, und bald darauf diese wunderbare Inselstadt, diese Biberrepublik betreten und besuchen sollte. So ist denn auch, Gott sei Dank, Venedig mir kein bloßes Wort mehr, kein hohler Name, der mich so oft, mich den Todfeind von Wortschällen, geängstiget hat. (*IR*, 69)

It seems as though Goethe would agree with Platen's insistence on firsthand experience. He continues with a recollection of a model of a gondola his father brought back from his own voyage to Venice and reports on his accommodations and punctuates his preface with the following:

> So wohne ich und so werde ich eine Zeitlang bleiben, . . . bis ich mich am Bilde dieser Stadt satt gesehen habe. Die Einsamkeit nach der ich oft so sehnsuchtvoll geseufzt, kann ich nun recht genießen, denn nirgends fühlt man sich einsamer als im Gewimmel, wo man sich allen ganz unbekannt durchdrängt. In Venedig kennt mich vielleicht nur Ein Mensch, und er wird mir nicht gleich begegnen. (*IR*, 69)

The visual sense is privileged here as throughout the *Italienische Reise:* the poet describes the need to load his memory with sights and scenes as if fuel for his future thoughts. Goethe, having assumed an incognito, anticipates the continued positive potential of solitude and anonymity. These images strongly preoccupied Platen during his own Venetian stay as revealed in the *Sonette aus Venedig.*

On many levels Goethe's Venetian narrative is a microcosm of his entire stay in Italy. His reports from Venice foreshadow his many interests that will vie for his attention throughout the following twenty-two months. His first ever encounters with the sea spark his scientific curi-

osity; he visits the theater and opera; views paintings by Titian and
Veronese; but above all, Goethe seems captivated by the architecture,
particularly that of Palladio. The only thing missing from Venice is, of
course, the classical past, although a collection of copies of ancient
statuary elicits his interest. Impatience for the things Venice hints at
will lead the German poet away after just 18 days. In the end Venice is
less important for what it is than for what it designates, the beginning
of a journey, the initial phase of discovery.

Platen receives and reworks the poetic images of Italy and Venice
propagated by Goethe. His title, *Sonette aus Venedig,* lacks the integrated point of view claimed by Goethe in his choice of the *Römische
Elegien* and *Venezianische Epigramme* in which the adjectival use of the
city's name implies that the poems themselves will assume the characteristics of the setting. Goethe's titular stance of assimilation, whether
or not mirrored in the actual content of the cycles, stands in strong opposition to the sense of the *Sonette aus Venedig* as poems issued as an
outsider's views on the city.[30] Although a mere glance at the titles of
these three poetic cycles, all of which privilege a specific type of poetry
and an Italian city, would surely suggest a likely affinity between the
Sonette and the *Epigramme,* I recognize the strongest association at
work between Goethe's *Römische Elegien* and Platen's *Sonette aus Venedig.* The bold narrative stance and coherence of both cycles clearly
supports this claim. The *Römische Elegien,* although strongly influenced
by Goethe's own experiences in Italy and his new-found life in Weimar,
are clearly fictional. In much the same way, Platen's cycle projects narrative closure and can be read as informed autobiographical fiction.
Goethe's *Venezianische Epigramme,* in contrast to the others, tackle a
far broader range of issues, lack their overarching narrative unity and
positive imaging of Italy, and present a far more cantankerous, less enthusiastic traveler.

A reading of the *Sonette aus Venedig* as a whole privileges an underlying narrative structure and coherence to the cycle in order to situate
the poet's main concerns. I consider all sixteen of Platen's original sonnets as well as the variant readings created by the omission of the fifteenth and sixteenth sonnets and the addition of the seventeenth.
Surprisingly little critical attention has been focused on the unity of the
Sonette aus Venedig as a cycle of poems, a phenomenon that likely results from the prevalent critical view that promotes form and structure
over content in Platen's work. Jürgen Link follows such a line of argu-
mentation when he concludes that Platen's mastery of the sonnet form
in the *Sonette aus Venedig* was made possible by the lack of a personally

informed world in Platen's figuration of Venice. According to Link, the suppression of the personal thus resulted in an isomorphic relationship between the poetic structure and the city of Venice (165). Although Platen de-emphasizes the personal, especially through his own editorial decisions, his dualistic construction of Venice does indeed make room for the expression of the self, albeit within the confines of the poetic imagination. Corbineau-Hoffmann's recent discussion of Platen's cycle also underlines the subjectivity of Platen's poetic figuration of Venice. In contrast to Link's reference to the affinity between form and city, she accurately sees a connection between self and city (173). She posits a reading, albeit too brief, which identifies in the sonnets the elements of a traditional prose travel narrative (arrival, stay, and departure), but sees in the sonnets the "Verlauf und Vollzug eines innerem Vertraut-werdens mit der Stadt" (180)[31] that is absent from many touristic prose descriptions of Venice.

Both the *Römische Elegien* and the *Sonette aus Venedig* are autobiographical to the extent that each presents the experiences of a traveling German poet to an Italian city, a role assumed by both Goethe and Platen. In turn, each of these travelers reflects upon his craft while abroad; they consider the appropriate use of their vocation as the poetic cycles at times assume a metapoetic stance. Most striking is the authors' conflations of great historical pasts and their contemporary times. In Platen's view, the Venice he encounters, occupied by the Austrians, casts but a shadow of the pre-Napoleonic glory experienced by Goethe's generation. The poet extrapolates this colonial oppression to the moral, social, and aesthetic realms of experience. On the broadest level, Platen's Venice is characterized by a tension between the contemporary city his poetic narrator encounters and that of the past, represented either in Renaissance Venetian painting or in the memory of the great Republic. Similarly, Goethe's poetic traveler ventures to Italy only to find himself traversing the boundaries between ancient and modern Rome. The authors could easily rely on their readers' accessibility to these historical memories. The elected poetic form of each group is derivative of the privileged historical epoch, the classical elegy and the Renaissance sonnet. The literal and symbolic isolation provided by the geographic situation of Venice or the walls around Rome delimits the northern travelers' experiences and, equally important, also protects their identities. One striking difference in the poets' insistence on the past is the political charge of Platen's denial of reality.

Although both poetic protagonists are clearly travelers from abroad, these works present scant detail of their journeys to Rome and Venice.

The *Elegien* begin some time after the fictional poet's arrival in Rome. Throughout Goethe's cycle, his traveling poet occasionally contrasts his northern European home with his southern refuge in a way that does not cast him as an outsider in Rome; to the contrary, it serves to question his status as a German. Platen's traveler completely banishes thoughts of his home from his reflections: the contrast of home and abroad disappears, replaced by the opposition of seemingly contentious images of Venice. Like the *Taugenichts* approaching Rome, Platen's traveler describes his emotional approach to Venice, a place so greatly invested with history and tradition that it arouses fear, not excitement. The first three sonnets each describe Venice through a limited and unique visual perspective: the first through the city's monuments and architecture of the past, as observed from the approaching ship; the second with its bird's eye perspective, looking down from St. Mark's tower; and the third with the reflection of the city in the surrounding waters, the observer looking out and down. The overwhelming visual program of the cycle is established through the opening words of "Mein Auge" (I: 1).[32] Clearly influenced by the dramatic ocular impact of the northern Italian city, Platen attempts to translate this into the medium of ekphrastic poetry.

The three varying points of view in the opening poems sketch for the reader a multifarious Venice. With a sigh of relief, the poetic voice declares at the opening of the fourth sonnet: "Nun hab ich diesen Taumel überwunden" (1). The speaker confesses that he has overcome the frenzy of Venice, not by means of these various lenses, but rather through the assistance of a guide, a friend; although the reader assumes that this must be a *cicerone,* the traditional guide engaged at various points along the Grand Tour, the final line of the sonnet reveals the companion to be Giovanni Bellini (1431–1516), a Venetian painter of the early Renaissance. The introduction of the figure of the male guide foreshadows the role of the contemporary friend, who in turn plays a role parallel to that of Faustina in the *Römische Elegien.* By enlisting an imagined guide, the poet banishes the contemporary populace of Venice, described earlier as "ein frohes Völkchen lieber Müßiggänger" (III: 9). The respective Italian cities are occupied, for the most part, not with contemporary residents, but rather with the spirits of other epochs, with ancient gods and Renaissance painters. In a politically charged gesture, Platen replaces the actual occupying forces of Venice, the Austrians, with these other inhabitants. The most important of the contemporary inhabitants are the travelers' lovers, each a native Italian, a child of the city in question.

Once having established his bearings in the city with the help of his metaphorical guide, the speaker can pronounce that "Venedig liegt nur noch im Land der Träume" (V: 1). This politically motivated sonnet acknowledges only a mythologized citizenry and the man responsible for their Republic's demise, Napoleon. The visitor must be content with the partially eroded signs of the great Venetian ancestors left on the Doges' tombs. Within the first five sonnets, Platen introduces all the subsequent themes of the cycle and shapes his Venice out of a strikingly limited vocabulary and repertoire of images. The traveling poet retreats into this *Land der Träume,* a purely interior and psychological world, which will then be summoned in various guises. This realm recalls the alternative state of being constructed within Goethe's *Römische Elegien* into which the traveling German poet flees.

In both cycles these divergent figurations of a fictional city are mirrored in the separation of day and night, and their respective activities. Goethe's poet plays the part of the respectable traveler by day, taking in the sights and reading the ancient writers; he visits his lover by night. He is unable to acknowledge her presence while at a wine tavern among other German travelers (XV).[33] In a reversal of Goethe's paradigm, Platen generally represents his imagined Venice in the daylight hours during which his protagonist retreats into interior spaces to admire Renaissance painting. It is at night that he finds himself among the throngs on St. Mark's Square when the contemporary Venetians, who are a distraction by day, become interesting.

Platen's surrogate Venice is first evoked in the example of the Renaissance painters who occupy the central portion of the cycle as any attempt at mimetic representation of the nineteenth-century city is abandoned. It is implied that the political freedoms of the Republic of Venice enabled the creation of the Renaissance masterpieces. In the sixth sonnet, the later Renaissance painters, Titian (1488/90–1576), Pordenone (1483–1539), Giorgione (1478?-1510), and Veronese (1528–1588), convene, but only Titian's *Mariä Himmelfahrt* (Maria's Ascension) is directly cited. Platen's description fails to evoke the image in the reader's mind: the poet merely recounts that clouds hover around Mary's feet. Moreover, in a strikingly anti-Christian gesture, the poetic observer supplants her with the figure of Titian, himself striving toward the heavens. The achievement of the individual (Titian) is valued over the religious content of his work. Such anti-Christian sentiment in Platen's cycle is reminiscent of Goethe's own attitude in his *Venezianische Epigramme.*

Interestingly, Platen chose to eliminate the seventh sonnet, "Der Canalazzo trägt auf breitem Rücken," from his ultimate collection. Upon reconsideration, the sonnet's primary concern with the Renaissance architecture of Venice did not fit into the broader aesthetic project of the cycle, represented elsewhere with reference to painting and less often to sculpture. Although the privileged architectural harmony of "Tiefsinn und Schönheit" (14) parallels the poetic project of the Renaissance sonnet, Platen's very model, the inclusion of the sonnet would undermine the poet's overall venture. This realm of architectural grandeur, here included in the *Land der Träume,* does not admit decay and decline. The litany of famous palazzi along the Grand Canal included in "Der Canalazzo trägt auf breitem Rücken" places the highest value on "Kraft," "Ebenmaß," and "Prunk" (4). In historical reality, however, the exterior buildings are witnesses to the passing of time and partakers in the history of Venice. By 1824, showing evidence of grave decay, the palazzi are the ruins of Venice. The paintings privileged by Platen's narrating traveler, contained within frames, protected within the walls of closed structures such as churches, are therefore untouched by politics and history. The removal of an architectural sonnet by Platen will further distinguish his work from its most famous predecessor: Goethe especially favored the architectural works of Palladio in his descriptions of Venice from the *Italienische Reise.*

The next six sonnets continue to emphasize Platen's concern with the visual arts, albeit with an intermingled reference to Venice's fall: "das ew'ge Leben" (XI: 1) and "goldne Zeit" (XII: 12) exist only within the frames of the painting. The opulent personification of Venice "als stolzes Weib mit goldenen Gewändern" (VIII: 10) in Veronese's *Venetia*[34] (see figure 3) stands in sharp contrast to Platen's allusion to the fall of the great Republic and is specific to the long tradition of the female personification of the city as *La Serenissima.*[35] Paintings give way to sculpture in order to reintroduce the contemporary public:

> Doch um noch mehr zu fesseln mich, zu halten,
> So mischt sich unter jene Kunstgebilde
> Die schönste Blüte lebender Gestalten. (IX: 12–14)

With these lines, Platen slowly orchestrates the entrance of the *Freund.* The study and admiration of the visual arts facilitates the full appreciation of the modern living inhabitants of Venice.

"Hier wuchs die Kunst wie eine Tulipane" (X: 1) ascribes an organic development to Venetian art; however, the tulip, the scentless flower, carries with it an artificial-like quality, which will coincide with the poet's attention to the absence of the natural world in Venice later in the cycle.[36] The eleventh sonnet ends with reference to three paintings, and again the gesture is reduced to cataloguing. Platen toys with the religiosity of St. Barbara and Tobias; by singing their praises, he does not spread the Gospel as a missionary, but rather propagates in his sonnets the Renaissance cult of the artist. His continued use of identifiable Renaissance painting recalls the eleventh elegy in which Goethe describes his collection of plaster casts of well-known classical statuary: the small representations of gods, both major and minor, are listed and described in a cursory fashion. This gesture is emblematic of Goethe's preference for the plastic arts throughout the cycle, the genre most closely associated with ancient Greece and Rome. Platen's vague descriptions of the paintings lack any humanizing aspect whatsoever. His aim is not to make the figures depicted more accessible, but rather to mirror the attraction and fascination derived precisely from their sublime inaccessibility and remoteness, as captured by the gifted painters of the Renaissance. In contrast, Goethe's descriptions of the ancient gods in mere plaster copies are almost human:

> Jupiter senket die göttliche Stirne und Juno erhebt sie,
> Phöbus schreitet hervor, schüttelt das lockige Haupt;
> Trocken schauet Minerva herab und Hermes der leichte,
> Wendet zur Seite den Blick, schalkhaft und zärtlich zugleich.
>
> (XI: 5–8)

The statues appear animated and fully present; in fact, they seem to participate in the poetic *tableau*.

Platen's insistence upon the visual program culminates in the twelfth sonnet, "Zur Wüste fliehend vor dem Menschenschwärme," which begins with an eight-line description of Titian's "Johannes in der Wüste"; however, despite its length, it is less an ekphrasis than an explanation of the painting's mood and the apparent emotional response of the viewer. There is no mention of color or technique, for example. Platen writes:

> Zur Wüste fliehend vor dem Menschenschwarme,
> Steht hier Johannes, um zu reinern Sphären
> Durch Einsamkeit die Seele zu verklären,
> Die hohe, großgestimmte, gotteswarme.

Voll von Begeisterung, von heil'gem Harme
Erglänzt sein ew'ger, ernster Blick von Zähren,
Nach jenem, den Maria soll gebären,
Scheint er zu deuten mit erhobnem Arme. (XII: 1–8)

In his final sublimation of religious content, Platen's treatment of a highly Christian religious figure is immediately secularized as the poet elevates Titian to the status of a god:

Wer kann sich weg von diesem Bilde kehren,
Und möchte nicht, mit brünstigen Gebärden,
Den Gott im Busen Tizians verehren? (XII: 9–11)

This apotheosis serves as the culmination of the poet's discussion of painting.

The thirteenth sonnet officially leads the reader out of the exclusive realm of painting and widens the cycle's concerns to include the contemporary city as well as its republican past. Venice, completely devoid of nature with the exception of its surrounding waters, is therefore a strange precursor to the twentieth-century metropolis. City poetry appealed to a poet like Platen, who strove to counter the Romantic tendencies of his generation. Platen writes:

Hier seht ihr freilich keine grünen Auen,
Und könnt euch nicht im Duft der Rose baden (XIII: 1–2)

In an interesting disjunction, Platen commented in his diary on 29 October 1824 about the lack of green in Venice and his eventual longing for it:

Ich fühle nun wohl, daß meine Stunde herannaht, Venedig zu verlassen. Eine gewisse Sehnsucht nach der Natur stellt sich ein, und der Besuch der Giardini ist mir zum Bedürfnis geworden. (*PT*, 716)

Platen's poetic alter-ego does not recount a visit to a garden, but rather recalls the attractive Venetians, especially female, who fill St. Mark's Square in the evenings (XIII: 5–11). Human nature replaces nature. The emphasis on the Venetian women is read as an extension of the nearly mythical status of Venice as the most serene woman and of the resulting images such as Veronese's.

The fourteenth sonnet explicitly reintroduces the admired friend, now as a lover, a Venetian, and a contemporary of the traveler. The absorption into the world of art has made this love possible. The ultimate sublimation is situated in the opening line: "Weil da, wo Schönheit waltet, Liebe waltet" (XIV: 1). Where republican ideals once flourished, beauty and love now govern. The tone, however, is one of resignation as the narrator already speaks of the inevitable impossibility of maintaining even a requited love. The subsequently withheld fifteenth sonnet further intensifies the speaker's identification of his friend with the city of Venice. Platen again alludes to the female allegory of Venice; she raised and nurtured the speaker's friend as a mother does a child:

> Dich aber hat Venedig auferzogen,
> Du bleibst zurück in diesem Himmelreiche,
> Von allen Engeln Gian Bellins umflogen (XV: 9–11)

The spirits of the former world will protect the native inhabitant of the latter, as Venice, the realm of dreams, is conflated with the traveler's contemporary Venice: neither can accommodate the outsider permanently. As the serene backdrop for a relationship, Venice is ultimately indifferent to the lovers. In contrast, the *Römische Elegien* tell of a relationship sanctioned by Faustina's mother, who aids in their obfuscation. Goethe's traveler's affair with the young Roman woman both literally and figuratively embodies the union of the ancient with the modern, the North with the South:

> Mutter und Tochter erfreun sich ihres nordischen Gastes,
> Und der Barbare beherrscht römischen Busen und Leib (II: 27–28)

Whereas he sees himself as a worthy successor to the ancient citizens of Rome, Platen's traveler can only dream of living up to the Renaissance models he finds in Venice.

It is vital to bear in mind that this sonnet (XV), when restored to its original position in the cycle, decisively reveals Platen's narrative intention that his poetic protagonist would depart Venice. Along with the following sonnet, "Was läßt im Leben sich zuletzt gewinnen?" it constitutes Platen's original closure to the cycle; however, both were omitted from post-1825 editions of the cycle. The visitor prepares for retreat by revisiting his favorite places:

> Eh mir ins Nichts die letzten Stunden rinnen,
> Will noch einmal ich auf und nieder wallen,
> Venedigs Meer, Venedigs Marmorhallen
> Beschaun mit sehnsuchtsvoll erstaunten Sinnen. (XVI: 5–8)

The ultimate tone of the fall of Venice prevails as the reflective qualities of the waters are called into question. Now the traveler admits that they reflect what is, not what once was:

> Das Auge schweift mit emsigem Bestreben,
> Als ob zurück in seinem Spiegel bliebe,
> Was länger nicht vor ihm vermag zu schweben (XVI: 9–11)

Within Platen's original conception, the initial image of the eye also punctuates the cycle, forming a frame of visual emphasis around the cycle:

> Zuletzt, entziehend sich dem letzten Triebe,
> Fällt ach! zum letztenmal im kurzen Leben,
> Auf jenes Angesicht ein Blick der Liebe. (XVI: 12–14)

Departure means one last glance at the city and the lover as well as the last loving gaze upon the traveler's face. By removing these two sonnets from the original series, which, after all, was self-published in a limited edition and therefore not well-known to a wider audience, Platen eradicates much of the intensely personal from the cycle, a strategy he likely perceived as helpful in bringing him the praise and validation his earlier work had not elicited.[37]

Added to the sonnets for their 1828 inclusion in Platen's collected poetry, "Wenn tiefe Schwermut meine Seele wieget" ostensibly provides a different kind of closure to the then reduced cycle of the *Sonette aus Venedig*. With the fifteenth and sixteenth sonnets removed, Platen's insistence upon departure from Venice and the demise of the *Land der Träume* is aborted. Although the narrator apparently remains in Venice, a happy ending is not ensured; he is now completely alone, without painterly guide or friend. The ultimate gesture of looking out, away from the city, toward the sea, emphasizes the traveler's status as an outsider in Venice and the impossibility of assimilation. The sight of the water recalls to the visitor the historical memory of the symbolic wedding of the city to the sea, celebrated annually by the Doge, who would drop a ring into the water.[38] The traveler's *Blick*, like the Doge's ring, disappears out into the sea. The city is ultimately unable to appreciate the visitor in a reciprocal fashion; the love for Venice remains equally unrequited. Finally, however, Platen's traveler does not dream of returning to his unnamed homeland; instead he is brought back to the realities of Venice by the call of the gondolier. Platen himself must have felt isolated and cut-off while in Venice, but in a safe, protected manner as he stayed longer in Italy than he had planned: he was arrested after his return to Germany for unauthorized extension of his military leave.[39]

Platen's Venice is literally the amalgamation of multiple images, including paintings; however, the spectator merely refers to individual works of art, hardly describing them in any detail. The poet lives up to his dedicatory proclamation: only one who has been to Venice can truly understand the *Sonette*, that is, only one who has seen the same views. Above all, the poems should evoke an emotional memory, which, in the end, can be derived only from personal experience. Despite his emphasis on the visual, Platen's description of Venice is nearly as unmimetic as the elegiac Rome crafted by Goethe. The vague references to Renaissance paintings, often by name alone, to a certain degree parallel Goethe's own reliance upon classical topoi, authors, and gods. Grandeur and sublimity are celebrated, but without a heavy reliance upon detail. Bellini, Platen's poet's main guide through Venice, fulfills much the same role as Goethe's Amor. Platen's particular conceit is that his Venetian experience is typical, his emotional response, standard. Although he believes that he has partaken of Venice in the appropriate ways, he ultimately chooses to edit individuality and personality from the *Sonette aus Venedig*. In addition, any ekphrastic goal the reader might infer, although not promised by the author, remains unachieved.

The closing lines of the *Sonette* call to mind the greatest difference in the two poet's constructions of Italian cities, as exemplified at the close of Goethe's first elegy:

Eine Welt zwar bist du, o Rom; doch ohne die Liebe
Wäre die Welt nicht die Welt, wäre denn Rom auch nicht Rom.
(I: 13–14)

Despite all of its historical and cultural merit, the traveler's experience is ultimately defined by his love affair with an Italian woman. His appreciation of the city's tradition informs his affection, and the relationship in turn deepens his knowledge of Rome. This same interdependency is embodied in the anagram Roma — Amor.

Both Platen and Goethe present narratives of a love affair; however, both instances call into question the viability of the continuation of the relationships. Although the *Sonette aus Venedig* is far more indirect in its depiction of a liaison (for example, in contrast to the naming of Faustina and her speaking role in the *Römische Elegien,* the object of Platen's attention remains nameless and voiceless), the poems cast doubt on its continuation in a remarkably more pointed manner. Not only does the author ultimately delete the strongest allusions to such an affair, but also the traveling poet of the narrative clearly acknowledges the temporary status of the relationship, which is inextricably linked to the mythical landscape of Venice. In the *Elegien* the well-maintained façade of the happy Roman affair is rarely jeopardized: in the eighteenth poem the traveler confesses his fear of contracting venereal disease. Although the lovers are afraid of being discovered, or betrayed, for example, by the barking Roman dogs, or by Faustina's uncle, their love is seldom questioned.

Whereas Platen's cycle remains devoid of irony, the ultimate gesture of Goethe's *Römische Elegien* playfully teases the reader. Self-referentially, the traveling German poet acknowledges the ultimate irony, the fictional boundaries imposed upon the narrative by its poetic structure. The poet confides his secret to the hexameter and pentameter, but it is he who will finally betray the relationship through the implied publication of the poetry:

> Und ihr, wachset und blüht, geliebte Lieder, und wieget
> Euch im leisesten Hauch lauer und liebender Luft,
> Und wie jenes Rohr geschwätzig, entdeckt den Quiriten
> Eines glücklichen Paars schönes Geheimnis zuletzt.
>
> (XX: 29–32)

The traveler of the *Sonette aus Venedig*, voluntarily confined in an imaginary realm, recognizes the incompatibility of his multiple Venices. Platen only introduces his fantasy after the Venetian context, despite its duality, has been firmly established. In a vastly different strategy, Goethe's poetic narrative begins with the relationship to both lover and to ancient Rome firmly in place. Mutually definitive, one does not facilitate the other.

Homosexual relations were illegal in Germany during Platen's lifetime. Because of its freer social and legal climate, Italy was generally recognized as a country more tolerant of such behavior. Goethe commented on the "extraordinary phenomenon" of the display of homosexual love in an oft-cited letter from Rome to Duke Carl August (*ISR*, 365, 29 December 1787). Bumm comments on the prevalence of male prostitution in Venice and speculates that Platen's first stay in Venice coincided with his sexual initiation (*PB*, 342). This is pure conjecture since Platen did not discuss any sexual relations in his diaries or letters at any time during his life. Although writing about the late nineteenth century, John Pemble remarks that "in Venice homosexuality was especially associated with Germans" (49). The free sexual climate of Venice was a remnant of the days of the Republic. G. S. Rousseau argues for a reconsideration of the Grand Tour in terms of its eighteenth-century British participants' sexual proclivities, which he sees as predominantly homoerotic.[40] Whereas the first of Goethe's elegies sets the tone of the cycle by signposting the emphasis on love and introducing the centrality of the covert sexual liaison, Platen disguised the sexual content of the *Sonette aus Venedig,* eventually editing the most direct references to a male lover from the cycle. The raw sexual honesty of Goethe's cycle stands in sharp contrast to the secret nature of the relationship in Platen's sonnets. The object of the traveler's love, then, can be identified as the city of Venice, which, as stated above, has a long tradition of being allegorized as a woman. Thus, Platen veils the true autobiographical circumstances that surely informed his work. His diaries speak of his friendship with a young Venetian nobleman named Priuli (*PT,* 714). In a further intensification of the poet's obfuscation of reality, Platen privileges his encounters with the great Italian painters, evoking the cult of male friendship so prevalent during the late eighteenth century. Simon Richter argues that the dominant culture of the Age of Goethe was, what he terms, homosocial. Regardless of a man's sexual orientation, at that time cultural life was characterized by a neoclassical "male heroic friendship."[41] Richter marks the end of the period, which not only tolerated, but also as he sees it, cultivated homoerotic expression, around 1806 when conservative nationalism rose amongst the Romantics to counter enthusiasm for Napoleon (38). Platen would find himself two decades later in the even more conservative and repressed milieu of Restoration Europe.

Platen's various editorial strategies serve him well in forming socially acceptable substitutions for explicit male homosexual reference. Platen reinforced this sublimation with one further element that can be located in the content of Renaissance Venetian painting. The paintings presented in the *Sonette aus Venedig* are, with two exceptions, of Christian religious content. In total, Platen names five paintings and one sculpture of religious significance.[42] In addition, he refers to one historical painting[43] and one allegory of Venice.[44] Although the majority of this list consists of male figures, they are not charged with latent homoerotic content. The Renaissance ideal of female beauty finds its highest form of expression in religious painting, notably representations of the Madonna as well as in mythological figures such as Botticelli's *Birth of Venus* and Raphael's *Galatea.* The status of male figurations such as Michelangelo's *David* is indisputable; however, the Venetian school

generally upheld a model of female beauty in contrast to that of men
and boys so dominant in classical Greek sculpture, and to some extent,
prevalent in Florentine art of the Renaissance. Without citing specific
examples, Camille Paglia supports this view in her discussion of Renaissance art:

> Beautiful boys, everywhere in Florentine art, rarely appear in Venetian
> painting, which is full of luscious female nudes. Mercantile Venice did
> not seethe with philosophers and crackpots, like Florence. In art,
> fleshy Venetian women, half-Oriental odalisques, relax in cordial land-
> scapes — a far cry from Leonardo's abandoned rock quarries. Venetian
> personae and Venetian landscape are equally heterosexual. Venice's
> appreciation of female beauty allowed acceptance of rather than resis-
> tance toward nature. Was this not the result of the city's unique physi-
> cal character? Venice, veined by water, is in placid relation to marine
> nature. Its people and artists imaginatively internalized female fluidity,
> the prime chthonian principle. The Renaissance City of Art, a triumph
> of architectural ingenuity, was its own balance of Apollonian and
> Dionysian and did not need to explore these ideas in painting.[45]

Although I do not agree with Paglia's overarching delineation of Venice as embracing nature, especially in application to Platen's portrayal,
her statement is thought provoking. Her insistence upon the female-
ness of elemental water bolsters the allegorization of Venice as a
woman. Platen's poetic allusions to Venice as a woman and a mother
further compound this view. Platen's emphasis on a much less sexually
charged religious style of painting within the *Sonette aus Venedig* is
quite striking, especially if contrasted with much of his other work. By
no means does Platen erase all homoerotic perceptions from this work,[46]
but manifest in his authorial and editorial decisions is what for the poet
amounts to a minimal devotion to male imagery. Again, this move can
be read as an appeal for a broader reading public and critical acceptance
in the face of an increasingly repressed, conservative, bourgeois sensi-
bility found in late 1820s Germany. The biographical details of Platen's
first journey to Italy only intensify the irony of the eventual critical reception of the *Sonette aus Venedig*. His greatest success, both popular
and critical, would emanate from the strong authorial suppression of
personality, individuality, and emotion in a literary work penned and
set in a city famous for its sexual and moral freedoms.

Imagological literary texts are usually less concerned with their apparent national object than with a variety of other issues. Platen's *Sonette aus Venedig* ultimately have less to do with Venice than with the
poet's search for identity and acclaim, a program not unlike that of

Goethe's *Italienische Reise,* in which the experience of the foreign is seen by the traveler as a preparation for the life to be lived once back at home. These are also matters addressed in the *Römische Elegien,* present in the traveling poet's struggle between vocation and love. In one instance, Amor chides the German for not spending enough time working on his poetry (XIII), while in another Fama and Amor quarrel over the poet's existence (XIX).

Platen projects his own aspirations onto the Renaissance painters praised within the *Sonette aus Venedig.* They assume the status of role model, although he will not emulate them in their medium, but rather in poetry. Unlike Goethe, Platen did not harbor any desire to become a visual artist: his goal is to achieve what the masters have achieved, but with words, not paint. In allying himself with them, Platen plays the part of epigone. He wavers in tone between the extremes of noncompetitive conciliation and boundless ambition. In the sixth sonnet, the traveler recognizes the accomplishments of a number of painters who, during their lifetimes, battled for superiority. He admonishes Titian to reconcile with Pordenone and then both to recognize the work of Giorgione and Veronese:

> Dir fast zur Seite zeigt sich Pordenone:
> Ihr wolltet lebend nicht einander weichen,
> Im Tode hat nun jeder seine Krone!
>
> Verbrüdert mögt ihr noch die Hände reichen
> Dem treuen, vaterländischen Giorgione,
> Und jenem Paul, dem wen'ge Maler gleichen! (VI: 9–14)

Platen's ambition and hyperbolic self-praise are well documented, yet here his poetic alter ego recognizes the vanity of such conceit. In the ninth sonnet the spectator declares that Venice and its art inspires him to greatness:

> Im Tiefsten fühl ich meine Seele brennen,
> Die Großes sieht und Großes will erreichen. (7–8)

Subsequently, artistic endeavor supplants religious fervor, and the sublimation is mirrored in the replacement of all earthly desires by artistic success and achievement:

> Um Gottes eigne Glorie zu schweben
> Vermag die Kunst allein und darf es wagen,
> Und wessen Herz Vollendetem geschlagen,
> Dem hat der Himmel weiter nichts zu geben! (XI: 5–8)

Unfortunately for Platen, both artistic recognition and requited love would continually elude him. The period preceding his trip to Venice is marked by the author's increasing frustration with his failure to have his dramatic works produced on the German stage. His search for an audience that would provide him with response and validation was lifelong. The strong instances of Platen's concern with poetic acclaim demand a second consideration of the closing line of the first sonnet: "Soll ich ihn wirklich zu betreten wagen" (14). Not only does the approaching traveler fear the weighty history of Venice, but also the imposing tradition of German writers who captured Italy in words. A cycle of sonnets presents an alternative to a possibly superfluous prose travel narrative.

The single reference to the traveler's vocation and most direct self-referential instance within the *Sonette* is found at the close of the eighth sonnet at the approximate midpoint of the cycle:

> Nun steht ein Dichter an den Prachtgeländern
> Der Riesentreppe staunend und bezahlet
> Den Tränenzoll, der nichts vermag zu ändern! (VIII: 12–14)

Here the poet's work is intimately entwined with the conflicting images of Venice confronting the visitor. Art alone may win God's glory, but the emotions of the artist, no matter how heartfelt, cannot change the course of history. The only possible reconstruction of the glorious past of Venice resides within the boundaries of poetry. In the final sonnet Platen's traveler makes one final reference to his search for poetic acclaim:

> Dann blick ich oft, an Brücken angeschmieget,
> In öde Wellen, die nur leise zittern,
> Wo über Mauern, welche halb verwittern
> Ein wilder Lorbeerbusch die Zweige bieget. (5–8)

Laurel, the sign of poetic superiority, a wreath of which is worn upon the head of Overbeck's *Italia* and is bestowed upon Madame de Staël's *Corinne* after she triumphantly performs her improvisation atop the Capitol,[47] grows wild over the decaying walls of Venice. Platen's traveling poet catches a glimpse of the abandoned, untended laurel in a decrepit garden, a reminder of the neglected responsibilities of the keepers of poetic posterity: publishers, critics, readers, and theatrical producers.

It is not inconsequential that Platen's most recognized individual poem, "Tristan," was composed in January 1825 shortly after the poet's return from Venice. Here Platen continues to deal with the theme of beauty and takes on a number of the issues raised in the *Sonette aus Venedig*:

> Wer die Schönheit angeschaut mit Augen,
> Ist dem Tode schon anheimgegeben,
> Wird für keinen Dienst auf Erden taugen,
> Und doch wird er vor dem Tode beben,
> Wer die Schönheit angeschaut mit Augen! (*P*, 69)

In a far more drastic expression than in the *Sonette aus Venedig*, here the sight of beauty can prove fatal.

In September 1826 Platen returned to Italy, where he would stay, with the exception of two brief visits to Germany, until his death in December 1835. He confesses his apprehension upon crossing into Italy and reveals himself to be uncharacteristically realistic and insightful in the following diary passage:

> ich fühle mich sehr melancholisch gestimmt in diesen Gebirgen und ich fürchte auch, daß das Glück in Italien so wenig wohnt als anderwärts. Heute habe ich wenigstens den Brenner überschritten und die ersten Vorboten einer südlichen Natur gesehen. Etwa eine Stunde von hier teilten sich die Straßen. Auf der einen Tafel las man: nach Italien! Auf der anderen: Nach dem Pusterthal! Ich weiß nicht, ob ich nicht lieber den Weg ins Pusterthal eingeschlagen hätte, so gleichgültig scheint mir in diesem Augenblicke, wonach ich mich so sehr gesehnt habe. (*PT*, 800)

The poet recognizes the nearly unfulfillable expectations he carries with him as echoes of Goethe, who twice aborted a journey south, again ring true. Platen's earlier visit to Venice had confirmed for him the transitory nature of beauty, love, happiness, and critical acclaim.

Figure 4. Engländer in der Campagna *(The English in the Campagna, 1835–1836) by Carl Spitzweg. Reproduced with the permission of the Staatliche Museen Preußischer Kulturbesitz, Alte Nationalgalerie, Berlin.*

6: Subverting Tradition: Heine and the German Myth of Italy

BORN NINE YEARS AFTER GOETHE'S RETURN to Weimar, Heine, like Eichendorff and Platen, was a member of the first post-French Revolution generation that matured during the tumultuous years of the Napoleonic Wars and reached adulthood at the time of the Restoration. The factors that intervened in the forty years between Goethe's trip and the publication of his account of it also inform Heine's own experiences south of the Alps and illustrate the greatest differences between the two men. Heine evokes in his own work not only the genre of German-language travel writing, specifically those texts concerning Italy, whose "Zahl ist Legion,"[1] but also and most especially Goethe's *Italienische Reise*. Goethe's apparent lack of concern for contemporary politics alienated his representation of Italy from this younger generation of travelers and left him vulnerable to challenge and sharp criticism that culminate in Heine's trilogy of *Reisebilder* (Travel Pictures, 1829, 1830, 1831) from Italy, cited today primarily as examples of Heine's political engagement and reinvention of the genre. The *Reise von München nach Genua* (Journey from Munich to Genoa) adheres most closely to the form of a *Reisebericht*. The second and third parts of the trilogy are most widely known not for Heine's depiction of Italy, but rather for his scathing attack on August von Platen in *Die Bäder von Lucca* (The Baths of Lucca) and the strong assault on organized religion that dominates *Die Stadt Lucca* (The City of Lucca).

Goethe's and Heine's journeys, though, are not entirely incomparable; both fled an increasingly uncomfortable environment amidst concerns for their future careers. After spending eight months in Munich, preoccupied with campaigning for a university professorship, Heine left for Italy on 4 August 1828 in the hopes of receiving news of such an appointment while away.[2] The first legs of Heine's trip are identical to Goethe's. In fact, the older poet spent one day in Munich before impatiently setting out for Italy. Both Goethe and Heine took the Brenner Pass after visiting Innsbruck and then moved on to Bolzano and Trento. Unlike Goethe, Heine avoided a detour to the lake region of northern Italy, but their routes converge again in Verona, a stop of significance to each. From this point the two travelers headed in decidedly different directions. Goethe went east toward Venice and then south-west toward Rome via Florence, whereas Heine traveled west through Milan and then further southwest to Lucca via Genoa. After his three-week stay in and around Lucca, he proceeded back to Germany via Florence, Bologna, Ferrara, Padua, and Venice, all of which are no-ticeably absent from his discussions. Heine returned to Germany in haste, still awaiting word on possible employment in Munich after re-ceiving news of his father's rapidly deteriorating health.

Heine lacked Goethe's latent desire to visit Italy as well as encour-agement from a father figure to make such a journey. From its incep-tion, he viewed the trip as an intermediate waiting station and as fodder for further literary and journalistic work. The two years preceding his journey saw the gradual establishment of his reputation as an important writer as well as the publication of *Die Harzreise* (The Harz Journey) in 1827 and *Die Nordsee* (The North Sea), in three installments, in 1827 and 1828. The first two volumes of the *Reisebilder* comprise the foun-dation of Heine's relationship with Campe and with his audience. Be-cause the publisher anticipated material for another volume of *Reise-bilder,* Heine drafted the first of the pieces on Italy while still abroad. The greater portion of it appeared in a serialized form in Cotta's *Mor-genblatt* shortly before the author returned to Germany. Heine's pre-ferred shorter style certainly lent itself to serialization and provided the author with much needed cash as well as with an outlet for continued dialogue with his growing audience. The *Reise von München nach Ge-nua* saw its first book publication in 1830 in *Reisebilder III,* along with *Die Bäder von Lucca. Die Stadt von Lucca* appeared approximately one year later in early 1831 in *Nachträge zu den Reisebildern.*[3]

It is productive to speculate on the more abstract reasons for Heine's affinity for these *Reisebilder.* At the time of Heine's journey, this is simply what a well-educated, literary-minded traveler was expected to do — write about his experiences abroad. His precarious financial situa-tion did not allow a lengthy *Bildungsreise* in the eighteenth-century style; however, had money been available, Heine surely would not have been interested in what, in his opinion, had become an outmoded, in-deed misguided endeavor. Of course, it was not this traditional role that Heine sought for himself. Instead, he became increasingly aware that the genre had outgrown its conventional definition and bounda-ries; it was in need of renewal, if not radical revision and in it he seems to have found the perfect medium for his views. Upon reading the es-says on Italy, the form's aptness as a vehicle through which he would be able to approach the subject of Goethe is immediately visible.

The tripartite structure of these separate, yet interrelated texts is intentionally reminiscent of Goethe's own *Italienische Reise*.[4] In his overall project, though, Goethe strived for a unified whole, a goal that clashes greatly with the deliberately fragmentary status of Heine's prose. Heine's texts are loosely linked only by their supposed Italian setting; the few recurring fictional characters appear in only the second and third installments. The texts' unity resides principally in the author's overarching political and cultural agendas, and the surface appearance of each essay as a *Reisebild* decreases sequentially throughout the series. The title *Reise von München nach Genua* undeniably accents a supposed relation to more traditional exponents of the genre. Heine specifically invokes the example of Goethe's *Italienische Reise* and emphasizes the process of travel, which for Goethe was synonymous with personal development; however, in singling out the origin and distinction, Heine diminishes the importance of grand concepts of both travel and Italy. The omission of Italy from the title contributes to a more utilitarian concept of travel as simply a means of getting from one place to another. Heine's choice of titles for the second and third essays casts further aspersions on an older model of travel as a means for education: it highlights a particular location, a rather historically insignificant location at that, when compared to the emotionally charged loci of Venice, Rome, Naples, and to some extent even Florence. Instead, Heine sets his subsequent texts in the town of Lucca and at its nearby bathing resort, Bagni di Lucca, where he spent most of September 1828.

The spas of Lucca were a popular nineteenth-century destination for well-to-do travelers, not a group with which Heine readily identified, although in more recent years he had grown accustomed to visiting the seashore.[5] By emphasizing the relatively insignificant Lucca in his own work, Heine deprecates Goethe's emphasis on Rome in the *Zweiter Römischer Aufenthalt*. Rome is a destination, it should be noted, that Heine consciously leaves out of his own Italian itinerary: this avoidance was surely a strong statement against Goethe and the tradition he had come to represent. This strategy of rewriting and limiting the classic Italian itinerary negates Goethe's expansion of his own father's journey through the sea voyage to Sicily.[6]

The initial response to the first two volumes of the *Reisebilder* was overwhelmingly positive; however, as the author strayed more and more from the traditional conception of such a text in each volume, critical opinion waned. Because of its attack on Platen, *Die Bäder von Lucca* became the focus of countless reviews, which generally followed one model: the denunciation of the attack without reference to the issue of homosexuality, and of course, contrary to Heine's intentions, the occasional defense of Platen's talents (*RB,* 1097). Certainly, the existence of such a scandal broadened the recognition factor of Heine's name, but such infamy was not accompanied with the respect and positive recognition he had hoped for at home. Ensuing political changes in Europe, especially the July Revolution, influenced the reception of *Die Stadt Lucca* in a more positive way, anticipating Heine's work on Germany (*RB,* 1494). Although the Young Germans would emulate the style of the *Reisebilder,* adopting prose as their preferred medium, the effects of the scandal lingered. The deaths of both Platen in 1835 and Immerman in 1840 again brought the conflict to the forefront. Throughout the 1830s Heine was recognized largely as the author of nonfiction: whereas Heine's *Buch der Lieder* (Book of Songs, 1827) sold surprisingly few copies in the 1830s, his *Reisebilder* were quickly issued in a second edition in 1837. During the 1840s, the popularity of the art song facilitated a new-found attention to Heine's poetry, so that by the time of the 1848 revolutions, Heine's reputation was based largely on his lyric poetry.[7] Interest in the *Reisebilder* was negligible until the early decades of the twentieth century.[8] The first real critical attention would come in the 1920s; as is well known, however, such interest came to a near halt until the postwar era and would not accelerate rapidly until the 1960s.[9]

There exist vast amounts of modern scholarship on Heine's corpus of *Reisebilder.* Peter Brenner reports that these works are among the most often studied German-language travel reports; in fact, he claims, the amount of secondary literature on them far exceeds that regarding Goethe's *Italienische Reise.*[10] Because the *Reisebilder* are dominated by Heine's political concerns, it is not surprising that this body of work attracted so much critical attention after 1968.[11]

Counter to Eichendorff, who applied a fictional model in the guise of autobiography for his reworking of Goethe's *Italienische Reise,* Heine assumes an ostensibly autobiographical stance, which, upon closer reading, reveals itself to be largely fictional. While the reality of contemporary Italy is hardly of interest to a Romantic writer like Eichendorff, an occupied Italy is Heine's primary focus: the urgent immediacy of the texts is palpable. Unexpectedly though, this reality remains, for the most part, general and vague, simultaneously confounded with the more fictional aspects of the texts. Unlike Goethe, who, despite his editorial revision, does maintain identification with the narrator throughout, Heine purposefully creates a fictional, pseudo-autobiographical voice to lead the reader through his Italian exploits.

In place of Goethe's actual incognito, Heine posits an authorial disguise in his choice of the fictionalized narrator who describes himself only one time in *Die Bäder von Lucca*, as "Johann Heinrich Heine, Doktor Juris" (*B*, 96). This dismissal of mimetic representation applies not only to the persona of the first-person narrator, but is also projected onto any historically accurate events depicted in the texts. As the scholarship has revealed, much in Heine's essayistic prose simply did not occur as presented, if at all.[12] Heine's extant correspondence from Italy is small, but significant in casting light on his experiences. It underlines the fact that, despite some similarity between his actual journey and that of the fictionalized narratives of his three *Reisebilder*, he viewed the essays primarily as vehicles for challenging the cultural and political establishment in Germany and not as traditional exponents of the genre. Whereas Goethe's *Italienische Reise* can be viewed as a part of his elaborate teleological, autobiographical project for which a dominant sense of self is surely mandatory, Heine is concerned far less with even an approximation of self. The guise of autobiography does little to obscure his preoccupation with the greater political issues of his day. Thus, self-representation is relevant to the author only in its capacity to elucidate his reactions and responses to such broader concerns inherent in various Italian experiences. Jeffrey Sammons considers the status of reality and imagination in Heine's works:

> [Heine] never acknowledged the priority of fact and event over imagination, and therefore it was never his interest to record and recollect with precision, to empathize, to turn observation into narration. Categories were more important to him than contingencies and, as he was an imagist rather than a historian of his time, so he was not a narrative historian of himself. Consequently nearly everything he has to say about himself, and especially his own early life, is instrumental, poetically and argumentatively, and only incidentally reminiscent.[13]

Many of Heine's works are characterized by this pervasive insistence upon a clearly constructed personal and historical subjectivity, the aspect of the *Reisebilder* that most decidedly distinguishes them from their predecessors. By all accounts then, the greatest differences between Goethe's and Heine's texts lie in their specific authorial intentions and points of view.

In *Die Nordsee. Dritte Abtheilung* (The North Sea. Third Part, 1827), Heine opposes what he sees as Goethe's conceit of objectivity in the *Italienische Reise*. Sixteen months prior to his own visit to Italy, Heine declares that traveling to Italy is not necessary and that experience would prove to validate his earlier perceptions of Goethe's work:

In dieser Hinsicht möchte ich am liebsten aufs Goethes italienische Reise hindeuten, indem wir alle, entweder durch eigne Betrachtung oder
durch fremde Vermittelung, das Land Italien kennen, und dabey so
leicht bemerken, wie jeder dasselbe mit subjektiven Augen ansieht, dieser mit Archenhölzern unmuthigen Augen, die nur das schlimme sehen,
jener mit begeisterten Corinnaaugen, die überall nur das Herrliche sehen, während Goethe, mit seinem klaren Griechenauge, Alles sieht, das
Dunkle und das Helle, nirgends die Dinge mit seiner Gemüthsstim-
mung kolorirt, und uns Land und Menschen schildert, in den wahren
Umrissen und wahren Farben, womit sie Gott umkleidet.[14]

Heine, the most subjective of writers, ridicules Goethe's supposed objectivity, although readers today automatically question the possibility
of objectivity in autobiography. Heine acknowledges the strong power
of literary texts in perpetuating imagological myths, both positive and
negative. Most striking here is his recognition of Goethe's sometimes
negative figuration of Italy, a vital factor, often overlooked or misread.
In this instance, then, he challenges the prevalent reception of Goethe's
work as much as the content of that work, his concern as much with
the audience as with the author to whom it responds. Heine will repeat
this sentiment with much of the identical imagery and vocabulary in the
Reise von München nach Genua, especially within his well-known evo-
cation of Mignon's song. Here he begins by comparing the song to the
author's later travel report: "Kennst du das Lied?" he asks the reader:

> Ganz Italien ist darin geschildert, aber mit den seufzenden Farben der
> Sehnsucht. In der italienischen Reise hat es Goethe etwas ausführlicher
> besungen, und wo er malt, hat er das Original immer vor Augen und
> man kann sich auf die Treue der Umrisse und der Farbengebung ganz
> verlassen. (*R*, 61)

Heine at first appears to validate Goethe's credibility as a traveling observer, yet as a reader he distinguishes between the imagined landscape
of the earlier poem and the reality that the *Italienische Reise* purports to
uphold. He draws attention to the uniqueness of his own presentation;
he promises no allegiance to the mimetic principle, but rather subscribes to the opposite impulse. Referring to the *Nordsee III* excerpt,
cited above, he continues:

> Ich finde es daher bequem, hier ein für allemal auf Goethes italienische
> Reise hinzudeuten, um so mehr da er, bis Verona, dieselbe Tour, durch
> Tyrol, gemacht hat. Ich habe schon früherhin über jenes Buch gespro-
> chen, ehe ich den Stoff den es behandelt, gekannt habe, und ich finde
> jetzt mein ahnendes Urtheil vollauf bestätigt. (*R*, 61)

Heine simultaneously participates in and belittles the prevalent view of Goethe as a thoroughly intentional mimetic writer. During his long career, Goethe's audience believed whole-heartedly that the writer's ambition was to be purely mimetic. Heine himself vacillates on the spectrum of literary objectivity: he calls to task Goethe's apparent mimetic intent, yet proposes to show the true condition of Restoration Italy, albeit in perhaps less than objective terms. In *Nordsee III* Heine anticipates the radical refunctioning of the genre he will put forth three years later where he mocks Goethe's presumed accomplishment as a poet of nature:

> Goethe hält ihr [der Natur] den Spiegel vor, oder, besser gesagt, er ist selbst der Spiegel der Natur. Die Natur wollte wissen, wie sie aussieht, und sie erschuf Goethe. (*R*, 61)

In his revisionist attempts Heine no longer ponders the impossibility of objectivity, but rather upholds the irrelevancy of any attempt at it.

Karl Immerman recognized Heine's radical challenge to the tradition of travel narratives, evidenced in a letter to Heine:

> Eine italienische Reise noch zu schreiben, wobei Einem keine frühere einfällt, will etwas sagen, und dieses Etwas, was hier ein sehr Vieles ist, haben Sie geleistet. Wenn die früheren Reisenden das Land theils durch die Naturbrille, theils durch die Kunstbrille, theils durch die schwärmerische Brille angesehen haben, so betrachteten Sie es zuerst mit dem innigen Blicke des Mitleids. Der ganze tieftragische, romantische Eindruck des Landes tritt mir viel eindringlicher aus Ihrem Buche zum Geist und zum Herzen, als aus dem rhetorischen Compendio der Staël. Die Posse der Verzweiflung, welche man seit Jahrhunderten das königliche Weib Hesperia, blutend und zerfleischt, behangen mit einer Narrenjacke, durchspielen läßt, haben Sie in ihrer wehmüthigsten Bedeutung aufgefaßt. Ich danke Ihnen herzlich für das Buch und für die Zueignung.[15]

Such contemporary comments did much to establish the prevalent critical view of the opposition between Goethe and Heine as one of objectivity versus subjectivity. Jost Hermand compares Heine's journey with Goethe's account of the same places in Italy from the earliest volume of the *Italienische Reise*. He locates an analogous relationship between Goethe's affirmation and Heine's rejection of Italy. Hermand aptly rephrases the limits of their differences, concluding:

> Wichtig ist Heine nicht die Natur, sondern in erster Linie der Mensch und seine Geschichte. Und in dieser Form der Subjektivität ist er wesentlich objektiver als Goethe. (167)

He finds rather two different forms of objectivity, Goethe's "eine na-
turwissenschaftliche" and Heine's "eine historische" (148).

Nearly all discussions of any aspect of Heine's trilogy on Italy include at least a passing reference to his written challenge to Goethe.
Many critics refer to Heine's lifelong ambivalence toward both the
historical and literary figures of Goethe, but George F. Peters has
delved into it in greatest depth in his *"Der große Heide Nr. 2."* He
identifies four levels of Heine's reception of Goethe. First is the formal
level on which Heine makes overt, direct comments about his views on
Goethe. Such statements often veil the second, more ambiguous level.
These personal feelings range from admiration and awe to the more
negative ones of "insecurity, jealousy, and at times hatred toward
Goethe, feelings which he seeks to combat by means of humor, irony
and sarcasm."[16] The next level is described as a play with Goethe's texts,
encompassing both obvious quotes and more disguised parodies and
transformations. The fourth and deepest level of Heine's reception is
Heine's reaction to "Goethe's artistic principles in general" (56). Peters
demonstrates this last level with lengthy analysis of Heine's poetry in
regards to his predecessor; most specifically, he posits Heine's *Neue
Gedichte* (New Poems, 1844) as such a response to principles embodied
in Goethe's *West-östlicher Divan*.

Throughout his study Peters clearly maps out the course of Heine's
reception of Goethe. He does not promote a discernible development
in it, but rather accentuates its almost cyclical structure (93), stressing
above all the need to distinguish between Heine's view of Goethe, the
historical figure, and his view of the earlier poet's works. Peters rightly
emphasizes Heine's defense of Goethe in his famous review of Wolfgang Menzel's *Die Deutsche Literatur* (German Literature, 1827, 1836).
In that text, where Heine made his oft-cited statement about the end
of the *Kunstperiode*, Heine clearly separates his views on Goethe, the
man, from the influence he exercised over literary developments. The
first book of *Die Romantische Schule* (The Romantic School, 1836) is
also crucial in understanding Heine's views on Goethe as it is largely
motivated by the need to come to terms with the significance of
Goethe's death for German literature. Peters writes:

> Heine manages at one and the same time to confirm in sharp, unam-
> biguous language the demise of the fateful *Kunstperiode* while elevat-
> ing its founder and ruler to the status of an immortal Greek god. By
> shifting the blame for apoliticism to the ill-defined Goetheaner, Heine
> rescues Goethe and the Goethean works from the sinking ship of the
> classical-romantic era; having done so, however, he is not quite sure

what to do with them, except to leave the works standing in the garden of literature as exemplary models of aesthetic wholeness. Heine
essentially manages to dismiss Goethe politically, in accord with his
own deeper artistic instincts. (86)

He will, however, not be able to dismiss Goethe's political abstinence
within his Italian *Reisebilder* to which Peters devotes surprisingly little
time. He calls attention to the major, direct references to Goethe, especially in the *Reise von München nach Genua*, but does not acknowledge
what he would consider the many second and third-level references to
Goethe and his *Italienische Reise*. He astutely concludes that the *Reise
von München nach Genua* is not a parody of Goethe's famous text, but
an attempt to surpass him (165). While Peters is right to emphasize
Heine's success in at least temporarily escaping the shadows of Weimar,
he underestimates the extent to which Heine seems to enjoy parodying
Goethe.[17] Peters does not go so far as to posit *Die Bäder von Lucca* and
Die Stadt Lucca as further examples of Heine's rewriting of Goethe and
the genre, although they obviously are.[18]

The three Italian *Reisebilder* reflect a progressive intensification of
authorial intent: however, as Heine turns increasingly away from the
model of a *Reisebild*, the orientation on Goethe remains intact, albeit
obscured. Much of Heine's appropriation and reworking of Goethe's
perceptions of Italy is indeed less apparent than previously acknowledged. These seemingly quieter references are evidence of the great
extent to which Goethe's text informs Heine's as well as the revolutionary subversion of the tradition he associates with the *Italienische
Reise*. Just as Goethe's father is the implied reader throughout much of
the *Italienische Reise*, Goethe, here to be read as both the, although
still living, already historicized figure and the traveler of the *Italienische
Reise*, accompanies Heine throughout his relatively brief but strong
foray into northern Italy. On the surface Heine continually reminds the
reader about Goethe's representation of Italy in an often hyperbolic
way; this deceptive accentuation serves to disguise even further the
deeper references. The areas with which Heine challenges the German
myth of Italy and Goethe's association with that myth are the issues
which could be said to grant some unity to the texts on Italy as a group:
self-referential discussions of the genre of travel writing and the status
of the traveler within the three essays; an ongoing discourse on nature;
and a multi-faceted consideration of the Italian people, society, politics
and history, which culminates in Heine's rejection of the prevalent
cultural orientation on classical Greece and Rome.

Throughout the trilogy Heine carries out a metadiscussion of the genre of travel writing and its subgenre of German reports on Italy. Heine most directly addresses Goethe's *Italienische Reise* in the *Reise von München nach Genua*. In addition, he refers to other exponents of the genre such as Lady Morgan's *Italy* and Germaine de Staël's *Corinne ou l'Italie*. Interestingly, Heine lumps together all types of books on Italy: alongside Goethe's text, he places a straight travel narrative and a novel. By citing the fact that so many northern Europeans have written on Italy, Heine minimizes even the appearance of contributing to that genre, and instead, draws attention to his own drastically divergent program. Likewise, he demonstrates that Goethe is far from being the only writer on Italy.[19] In *Die Bäder von Lucca*, as Heine turns full force to his Platen polemic, he further ironizes the genre and his own subversive intent:

> Es giebt nichts Langweiligeres auf dieser Erde, als die Lektüre einer italienischen Reisebeschreibung — außer etwa das Schreiben derselben — und nur dadurch kann der Verfasser sie einigermaßen erträglich machen, daß er von Italien selbst so wenig als möglich darin redet. Trotz dem, daß ich diesen Kunstkniff vollauf anwende, kann ich dir, lieber Leser, in den nächsten Capiteln nicht viel Unterhaltung versprechen. (*B*, 113)

Similarly, *Die Stadt Lucca* also lacks the structural prerequisites for a travel report. Its disparaging representation of the procession on the eve of the Exaltation of the Holy Cross contorts the custom of representation of cultural and religious festivities in the genre such as Goethe's *Römisches Carneval,* all in the service of a political agenda. The setting is pertinent only in its ability to elicit or substantiate broader themes.

Closely connected to Heine's metadiscussion of the genre in which he purports to participate is the self-perception of the narrator as traveler and his observations on traveling and other travelers. These remarks severely discredit the long-standing tradition of the *Bildungsreise*. In fact, in extreme contrast to self-edification and maturation, the promised ends of this eighteenth-century paradigm, Heine's travelers occasionally cast a dubious light on their own sanity. Upon making the decision to travel south, the narrator of the *Reise von München nach Genua* can utter "kein vernünftiges Wort"; he is reduced to constant "tirilieren" as he duplicates the response of the philistine with whom he spoke in Munich (*R*, 26). Upon meeting his old Irish acquaintance, Mathilde, Dr. Heine, the traveler, responds to her inquiry into his condition:

Ueberall wohin ich kam, wußt ich mich um die Tollhäuser herumzu-
schleichen, und ich denke, es wird mir auch in Italien gelingen. (*B*, 85)

His travel is motivated by the need to avoid the insane asylum. The
irony becomes clear as the narrative unfolds; the spa guests in Lucca are
hardly balanced; the spa is very nearly a *Tollhaus* itself. It is not the
Italians who are crazy, but rather the foreigners who flock there.

Dr. Heine comments on various established practices in European
travel throughout the *Reise von München nach Genua;* for example, in
Trento, the narrator exchanges fruit with the *Obstfrau* in lieu of *Emp-
fehlungsbriefe* (*R*, 43), and offers useful, practical advice to his reader:

> Aber reise nur nicht im Anfang August, wo man des Tags von der Son-
> ne gebraten, und des Nachts von den Flöhen verzehrt wird. Auch rathe
> ich dir, mein lieber Leser, von Verona nach Mayland nicht mit dem
> Postwagen zu fahren. (*R*, 63)

Here the split nature of travel literature is evident: many readers will
co-opt such works, looking to them for the practical advice of a guidebook. In place of an embellished, poeticized view, the reality of northern Italy in August dominates: thieves, dust, and fleas. Only in Trento
does Heine's narrator hint that he stands out in the Italian setting with
the sound of his boots (*R*, 42). In this most subtle reference, Heine
alludes to Goethe's report from Verona that his boots announced his
nationality; he quickly switched to shoes and socks (*IR*, 55, 17 September 1786). Differences in appearance cannot mask deeper tem-
peramental characteristics. Heine's alter ego rejects the concept of a
tour guide, declaring:

> mein Herz ist der beste Cicerone und erzählt mir überall die Geschich-
> ten, die in den Häusern passirt sind, und bis auf Namen und Jahrzahl
> erzählt es sie treu genug. (*R*, 60)

Fiction proves to be more interesting and useful than any approximation of truth. Upon arriving in Verona, Heine establishes his traveler as
the successor not of Goethe, or any other of his recent contemporaries,
but rather of the "germanische Wandervölker" (*R*, 55). He thus draws
a much longer connection to the earliest of German travelers and
sharply criticizes his more recent predecessors by disassociating himself
from the likes of Winckelmann and Goethe.

Implicit in Heine's own debate about the status of travel writing as
a valid genre is a preoccupation with the concept of imitation and copy.
The idea of *Nachahmung*, of course, was a prominent topic in late
eighteenth- and early nineteenth-century discussions of aesthetics and

had become a tenet of classicism. On a more practical level, one imagines travelers sketching the sights they visited. Heine redefines these associations by labeling all human beings, himself included, as "Copien
von längstverschollenen Menschen" (*R*, 79). Portraits of the famous
women of Genoa are seen as cheap copies of the real thing, imitations
of long-since departed originals. Such comments point out the suspect
objectivity posited by the traditional exponents of the genre of travel
writing: the elusiveness of authenticity renders imitation futile. In *Die
Bäder von Lucca,* the narrator briefly expresses the wish to commission
an etching of his beloved Franscheska, but then changes his mind:

> wie andere Reisende ihren Werken noch besondere Karten von histo-
> risch wichtigen oder sonst merkwürdigen Bezirken beyfügen, so
> möchte ich Franscheska in Kupfer stechen lasen. Aber ach! was hilft die
> todte Copie der äußern Umrisse bey Formen, deren göttlichster Reitz
> in der lebendigen Bewegung besteht. Selbst der beste Maler kann uns
> diesen nicht zur Anschauung bringen; denn die Malerey ist doch nur
> eine platte Lüge. (*R*, 104)

Dr. Heine shuns the eighteenth-century, almost colonizing, impulse to
collect while abroad and mocks the legions of northern painters who
flocked to Italy for study. The closest representation he can imagine
of Franscheska is a Venus sculpted by Canova, which in his fantasy
might come to life, but yet this too remains nothing but a cold marble
imitation. In a similar vein, Heine will accuse Platen throughout *Die
Bäder von Lucca* of pretentious poetic imitation. The concept of imitation takes on a sharply critical element in *Die Stadt Lucca* as the narrator describes "die Originalgesichter der katholischen Pfaffen," visible
only in Italy. Their German counterparts are mere "schlechte Nachah-
mungen, oft sogar Parodien der italienischen" (*S*, 165). In the omnipresent contrast between Germany and Italy, it is not Italy, but rather
the Italians, who are endowed with a latent authenticity that history has
betrayed. The Austrian occupation of northern Italy squelches Italian
identity. Heine's revolutionary urges reside disguised under the wraps
of imitation.

The most specific and pointed remarks about traveling in Italy are
presented in *Die Bäder von Lucca* and are most often relegated to the
mouth of a character other than the narrator, usually Hyazinth.[20] The
former Hirsch, lottery collector from Hamburg, has journeyed to Italy
in the service of Gumpelino, he claims, for the sake of *Bildung;* yet Italy
seems to hold little charm for him:

> Ach, in bin jetzt in Italien, wo die Zitronen und Orangen wachsen; wenn ich aber die Zitronen und Orangen wachsen sehe, so denk ich an den Steinweg zu Hamburg, wo sie, ganzer Karren voll, gemächlich aufgestapelt liegen, und wo man sie ruhig genießen kann, ohne daß man nöthig hat, so viele Gefahr-Berge zu besteigen und so viel Hitzwärme auszustehen. (*B*, 93)

Here the originals, or rather the fruit in its natural setting, seem inauthentic. Hyazinth, continually plagued by discomfort and fear, harbors distrust for the Italians. In a reversal of the typical *Sehnsucht nach Italien*, he longs to return to Hamburg, though there too, his status as reformed Jew bars him from assimilation. In fact, he later chides the narrator, who, had he won the lottery, could have stayed home rather than travel, a statement certainly counter to the modern association of leisure travel as a desirable, negotiable, status-building commodity:

> Hätten Sie nur zuletzt 1365 statt 1364 gespielt, so wären Sie jetzt ein Mann von Hundert tausend Mark Banko, und brauchten nicht hier herumzulaufen, und könnten ruhig in Hamburg sitzen, ruhig und vergnügt, und könnten sich auf dem Sofa erzählen lassen wie es in Italien aussieht. (*B*, 110–11)

Hyazinth, whose views are certainly derivative of prevalent early nineteenth-century stereotypes of Italy, unmasks the reality of many journeys; yet he criticizes the observed land in a disengaged and quickly dismissive fashion in contrast to the eponymous narrator, who is critical in an almost regretful way.

The figure of Gumpelino, the banker from Hamburg, has literally acquired his new-found religion through travel: he purchased his own chapel in Rome. He presents himself as the product of education acquired through travel, but is oblivious to the superficiality of that knowledge. He claims that he can identify all the paintings and their painters in the Uffizi Gallery in Florence, blindfolded, for he has apparently memorized their order (*B*, 94). His pupil, Hyazinth, is equally naive but far less pretentious; he recognizes value in the smallest amount of education, but has not realized the suspect qualifications of his teacher: "so ein bißchen Bildung ziert den ganzen Menschen" (*B*, 111): ultimately, it is Gumpelino who offers Heine's reader the most pedantic, philistine view of things in Italy. In *Die Bäder von Lucca* he declaims:

> Italien aber geht über alles. Wie gefällt Ihnen hier diese Naturgegend? Welche Schöpfung! Sehen Sie mahl die Bäume, die Berge, den Him-

mel, da unten das Wasser — ist nicht alles wie gemalt? Haben Sie es je im Theater schöner gesehen? (*B,* 94)

His is the most generic of description; such travelers come to Italy with their expectations strongly derivative of famous art works and travel book descriptions. Whereas Hyazinth would be satisfied with the staged version of Italy in Hamburg, Gumpelino is obliged to seek verification of those preconceptions in reality.

Although Hyazinth and Gumpelino are the most laughable of travelers, Heine, like Goethe, depicts the English travelers as the most inadequate. These British are the embodiment of intrusive tourists, replete with guidebooks and catalogues. The narrator of the *Reise von München nach Genua* frequently comments on English tourists he meets along his journey, and the most inept are surely those encountered in the *Hofkirche* in Innsbruck; they misread their guidebook and view the exhibited work out of order, thus misidentifying the statues of the princes and princesses in Austria with uproarious results. They wonder why Rudolf of Hapsburg wears women's clothing and Queen Maria sports armor and beard (*R,* 30). Implicit in this satire is also a critique of the far-reaching power of the Hapsburgs, which will become only more evident in Italy. The narrator establishes his supposed credibility as a seasoned traveler when he meets Tom, Miss Molly, and Miss Polly, whom he knows from an earlier trip to England. In fact, the British are omnipresent:

> sie sind jetzt in Italien zu zahlreich, um sie übersehen zu können, sie durchziehen dieses Land in ganzen Schwärmen . . . und man kann sich keinen italienischen Zitronenbaum mehr denken, ohne eine Engländerinn, die daran riecht, und keine Galerie ohne ein Schock Engländer, die, mit ihrem Guide in der Hand, darin umherrennen, und nachsehen, ob noch alles vorhanden, was in dem Buche als merkwürdig erwähnt ist. . . . [Man glaubt] eine elegante Völkerwanderung zu sehen. (*R,* 64–65)

Heine's description recalls Goethe's own critical remarks concerning the British in Italy and prefigures Carl Spitzweg's painting, *Engländer in der Campagna,* in which a *cicerone* points to the *Sehenswürdigkeiten* as an English couple looks on, clutching their guidebooks (see figure 4). Another woman appears to sketch the ruins in the far landscape as a disinterested porter holds an array of umbrellas, walking sticks, and jackets. These British tourists are overdressed for the hot scene: a dark, dusty, and parched landscape has superseded the lush vegetation of Tischbein's *Goethe in der Campagna.* Ironically, the Italy they observe is bland and unimpressive; it is their presence as outsiders that dominates the canvas.

In the *Reise von München nach Genua,* Heine's traveler recalls, in Goethean terms, his own psychological state before leaving Germany: "Es war damals auch Winter in meiner Seele, Gedanken und Gefühle waren wie eingeschneit . . ." (*R*, 24). Heine alludes to that most prevalent feature of German travelogues on Italy, the transformative power of a sojourn in the South. The benefits include restored health, renewed inspiration, and peace of mind. The decision to travel to Italy marks a change in emotional weather, and this, in turn, will be mirrored in the juxtaposition of Germany and Italy. Heine continues with the text's single most memorable passage:

> Endlich kam der Tag, wo alles ganz anders wurde. Die Sonne brach hervor aus dem Himmel. . . . Da begann auch in mir ein neuer Frühling, neue Blumen sproßten aus dem Herzen, Freyheitsgefühle, wie Rosen, schossen hervor. . . . Ueber die Gräber meiner Wünsche zog die Hoffnung wieder ihr heiteres Grün, auch die Melodieen der Poesie kamen wieder, wie Zugvögel . . . — nur weiß ich nicht, wie das alles kam. . . . Ich weiß nicht, aber ich glaube, auf der Terrasse zu Bogenhausen, im Angesicht der Tyroler Alpen, geschah meinem Herzen solch neue Verzauberung. Wenn ich dort in Gedanken saß, war mirs oft, als sehe ich ein wunderschönes Jünglingsantlitz über jene Berge hervorlauschen, und ich wünschte mir Flügel, um hinzueilen nach seinem Residenzland Italien. Ich fühlte mich auch oft angeweht von Zitronen- und Orangendüften, die von den Bergen herüberwogten, schmeichelnd und verheißend, um mich hinzulocken nach Italien. Einst sogar, in der goldenen Abenddämmerung, sah ich auf der Spitze einer Alpe ihn ganz und gar, lebensgroß, den jungen Frühlingsgott, Blumen und Lorbeeren umkränzten das freudige Haupt, und mit lachendem Auge und blühendem Munde rief er: Ich liebe dich, komm zu mir nach Italien! (*R*, 24–25)

Heine manipulates a number of the, by his time codified, German images associated with travel to Italy, ranging from references to Mignon's song and Roman mythology to Italian landscape, nature, and sensuality. In an anticipation of the Platen polemic, he derides those traveling poets and artists who seek inspiration, identity, and fame in southern Europe while hinting at the erotically, if not homoerotically, charged atmosphere of Italy.

The discourse on man's relation to nature clearly plays a programmatic role in Heine's ongoing challenge to Goethe and also sheds light on his relationship to the Romantics. Like Goethe, Heine frequently comments on the meteorological conditions of his journey that directly impact his constitution. As the distance from Germany increases, so too the narrator's health. The inhabitants' appearances and emotions reflect their cultural and natural surroundings. While Heine views this affinity between the contemporary Italians and nature positively, he remonstrates Goethe's objective representation of the natural world in the *Italienische Reise*. He will eclipse the conception of Goethe as the mirror of nature: Heine's alter ego now possesses the ability to converse directly with the natural world. In the sixth chapter of the *Reise von München nach Genua*, the green-tongued plants confide their stories to him (*R*, 26).

The inability of communication confronted Heine daily while in Italy: in his correspondence Heine commented with regret upon his own complete and tormenting lack of Italian language skills: "Ich versteh' die Leute nicht und kann nicht mit ihnen sprechen. Ich sehe Italien, aber ich höre es nicht. . . ." Of course, Goethe traveled confidently with good Italian-language skills. Heine's narrator manages to get by, but his admission of discomfort with the language discredits the conversations he reports from Italy and reinforces the constructed, fictional status of the prose. As he continues the above letter, Heine minimizes his alienation by introducing the very image of an empathetic, animated nature:

> Dennoch bin ich oft nicht ganz ohne Unterhaltung. Hier sprechen die Steine, und ich verstehe ihre stumme Sprache. Auch sie scheinen tief zu fühlen, was ich denke.[21]

Not only do the stones agree with his projected thoughts, they have internalized them emotionally as well.

Heine's texts, if read as travel reports, are surprisingly devoid of the expected lengthy descriptions of the natural world. The first such description in *Die Bäder von Lucca*, situated in the third chapter, is a case in point. Despite its catalogue of plants, it casts a generic impression:

> Weinreben, Myrtengesträuch, Geisblatt, Lorbeerbüsche, Oleander, Geranikum und andre vornehme Blumen und Pflanzen, ein wildes Paradies. Ich habe nie ein reitzenderes Thal gesehen. (*B*, 90)

Much like the Romantic descriptions of nature found in the *Taugenichts*, this scene is hard to picture. Again, it seems as though Heine could have drafted this setting without ever having left northern Europe. Unexpectedly though, his analysis of the scene assumes a strikingly Goethean character:

> Der Hauptzauber dieses Tals liegt aber gewiß in dem Umstand, daß es nicht zu groß und nicht zu klein, daß die Seele des Beschauers nicht

gewaltsam erweitert wird, vielmehr sich ebenmäßig mit dem herrlichen Anblick füllt, daß die Häupter der Berge selbst, wie die Apenninnen überall, nicht abenteuerlich gotisch erhaben mißgestaltet sind, gleich den Bergkarikaturen, die wir eben sowohl wie die Menschenkarikaturen in germanischen Ländern finden: sondern, daß ihre edelgeründeten, heiter grünen Formen fast eine Kunstcivilisazion aussprechen, und gar melodisch mit dem blaßblauen Himmel zusammenklingen. (*B*, 90)

Heine's narrator seems relieved that the mountains are harmonious and benign, not the mountains that confounded Eichendorff's *Taugenichts,* and grateful to have avoided the effect that Paestum, for example, had on his famous predecessor. Nature reflects the civilized art and music of the Italians, now obscured by political repression. When confronted with the Romantic alternative, Heine adopts Goethean relativized terms.

As part of this ongoing ironization of nature, Heine places emphasis on twilight throughout the trilogy. Although sunshine reigns prevalently in the earlier portions, dusk takes on an increasingly prominent role in the *Reise von München nach Genua:* by the thirty-second chapter, Heine approaches Genoa as night falls. The hot days of August have taken their toll on the traveler who now ascribes more positive attributes to the night. Most importantly, the use of twilight underscores the political and social reality of occupied, post-Napoleonic northern Italy; for example, in *Die Stadt Lucca* Dr. Heine conveniently arrives in Lucca at night during the torchlight Procession of the Feast of the Holy Cross, which, so depicted, is well-suited as the object of Heine's critique. The true nature of the Church becomes visible only in the severe contrast of candlelight at night. Goethe reported in November 1787, in a less critical manner, of a remarkable visit to the Vatican Museum to see the sculptural works illuminated by torchlight. He expounds at length on the advantages of such a tour; this method of illumination served to highlight the sublime aspects of works such as the Apollo of Belvedere and the Laocoön. (*IR*, 470–71). In Heine's work though, representation of art is subordinated to an understanding of the people.

This "romantische Naturbeseelung" (*RB*, 839) reaches its pinnacle in *Die Stadt Lucca*. This text exemplifies Heine's ultimate dismissal of both the Goethean and Romantic models of nature as a new *Gesprächspartner* enters the scene, the Apennine lizards, "mit ihren klugen Schwänzen und spitzfündigen Aeuglein" (*S*, 159). Because direct communication is possible with only some of nature, the Hegelian lizards teach the narrator a secret language so that he can communicate with the rest of the natural world (*S*, 160). This language facilitates mutual understanding between traveler and nature, a relationship denied him with the Italian people. Surpassing Goethe's ability to reflect nature, this traveler has earned the sympathy and understanding of his surroundings. Its inhabitants confide their secrets in him:

> O Natur! du stumme Jungfrau! wohl verstehe ich dein Wetterleuchten, den vergeblichen Redeversuch, der über dein schönes Antlitz dahinzuckt, und du dauerst mich so tief, daß ich weine. Aber alsdann verstehst du auch mich, und du heiterst dich auf, und lachst mich an aus goldnen Augen. Schöne Jungfrau, ich verstehe deine Sterne und du verstehst meine Thränen! (*S,* 160)

In an effort to challenge Goethe, Heine has assumed a typically Romantic posture of the assimilation of man and nature with one great difference: this comprehension is only possible through the means of an intermediary language. The most difficult communication, no longer unmediated, is attainable only through translation.

This interjection, though, is immediately jeopardized as the narrator embraces an artificial view of the Italian landscape (reminiscent of Gumpelino's):

> Das ganze Land ist dort so gartenhaft und geschmückt, wie bey uns die ländlichen Scenen, die auf dem Theater dargestellt werden; auch die Landleute selbst gleichen jenen bunten Gestalten, die uns dann als singende, lächelnde und tanzende Staffage ergötzen. (*S,* 163)

Like a scene out of Disneyland, a steam train might carry tourists through a Tivoli-like miniature Italy comprised of props, a Potemkin village with costumed workers. The final chapters of *Die Stadt Lucca* complete Heine's de-romanticization of nature: the traveler recounts a powerful childhood memory, that of reading Don Quixote aloud to the plants and animals around him. Because he was not yet able to read, all the naive creatures, innocent of irony, took each word for truth (*S,* 199). Shortly thereafter, however, the final chapter shifts to a melancholy tone of regret. Adulthood brings with it resignation:

> Das ist nun lange her. Viele neue Lenze sind unterdessen hervorgeblüht, doch mangelte ihnen immer ihre mächtigster Reitz, denn ach! ich glaube nicht mehr den süßen Lügen der Nachtigall, der Schmeichlerinn des Frühlings, ich weiß wie schnell seine Herrlichkeit verwelkt, und wenn ich die jüngste Rosenknospe erblicke, sehe ich sie im Geiste schmerzroth aufblühen, erbleichen und von den Winden verweht. Ueberall sehe ich einen verkappten Winter. (*S,* 200)

The emotional winter described upon departure has returned. Such statements retroactively call into question the earlier conversations with nature, both direct and mediated, and indicate conclusively that the South has not produced the desired curative effect, at least not a permanent one. Any refuge sought is now analogous to childhood, a transitory state that must be left behind, a distant memory. In the end it is a purely naive assumption that nature can share one's experiences and reflect one's disposition, a further sign of Heine's disassociation from the Romantics. These sentiments are primarily invoked to underline the pointedly political agenda of *Die Stadt Lucca* and the double alienation, both environmental and historical, the narrating traveler feels. In the overall framework of the trilogy, however, they also abrogate further the idealization of the Italian landscape within German literary iconography.

Heine's overall depiction of the culture and society of Italy, like that of nature, remains, with few exceptions, rather nonspecific. His apparent appropriation of the genre of travel literature, which by definition presupposes lengthy expository and descriptive passages, is deceiving: a broad portrayal of Italy and the Italians is subordinated to the greater authorial concerns. Through Dr. Heine's remarks, a picture of a decayed and decrepit Italy slowly emerges, an image that encompasses past, present, and future as well as the multiple histories of the land. The Italian people literally embody all that the country has endured: they are Italy's true ruins. The older female fruit vendor in Trento becomes a living statue, a memorial to the long history of Italy:

> ich konnte an jener lebenden Menschenruine noch viel mehr studieren, ich konnte die Spuren aller Civilisazionen Italiens an ihr nachweisen, der etruskischen, römischen, gothischen, lombardischen, bis herab auf die gepudert moderne. . . . (*R*, 43)

Unlike Platen, who aestheticizes his experiences with the Italians, Heine reverses the strategy and reads history on the people he meets. Similarly, an allegorized Italy is described in human terms, but, instead of the grand and glorious Renaissance figurations of a female Venice, Heine presents "[das] arme geknechtete Italien" (*R*, 49). Past glories and impressive achievements are diminished in the presence of this downtrodden group. The art of Raphael, the Renaissance, and the literature of Dante and Boccaccio are all absent from Heine's consideration. The singular such cultural phenomenon which interests the traveler is Italian music. In the *Reise von München nach Genua,* he discusses Rossini's *Barber of Seville* as "ein ächt italienisches Musikstück" (*R*, 48). In this one noteworthy exception, Heine admits the necessity of immediate and direct cultural experience, insisting that one can only appreciate Italian music, specifically the *opera buffa,* while surrounded by Italians. The music, in turn, incarnates that which the people cannot express directly:

> Dem armen geknechteten Italien ist ja das Sprechen verboten, und es darf nur durch Musik die Gefühle seines Herzens kund geben. All sein Groll gegen fremde Herrschaft, seine Begeistrung für die Freyheit, sein Wahnsinn über das Gefühl der Ohnmacht, seine Wehmuth bey der Erinnerung an vergangene Herrlichkeit, dabey sein leises Hoffen, sein Lauschen, sein Lechzen nach Hülfe, alles diese verkappt sich in jene Melodien, die von grotesker Lebenstrunkenheit zu elegischer Weichheit herabgleiten, und in jene Pantomimen, die von schmeichelnden Caressen zu drohendem Ingrimm überschnappen. Das ist der esoterische Sinn der Opera Buffa. (*R*, 49)

Heine's traveler discerns an affinity with Italy: the inarticulate foreigner visits the voiceless, occupied nation, allies himself with its inhabitants, and ironically attempts to speak for it, albeit in a foreign tongue. This political empathy intensifies throughout the trilogy.

Much of the criticism on Heine's Italian *Reisebilder* has focused on his political agenda. For Günther Oesterle, whose main concern is history and its representation within the *Reise von München nach Genua,* Heine's achievement resides in the "Poetisierung des Italiendiskurses," which

> eröffnet Dimensionen, die der gelehrte, gebildete, pragmatische Reisebericht nicht einzuholen vermag; [sie] ermöglicht 1. die Ersetzung der "alten Stereotypen" zugunsten neuer, zutreffenderer, zeitgemäßerer "Charakteristiken der Völker" und 2. die Gestaltung der Gleichzeitigkeit des Ungleichzeitigen.[22]

Heine forms his text as "das Wunschbild einer Einheit des Politischen und Ästhetischen," a condition that does not exist in Italy, but that will be put forth in Paris. Oesterle concludes that, for Heine, Paris does not represent the new Rome, but rather the new Florence where the artists of the Renaissance were not alienated from contemporary life (276–77). The role of the artist is infused with the political as the artist searches for a society in which his work can participate legitimately in the public debate. In contrast to Oesterle, other scholars have convincingly argued that Heine did subscribe to older, familiar national stereotypes.

Sammons interprets the use of such standardizations as evidence against the frequent critical view of Heine as a *Weltbürger,* citing the overriding fictional predominance of the Italian *Reisebilder.*[23] Heine has long been associated as a poet, if not *the* poet, of Europe, one whose dream of *bürgerliche Emanzipation* transcends national borders. Renate

Stauf's interest in this topic and her recent investigation into Heine's difficult relationship to the concepts of Europe and Germany are all the more thought-provoking due to its timely connection with European unity in the early twenty-first century. His representations of nationalities are not necessarily as progressive as many readers have assumed. Stauf locates the origins of Heine's ideas on nationalities in various late eighteenth-century concepts of national characteristics put forth, for example, by Herder and Schiller. Concerning the prose pieces on Italy, Stauf demonstrates how Heine uses the misery and suffering of an occupied northern Italy to represent the larger subject of Restoration Europe.[24] Because this Italian illness reflects a similar German ailment, "die deutsche Misere hat eine transnationale Dimension angenommen" (123). Thus, an Italian respite cannot cure German ills, for both countries suffer, and Italy has been devalued as a paradise. Like Sammons, Stauf correctly underscores the status of Germany as the informed focus of orientation in all of Heine's writings. An idealized Germany assumes the role of utopia alongside harsher reality (57). Heine posits an ideal Germany as the implied opposite of his cuttingly derogatory remarks regarding both contemporary Italy and Germany, a process Stauf identifies as ongoing throughout Heine's career.

It is vital to remember that Heine, although revolutionary in his redefinition of the form of the German-language *Reisebild,* does not stand alone in his politicizing tendencies. Guillaume van Gemert cites earlier examples of the politicization of German-language travel reportage, including Gottfried Seume's *Spaziergang nach Syrakus im Jahre 1802* (A Walk to Syracuse in 1802), Georg Forster's *Ansichten vom Niederrhein* (Views from the Lower Rhein, 1791), and Ludolf Wienbarg's *Holland in den Jahren 1831 und 1832* (Holland in 1831 and 1832, 1833). For van Gemert the *Reise von München nach Genua* situates Heine as a harbinger of Burkhardt's groundbreaking *Kultur der Renaissance in Italien* (Culture of the Renaissance in Italy, 1859), specifically in its insistence upon the status of the individual. Like Hermand, van Gemert suggests that perhaps Goethe and Heine are not completely incompatible. Since Heine's politicization of Italy is actually a projection more than a mimetic representation, van Gemert concludes that it, like the image of the *Italienische Reise,* is, above all, a mythos.[25]

Stefan Oswald includes just a small section on Heine in his study of the German *Italienbild* and upholds the impact of the political in Heine's ironic rather than parodic tendency. Heine's parody of Goethe's Mignon could easily have become a meaningless caricature, but is invested with the larger symbolic representation of Italy under Austrian occupation (*O*, 137). In fact, Oswald underscores that on his actual journey, Heine, like his traveling alter-ego, never actually left the sphere of influence of the Holy Alliance, that is, never reached an authentic Italy (*O*, 141).

The construction of the national Italian identities within Heine's trilogy is inextricable from his portrayal of women; nearly without exception, the Italians with whom the narrator establishes contact and converses are female. Concomitantly, these major fictional figures, except Mathilde, reveal something about their own sexuality. (It is inferred indirectly that perhaps in the past there existed a sexual relationship between Dr. Heine and Mathilde.) The narrator's itinerary, as outlined in the *Reise von München nach Genua*, could easily be recast as a list of the women encountered along the way. In Steinach, still barely on the northern side of the Brenner, the lovely Italian spinner, immediately reminiscent of Goethe's "Gretchen am Spinnrade," exhibits the first of those Italian eyes. Dr. Heine dreams of her and thinks of her along his journey: soon all the Italians are watching him with their "großen italienischen Augen" (*R*, 39). Waltraud Maierhofer traces the ongoing allegorization of women in late eighteenth- and early nineteenth-century German painting and literature, and posits Heine's intentional response to this tradition: both the visual and Heine's literary female representations tend toward nationally stereotyped characterizations. She broaches the latent sexuality found in the spinning girl in Trento as a product of male fantasy.[26] Dr. Heine focuses much attention on the *dicke Obstfrau* in Trento. The narrator recounts what is easily discernible as a thinly veiled sexual proposition from the Mignon-like *kleine Harfistin* (*R*, 50). In Genoa, it is not the living women who come to represent their city, but rather a gallery of portraits of the long-since deceased noble ladies of the town; the image of the *tote Maria* unifies the three texts.

At other times, these Italian women are contrasted with the English. In *Die Bäder von Lucca* Gumpelino's frustrated attempts to woo Lady Julia Maxfield build the framework for Heine's attack on Platen; the abstinent Hyazinth, who prefers money to love, offers Gumpelino his cure against love sickness, a laxative. Signora Lätizia, poised like the Sphinx and surrounded by her two *Galans*, is portrayed as a woman beyond her prime, a modern ruin herself, a ludicrous example of Italian sensuality. Surprisingly, Maierhofer unmasks Signora Lätizia as a possible refiguration of Emma Hart; with her two admirers, she is reminiscent of Hart surrounded by Hamilton and Nelson (163). Of the spa guests, only Franscheska and Mathilde reappear in *Die Stadt Lucca*.

Franscheska plays the most erotic role in the earlier text: foot fetishism is taken to its farthest extremes as she recounts the story of her love for Abbate Cecco using her naked feet as puppets. At the end of Franscheska's performance, her new-found admirer, the narrator, is granted permission to kiss and reclothe her foot with stocking and shoe. Maierhofer sees the dancer Franscheska as the narrator's "Wunschvorstellung von Weiblichkeit" (164), but neglects the vastly different image of Franscheska offered in the final Italian *Reisebild* where she remains the personification of piety and religious faith. This ongoing fictional narrative serves to amuse, shock, and intensify Heine's scathing critique of the Roman Catholic church: the narrator brazenly attempts to gain passage to Franscheska's room. In vowing to become Catholic for just one night, he is willing literally to embrace the personification of that religion (*S*, 175–76): however, he must settle for an electrical shock transmitted the next morning through holy water from his finger to hers. He does not comment on Franscheska's change in behavior after leaving the spa, but instead ascribes her actions to the ongoing religious celebration. She is the single Italian to play a major role within the narrative, yet we hear little from her. She is excluded from much of the dialogue in *Die Stadt Lucca* while the narrator and Mathilde converse in English. What the narrator does report on is her naiveté and ignorance concerning German history and geography. Notwithstanding the fact that Heine subordinates character development to the political program, he clearly means to draw attention to the hypocrisy he sees in the discrepancy between contemporary Italian life and the role of the Roman Catholic Church. Maierhofer convincingly suggests that Mathilde, actually quite masculine in her presentation, is used primarily as "ein Konstrukt . . . um Gespräche in Gang zu bringen, eine Maske für den Verfasser selbst" (164). This explains Mathilde's gender-neutral role in the final text of the trilogy.

Heine's own correspondence from Italy, in which he describes life like a true vacationer, reveals his predilection for Italian women:

> Diesen Brief erhältst Du aus den Bädern von Lucca, wo ich jetzt bade, mit schönen Frauen schwatze, die Appeninnen erklettere und tausenderlei Thorheiten begehe.[27]

This is nothing like the prevalent image of the conscientious Goethe, collecting and studying. His narrator openly expresses his affection for Franscheska within the pages of *Die Bäder von Lucca* and *Die Stadt Lucca*, whereas Goethe could only allude to his feelings for the unnamed *schöne Mailänderin* and erases any trace of intimacy. The spa's relaxed life is perhaps more reminiscent of the classical fantasy depicted in Goethe's *Römische Elegien*.

The memory of the ancient, pre-Christian world becomes for Heine and Goethe a common venue for sexual expression. In the *Römische Elegien* the northern European traveler visits late eighteenth-century Rome, but presents his love affair with a young Roman woman before the backdrop of appropriated Roman antiquity. The gods are summoned as safekeepers of their secret love. For Heine, the late Tuscan nights provide the closest substitute for the ancient world where fewer inhibitions reigned. In *Die Bäder von Lucca* the narrator confesses that further pleasures followed his attentions to Franscheska's foot:

> Und ich habe es weit gebracht in dieser Welt! Deß seyd mir Zeugen, toskanische Nächte, du hellblauer Himmel mit großen silbernen Sternen, Ihr wilden Lorbeerbüsche und heimlichen Myrten, und ihr, o Nymphen des Apennins, die Ihr mit bräutlichen Tänzen uns umschwebtet, und Euch zurückträumtet in jene besseren Götterzeiten, wo es noch keine gothische Lüge gab, die nur blinde, tappende Genüsse im Verborgenen erlaubt und jedem freyen Gefühl ihr heuchlerisches Feigenblättchen vorklebt. (*B*, 108)

The ancient gods, who witnessed the affair of the *Römische Elegien,* are no longer accessible to Heine; instead, the night skies are only a vague remnant of the authentic freedoms once upheld in classical antiquity. In the "gothische Lüge" Heine alludes to the inauthentic nature of Goethe's poetic construction of Italy. The tender rhythm of Goethe's hexameter is replaced by the shameful, blind, groping of a repressive post-Napoleonic Europe.

Italy had long been known for its atmosphere as a place where sexual mores were freer and inhibitions fewer. The promiscuity and lax morality of Italy stand in contrast to its association as the seat of the Roman Catholic Church, a disjunction not overlooked by Heine. Eichendorff . sublimates sexual desire. Female figures are disguised, mysterious, and sometimes frightening; a true consummation of love is achieved within the bonds of a Roman Catholic spiritualism and only after overcoming the many treacheries encountered in Italy. For Eichendorff, Italy does indeed represent a sensualistic threat, or temptation, that must be avoided at every turn. In a similar fashion the sensual side of Italy is ultimately aesthetisized by Platen as the affection for a male friend is projected onto visual representations of the allegorized female city. Direct reference to homosexual encounter remains veiled. Although Goethe appreciates the sensual aspects of Italy, he edits the overtly sexual, both personal and general, from his *Italienische Reise*. Sensuality is admitted only to the poetic realm, specifically to the *Römische Elegien* and, contemporaneous with the first two parts of the *Italienische Reise*, the *West-östlicher Divan*, a work that also appealed to Heine's orientalist interests. In contrast, Heine promotes a far more open discussion of his sexual exploits while in Italy: sensuality and its expression are an essential part of life that the Christian world has suppressed and, in psychoanalytic terms, that many of his contemporaries, including Platen, have repressed. Heine accommodates the sensual, in part to counter further Goethe's *Italienbild*. In his three travel essays on Italy, Heine subverts the Romantic sublimation of sexuality as well as Goethe's quiet anonymity and avoidance.

Sensualism is one of the most consequential and positive aspects of antiquity, which Heine resuscitates in his reception of German Grecophilia. Critics have dealt with this only in so far as it has been assigned the label sensualism in contrast to spiritualism, an opposition also mirrored in the concepts Hellenism and Nazarenism.[28] Regarding *Die Stadt Lucca*, Sammons has emphasized the priority of this sensual repression within Heine's program, other aspects of which, including his social radicalism, stem from the spiritualist repression of the politics of the time.[29] Heine and Goethe's compatibility regarding the Classical ends at the sensualist priority of that era. In fact, it is in his discussion of a long-since vanished classical society that Heine most forcefully and successfully challenges Goethe's contemporary political abstinence. Heine's one lengthy exegesis on the subject occurs within the narrator's visit to Verona, the most touristic stop on the itinerary of the *Reise von München nach Genua*. The ruins of the Roman amphitheater were the first that Goethe saw (16 September 1786) and anticipate his sometime ambivalent response to that which he will see in southern Italy. Goethe regrets that he cannot see and experience the massive structure filled with the masses as it was meant to be; instead he contemplates its overwhelming dimensions and its architectural simplicity. Heine, on the other hand, even during the performance of a contemporary *opera buffa*, is able and willing to imagine the structure filled with a cheering crowd as the gladiators battle and wild animals meet a bloody end. The contrast between past and present, Goethe and Heine, could not be greater:

> Die Spiele der Römer hingegen waren keine Spiele, diese Männer konnten sich nimmermehr am bloßen Schein ergötzen, es fehlte ihnen dazu die kindliche Seelenheiterkeit, und ernsthaft wie sie waren, zeigte sich auch in ihren Spielen der baarste, blutigste Ernst. Sie waren keine

große Menschen, aber durch ihre Stellung waren sie größer als andre
Erdenkinder, denn sie standen auf Rom. (*B*, 58)

For Heine, the amphitheater reifies ancient Rome. He strives to over-
turn the prevalent idealization of its culture and reveal the brutal, bloody
reality of its people. In doing so, he attacks Goethe's continued political indifference. It is not surprising to Heine that if one is blind to the
uglier side of a past reality, then one will choose, without qualms, to
ignore pressing contemporary political debates. Heine locates the last-
ing legacy of the Romans in their own propagation of a grand self-
image, a trait he likewise associates with Goethe and the promulgation
of his Italy:

> so sind die Römer groß durch die Idee ihrer ewigen Roma, groß überall
> wo sie in der Begeisterung dieser Idee gefochten, geschrieben und ge-
> baut haben. (*R*, 58–59)

Earlier, the narrator introduced his discussion of the amphitheater with
a similarly unflattering view of Rome, implying in this singular instance
that he might be heading in a similar direction:

> Und Rom? Wer ist so gesund unwissend, daß nicht heimlich bey diesem
> Namen sein Herz erbebte, und nicht wenigstens eine tradizionelle
> Furcht seine Denkkraft aufrüttelte? Was mich betrifft, so gesteh ich, daß
> mein Gefühl mehr Angst als Freude enthielt, wenn ich daran dachte,
> bald umherzuwandeln auf dem Boden der alten Roma. Die alte Roma
> ist ja jetzt todt, beschwichtigte ich die zagende Seele, und du hast die
> Freude, ihre schöne Leiche ganz ohne Gefahr zu betrachten. Aber dann
> stieg wieder das Falstaffsche Bedenken in mir auf: wenn sie aber doch
> nicht ganz todt wäre, und sich nur verstellt hätte, und sie stände plötz-
> lich wieder auf — es wäre entsetzlich! (*R*, 57–58)

These words recall Goethe's references to "klassischer Boden" and are
also strongly reminiscent of the Taugenichts's approach to Rome as he
treads in fear of the wandering heathen ghosts of antiquity. Because
Heine limited his journey to the North, the amphitheater is the most
significant ancient sight he describes. Like the stones of his correspondence, the amphitheater seems to converse with him, and like the fruit
seller in Trento, the ruins of Verona reflect Italy's long history. Verona
receives lengthy exposition and occupies a privileged position within
the pages of *Reise von München nach Genua;* yet, unexpectedly, the
narrator comments that the events recounted all took place on a single
busy day, which counters the months, totaling well more than a year,
which Goethe spent in Rome.

Heine's empathy with the condition of the Italian people, for example feeling the same ills, is mirrored in the narrator's description and identification of himself in classical terms. In a letter Heine writes:

> Bin ich doch selbst eine Ruine, die unter Ruinen wandelt. Gleich und Gleich versteht sich schon. Manchmal zwar wollen mir die alten Paläste etwas zuflüstern, ich kann sie nicht hören vor dem dumpfen Tagesgeräusch; dann komme ich des Nachts wieder, und der Mond ist ein guter Dolmetsch, der den Lapidarstil versteht und in den Dialekt meines Herzens zu übersetzen weiß. Ja, des Nachts kann ich Italien ganz verstehen, dann schläft das junge Volk mit seiner jungen Opernsprache, und die Alten steigen aus ihren kühlen Betten und sprechen mit mir das schönste Latein. Es hat etwas Gespenstisches, wenn man nach einem Land kommt, wo man die lebende Sprache und das lebende Volk nicht versteht und statt dessen ganz genau die Sprache kennt, die vor einem Jahrtausend dort geblüht und, längst verstorben, nur noch von mitternächtlichen Geistern geredet wird, eine todte Sprache.[30]

Again emphasizing the communicative aspect of travel, Heine confesses that it is only at night that he can converse with the past, and only in Latin. His correspondence again tends to fictionalization: commentators have documented the poet's ongoing difficulty with Latin. Much of his antipathy for the Roman heritage can also be traced to his study of the law, which around 1820 consisted mainly of the study of the history of Roman law, that Heine would have found ludicrously irrelevant to contemporary German society. Thus, the discomfort he feels regarding the ancient heritage of Italy is only intensified when he sees decay personified in contemporary Italians such as the fruit vendor. The lack of conscious historical recognition by the populace is no fault of its own.

Heine's response to ancient Rome is also interwoven with his complex reaction to German Classicism and its orientation on Greece. Robert Holub investigates Heine's reception of German Grecophilia, stressing that his responses to classical Greek culture were mediated largely through his predecessors, including Hegel, Schlegel, Schiller, and Goethe. Heine specifically abhors the principle of imitation because it presupposes the perfection of Greek art; however, he does not entirely reject the Greek heritage as did the Romantics. Instead, he appropriates what he considers to be its more positive tenets, especially the erotic, and questions how they might be applicable in his time.[31] Goethe is the personification of Hellenism in modern Germany so, for Heine, ambivalence vis-à-vis Goethe is mirrored in his ambivalence toward the classical heritage still embraced by many in the early nineteenth century. Just as Heine distinguishes between Goethe in the political and the aesthetic spheres, so does he bifurcate these aspects of the Greek tradition. He privileges Goethe's pagan neo-Hellenism over the devout and regressive Christianizing tendencies of the Romantics, Holub argues, because of his abhorrence of the Romantic alternative (73). There are, however, important aspects associated with paganism that Heine does not see fully developed in Goethe's work: here sensualism is also to be read as counter to Romantic spiritualism (75).

Italy, of course, was the place where Germans of the eighteenth and early nineteenth centuries, with few exceptions, could come closest to experiencing the ancient Greek heritage. In southern Italy one could visit the ruins of Greek civilization in loci such as Paestum and Sicily. One could see relics of Greece that had been transported to Rome, or the Roman copies of Greek art, considered to be as sublime as the originals. Therefore, it seems to me that in rejecting the outward remains of ancient Rome, Heine also dismisses Greece. It is in this context that Heine's avoidance of Rome becomes clear; in bypassing southern Italy, he rejects more than Goethe's model of travel. The fact that Heine decisively attacks the Roman Catholic Church from a small town like Lucca underscores, even more in his view, Rome's irrelevance on an Italian itinerary. In Heine's figuration, Lucca has supplanted Rome as the major clerical city of Italy. He selectively salvages the abstract principle of the social and sensual freedoms not easily read in the ruins of the amphitheater in Verona.

Heine's attack on Platen, an integral part of *Die Bäder von Lucca,* is relevant in this discussion of Heine's resuscitation of classical sensuality.[32] The literary battle does not actually touch upon either poet's images of Italy, nor does Heine in any way refer or respond directly to Platen's *Sonette aus Venedig.* In fact, the attack on Platen is contained completely within the bounds of the fictional story of Gumpelino and Hyazinth. Notwithstanding this apparent lack of direct relevance to an imagologic study of Italy, a certain degree of irony informs the literary context of the feud.[33] That Heine's attack, which primarily concentrates on Platen's suspected sexual orientation, is found within a text ostensibly offering a view of nineteenth-century Italy, is perhaps surprising in light of that country's long-standing recognition as a relatively safe destination for male homosexuals from northern Europe. One might prematurely jump to the conclusion that Heine's reaction to homosexuality is derivative of the Restoration equation of male friendship and beauty with immorality, as explicated in the previous chapter; however, upon an attentive reading it becomes clear that Heine does not dismiss Platen on moral grounds, but rather on the charge of a lack of authenticity. Platen represents for Heine merely the *schlechte Nachah-mung* of a real poet. Robert Holub explains that Heine saw Platen's homosexuality as a "mannerism," that is, inauthentic (107). Heine deals with both Goethe's and Platen's neoclassicism in different ways: for Heine, unlike Goethe's, "Platen's appropriation of this heritage . . . displays no redeeming qualities" (87). The sexual emancipation posited by Heine in his *Reisebilder* excludes homosexuality, which for Heine, at least in these three texts, remains just another example of repression. In Richard Block's description, Heine marks a turning point in the German fascination with Italy precisely because he decisively reveals the true impotence of the ideal that both Wickelmann and Goethe posited in their considerations of Italy. And as an extension of this and due to Platen's retrospective desire to be the Weimar poet's successor, the attack on Platen is read as an attack on Goethe.[34]

Interestingly, Stefan Oswald describes the extent to which, even in his least contentious text on Italy, the *Reise von München nach Genua,* Heine offended an already established literary tradition and symbol:

> Die konservative Kritik hat es Heine nie verziehen, eine italienische Reise als Mittel für die eigenen Zwecken benutzt zu haben. Es war die Profanation eines nationalen Heiligtums. (*O,* 141)

Oswald's remarks, when applied to *Die Bäder von Lucca* and *Die Stadt Lucca,* take on an increased intensity. For it is in these later texts that Heine uses the traditionally privileged, nearly sacred, genre of German-language prose on Italy as the forum for what became an embarrassing attack on a defenseless, homosexual poet and a revolutionary critique of religion. Alberto Destro searches for evidence of Italy at the end of Heine's trilogy and concludes:

> Und Italien? Das gibt es nicht mehr. Heine ist dahin zurückgekehrt, von wo er sich nie ernsthaft entfernt hatte, nämlich zurück zu seiner Welt, die in Deutschland ihren Mittelpunkt hat und von dortaus geistig die ganze Menschheit umfaßt. Die Italienreise war gleichsam eine große Lüge des Dichters — mit dem Kopf und dem Herzen war er niemals wirklich dort. Er hat sich aus dem Reiseerlebnis Italien lediglich ein paar Kulissen und Requisiten für seine faszinierenen poetischen Fiktionen nach Hause mitgenommen. Durch solche Fiktionen allein vermittelt er aber seine eigentliche Wahrheit.[35]

Destro emphasizes Heine's continual orientation on Germany during the Italian journey as well as the potential of subjective fictionalization. The final gesture of *Die Stadt Lucca,* the call of the citizens to arms (*S,* 205) is the literal step from Italy to France; it is the call to Heine's

German audience to shift the search for the integration of art and politics, now impossible in Rome, to Paris.

When reading a travel report on Italy, early nineteenth-century German readers expected to learn about landscape, climate, art, architecture, history, and increasingly, contemporary society: in short, an introduction to that country. The majority of the genre's readers were true armchair travelers and this was their means of safely experiencing the foreign. Heine addresses many of these issues in his three *Reisebilder,* but in a thoroughly innovative and unexpected way. Through these texts Heine upsets the traditional German literary image of Italy, creating for himself an entirely new and unique role as traveler, observer, and commentator. He ridicules not only the traditional *Bildungsreisende* of the eighteenth century, represented in his texts by Gumpelino and Hirsch, but also the new breed of travelers, the tourists, as characterized by the inadequate, guidebook-laden British. Heine, the author, and Dr. Heine, the narrator, fit into neither category. The traditional aspects of the genre of travel writing, which according to Chloe Chard include digression and hyperbole[36] are taken to new extremes; the primary aims of the earlier and now archaic Grand Tour, personal pleasures and improvements, are clearly unattainable.

Conclusion

THE RECEPTION OF GOETHE'S MULTIPLE IMAGES of Italy in the short period between the publication of the first volume of the *Italienische Reise* in 1816 and the poet's death in 1832 reveals the extent to which the cultural construction of the South had permeated German literary society. The process of the transmission of cultural memory within German letters cannot be divorced from the prevalent status of Goethe's two-year Italian sojourn and the resulting travel narrative. Thus, the reception of Italy is closely linked to the reception of Goethe's text, which is less a mimetic representation of Italy in the late 1780s than a response to the vast changes in Europe of the ensuing decades. The public's association of Goethe with a classical literary program, upheld in works such as the *Römische Elegien,* was responsible for the ongoing projection of such an agenda onto his Italian recollections; in other words, the public's expectations of Goethe's Italy long predate the *Italienische Reise.* This lives on in the ongoing identification of Goethe with Tischbein's famous portrait; the establishment of the Goethe Museum in Rome; and the presence of quotations from the *Italienische Reise* in German-language guidebooks and tourist brochures available throughout Italy. Counter to such expectations, there exists an ambiguity in Goethe's response to Italy; his less than positive reception of classical ruins, for example, anticipates the response of his successors.

The stance of each of the writers studied here vis-à-vis Goethe exemplifies their individual literary programs and agendas, and also reflects a progressive intensification of the political as well as an increasing detachment from the actual experience of Italy. An orientation on the past gradually shifts toward the present and future. As portrayed travelers, the characterizations also evolve: from the enthusiastic traveler, Goethe, to the disorientated, although fearless but naive Taugenichts; to the resigned traveler of Platen's sonnets; and finally to the reluctant and ambivalent Dr. Heine. They all partake in the quest for the authentic Italy. At times the South assumes the role of a screen onto which the foreign observer projects his desires and fantasies. For some, Italy displays the great cultural achievements of various historical epochs; for others, it reflects a depressing contemporary reality. Within the first decades of the nineteenth century, Italy plays both the parts of foreign prison and paradise. The multi-genre approach to this topic is decisively validated in the elision of fact and fiction throughout all of the works in question, whether primarily autobiographical prose, postured fictional autobiography, or poetry as well as in the authors' prevalent metadiscussions of travel narrative throughout many of these individual texts.

Eichendorff, who assumes a mocking, playful tone in parodying the *Italienische Reise* within his *Aus dem Leben eines Taugenichts,* is not intimidated by the Weimar poet's overwhelming literary presence. He neither embraces nor rejects Goethe's Italy completely, but rather adapts the form of the prose travel narrative within the bounds of fiction. His rendering of Italy, not a personal attack on Goethe, but rather a corrective response typical of the late Romantic movement, emphasizes the disorienting effect of Italy on the naive German traveler. The *Kavaliersreise,* as a rite of passage, represents the loss of self rather than *Bildung.* Travel accelerates toward tourism as social and political realities evolve.

The religious sublimation of sexuality upheld in *Aus dem Leben eines Taugenichts* is aestheticized by Platen in his *Sonette aus Venedig.* The grand journey through Italy is reduced to the experience of one isolated city so that the overwhelming frenzy of the Taugenichts's journey is avoided. Assimilation of the traveler is only possible within the elusive memory of the long-since vanished Renaissance. Platen's priority of form and literary-historical context, reminiscent of Goethe's own frequent poetic strategy, subordinates the expression of the personal. Unexpectedly, Platen's work addresses political concerns in a far more direct manner than Eichendorff's. His priority of the artistic achievements of the Renaissance in both poetry and painting displaces Goethe's presumed orientation on the Classical; however, where Goethe perceived an unforeseen ambivalence in his response to the ancient ruins of Italy, Platen evokes an overwhelmingly positive series of images from Venetian Renaissance art, which serve to shelter the traveler from the unpleasant reality of a decaying, occupied Venice. Platen's gesture, unlike that of the *Italienische Reise,* recalls that of Goethe's *Römische Elegien.*

Heine, who represents the most radical and political approach to the genre of travel narratives through the 1830s, extends the parodic tendencies of Eichendorff. His views on Italy are colored early on with a sarcasm and bitter irony that extend in large part to his difficult relationship with Goethe and Germany. Along with their sexual repression, the religious and aesthetic sublimation of the earlier writers is countered by Heine's overt sensualism. In spite of his myriad differences with

Goethe, Heine agrees with the privileged sensualization evident in classical literature and appropriated by Goethe in such works as the *Römische Elegien*. Heine's traveler adopts but a small portion of the standard Italian itinerary and self-consciously manipulates the audience's expectations of travel narrative. The resulting texts are so innovative that the reader must ask if Heine ever really saw Italy. His *Reisebilder* are the final anticipation of the coming age of tourism in the *Biedermeierzeit* and decisively signal the end of the *Kavaliersreise*.

Eichendorff, Platen, and Heine all partake in the formation of the German image of Italy after Goethe, yet one must conclude that they are far less concerned with Italy as a geographic and historical reality than with Germany and, most importantly, their own literary survival in that Germany. In the end, the search for Italy must be read as a search for self. The representation of either the self or a fictional protagonist as German traveler abroad is integral to the author's conception of Italy. Literary statement became a vehicle for the canonization of a cultural experience. After Goethe, who inherited and rewrote the tradition of Germans in the South, the path to literary success in Germany leads through Italy.

The evolving priority of Italy in the German imagination is mirrored in the visual arts as well. Tischbein's famous portrait froze Goethe in the Italian moment. The harmony of Overbeck's *Italia und Germania* is questionable in light of the Romantic portrayal of Italy. Like Heine, Spitzweg parodies the early tourists.

Although scores of travelers will continue to compose traditional travel diaries, both for public and private appreciation, the multifarious modes of representation of the 1820s prepare the way for continued variety in the German perception and conception of Italy. By 1834 Heine is not alone in his critical view; Gustav Nicolai's *Italien wie es wirklich ist: Bericht über eine merkwürdige Reise in den hesperischen Gefilden als Warnungsstimme für Alle, welche sich dahin sehnen* (Italy as It Really Is: A Report on a Strange Journey in the Hesperian Fields as a Warning for All Who Long to Go There), published in 1834, recounts the Prussian military officer's journey to Italy in the spring of 1833. Nicolai's subtitle indicates the mythological status of Italy within German culture; his singular purpose is to reveal the deception that has been propagated concerning the South. He refers to Italy as "das bis zum Ekel gepriesene Wunderland" and declares:

> Auch mir war Italien das Eldorado meiner Phantasie. . . . Allein als wir
> Italien erreicht hatten, sahen wir uns bald in unsern Erwartungen so

schmerzlich betrogen, daß wir uns fast zur Umkehr entschlossen hätten; nur die Hoffnung, das gelobte Land im tiefern Süden zu finden,
hielt uns zurück.[1]

Nicolai scolds Goethe and the Romantic writers of the "Nebelschwe-
belperiode" (4) for misrepresentation. But those whom he holds most
responsible for the disappointment encountered in Italy are those who
continue to write travel reports for profit and whom he suspects of
purposefully concealing the truth from their public. He posits the existence of many travelers who are afraid to challenge tradition, believing
that they somehow have failed or are not yet mature enough to appreciate Italy (7–8).

Just as Heine's work is a forerunner to more journalistic and less
poetic treatments of Italy, Platen's poetry precedes that of Meyer,
Nietzsche, George, and Rilke to come beginning in the 1870s as well
as the increasing concentration on Venice as the fin de siècle approaches. This fascination with decadence and decay will reach its culmination in Mann's *Der Tod in Venedig* (Death in Venice, 1912),
renewed again decades later in Wolfgang Koeppen's *Der Tod in Rom*
(Death in Rome, 1954).

The German fascination with things Italian continues to this day as
Italy remains one of the most popular destinations for vacationing
Germans. In a discussion of the growing economic and social problems
facing a reunified Germany, David Rieff considers the Germans' continued insistence on foreign travel in opposition to the traveling habits
of other Europeans:

> Their desire to go abroad is to a large extent fueled by a desire to
> leave their own country, and that urge to flight is itself an emblem of
> the profound discomfort so many Germans feel about the simple fact
> of their being German.[2]

Although Rieff does not comment specifically on their long-standing
predilection for Italy, he cites the lack of affinity some former West
Germans feel for their eastern counterparts:

> How much more comfortable it was to go to Italy and imagine one
> belonged there — indeed, when one returned, to assure visitors of the
> fact — than to walk down a Berlin street and, after an encounter with
> some ill-clad prole from Potsdam or Marzann, to realize that it was
> with Leipzig rather than with Florence that one shared a nation. (34)

Der Spiegel (The Mirror) recently reported on the large number of
German immigrants to warm southern European countries, estimating
that nearly 1,000,000 German citizens own property from Portugal to

Greece.[3] Although the historical and political circumstances are vastly different today than in the late eighteenth and early nineteenth centuries, this is not a new desire to flee. As Sigmund Freud famously declared in 1936, the deepest desires to travel are rooted in one's own dissatisfaction with home.[4]

The literary *Italienbilder* of the 1820s manifest a vast range of response to Goethe's experience of Italy, including incomprehension, avoidance, and rejection. In the *Italienische Reise* Goethe describes his long-burning desire to visit Italy as "eine Art von Krankheit" (*IR*, 135, 1 November 1786). For the Taugenichts, the South is far more confusing than rehabilitative. Platen is secure only within the vacuum of a historically regressive fiction. Sadly, he died in Sicily in 1835. Falsely believing to suffer from cholera, he fled further and further south, apparently overdosing on cholera medications. But it is Heine who decisively discovers that Italy cannot eradicate the "alte deutsche Schmerzen" (*R*, 46).

Appendix

Sonette aus Venedig — Comparison of Editions

Numbers = first edition of 1825		[Numbers in 1834 edition]
I.	Mein Auge ließ das hohe Meer zurücke	[XVIII]
II.	Dies Labryinth von Brücken und von Gassen	[XIX]
III.	Wie lieblich ist's, wenn sich der Tag verkühlet	[XX]
IV.	Nun hab ich diesen Taumel überwunden	[XXI]
V.	Venedig liegt nur noch im Land der Träume	[XXII]
VI.	Erst hab ich weniger auf dich geachtet	[XXIII]
VII.	<u>Der Canalazzo trägt auf breitem Rücken</u>	
VIII.	Es scheint ein langes, ew'ges Ach zu wohnen	[XXIV]
IX.	Ich fühle Woch' an Woche mir verstreichen	[XXV]
X.	Hier wuchs die Kunst wie eine Tulipane	[XXVI]
XI.	Ihr Maler führt mich in das ew'ge Leben	[XXVII]
XII.	Zur Wüste fliehend vor dem Menschenschwarme	[XXVIII]
XIII.	Hier seht ihr freilich keine grünen Auen	[XXIX]
XIV.	Weil da, wo Schönheit waltet, Liebe waltet	[XXX]
XV.	<u>Ich liebe dich, wie jener Formen eine</u>	
XVI.	<u>Was läßt im Leben sich zuletzt gewinnen?</u>	
	Wenn tiefe Schwermut meine Seele wieget	[XXXI]

Key for above:

Plain text:	included in first edition, 1825
<u>Underlined:</u>	deleted after first edition
Italics:	added in edition of 1828

1825 = Platen, *Sonette aus Venedig.* Erlangen: Heyder, 1825.
= dedication and 16 sonnets, numbered I–XVI
= self-published by Platen

1828 = Platen, *Gedichte.* Stuttgart: Cotta, 1828.
= 14 sonnets, numbered XIX–XXXII

1834 = Platen, *Gedichte.* Stuttgart: Cotta, 1834.
= 14 sonnets, numbered XVIII–XXXI
= *Ausgabe letzter Hand*
= identical to 1828 edition in selection and order

1839 = Platen, *Gesammelte Werke in einem Band.* Stuttgart: Cotta, 1839.
= 17 sonnets, numbered 26–42
= previously omitted sonnets added to end of 14 sonnet cycle

1910 = Platen, *Sämtliche Werke in zwölf Bänden: Historisch-kritische Ausgabe.* Ed. Max Koch and Erich Petzet. Leipzig: Hesse, 1910.
= 17 sonnets, restored to original order, numbered XVIII–XXIII, 26, XXIV–XXX, 34, 35, XXXI

1968 = Platen, *Gedichte.* Ed. Heinrich Henel. Stuttgart: Reclam, 1968.
= identical to Koch and Petzet, 1910.

1982 = Platen, *Lyrik.*, Ed. Kurt Wölfel and Jürgen Link. Munich: Winkler, 1982.
= 14 sonnets (identical to 1834 edition)
= + 3 omitted sonnets reprinted elsewhere in volume

Works Cited

Primary Works

Eichendorff, Joseph von. *Werke.* Ed. Wolfgang Frühwald, Brigitte Schillbach and Hartwig Schultz. 6 vols. Frankfurt am Main: Deutscher Klassiker Verlag, 1985–93.

Goethe, Johann Wolfgang von. *Italian Journey.* Ed. Thomas P. Saine and Jeffrey L. Sammons. Princeton, NJ: Princeton UP, 1989.

———. *Poetische Werke. Kunsttheoretische Schriften und Übersetzungen.* Ed. Siegfried Seidel. 22 vols. Berlin: Aufbau, 1960–1978.

———. *Sämtliche Werke, Briefe, Tagebücher und Gespräche.* Ed. Dieter Borchmeyer et al. 40 vols. Frankfurt am Main: Deutscher Klassiker Verlag, 1985–.

———. *Werke.* Ed. Erich Trunz. 14 vols. Munich: Beck, 1981.

Heine, Heinrich. *Heinrich Heine Säkularausgabe.* Ed. Nationalen Forschung- und Gedenkstätten der klassischen deutschen Literatur in Weimar and Centre National de la Recherche Scientifique in Paris. 27 vols. Berlin: Akademie, and Paris: Editions du Centre National de la Recherche Scientifique, 1970.

———. *Historisch-kritische Gesamtausgabe der Werke.* Ed. Manfred Windfuhr. 16 vols. Hamburg: Hoffmann und Campe, 1973–1997.

Platen, August von. *Gedichte.* Stuttgart: Cotta, 1828.

———. *Gedichte.* Stuttgart: Cotta, 1834.

———. *Gedichte.* Ed. Heinrich Henel. Stuttgart: Reclam, 1968.

———. *Gesammelte Werke des Grafen August von Platen in einem Band.* Stuttgart: Cotta, 1839.

———. *Lyrik.* Ed. Kurt Wölfel and Jürgen Link. Munich: Winkler, 1982.

———. *Sämtliche Werke in zwölf Bänden: Historisch-kritische Ausgabe.* Ed. Max Koch and Erich Petzet. 12 vols. Leipzig: Hesse, 1910.

———. *Sonette aus Venedig.* Erlangen: Heyder, 1825.

———. *Die Tagebücher des Grafen August von Platen: Aus der Handschrift des Dichters.* Ed. G. von Laubmann and L. von Scheffler. 2 vols. Stuttgart: Cotta, 1896–1900.

Secondary Works

Aldrich, Robert. *The Seduction of the Mediterranean: Writing, Art and Homosexual Fantasy.* New York, NY: Routledge, 1993.

Andrews, Keith. *The Nazarenes: A Brotherhood of German Painters in Rome.* Oxford: Clarendon, 1964.

Barolini, Teodolinda. "Giovanni Boccaccio." *Petrarch to Renaissance Short Fiction.* Ed. William T. H. Jackson and George Stade. New York, NY: Scribners, 1983. 509–34.

Battafarano, Italo Michele, ed. *Italienische Reise. Reisen nach Italien.* Trento: Reverdito, 1988.

Block, Richard O. *The Spell of Italy: The Goethe Effect and the German Literary Imagination.* Diss. Northwestern U, 1998. Ann Arbor, MI: UMI, 1998. 9832549.

Bloom, Harold. *The Anxiety of Influence: A Theory of Poetry.* New York, NY: Oxford UP, 1973.

Boerner, Peter. "Italienische Reise." *Interpretationen: Goethes Erzählwerk.* Ed. Paul Michael Lützeler and James E. McLeod. Stuttgart: Reclam, 1985. 344–61.

———. "National Images and their Place in Literary Research: Germany as seen by Eighteenth-century French and English Reading Audiences." *Monatshefte* 67 (1975): 358–70.

Boyle, Nicholas. *Goethe: The Poet and the Age.* 2 vols. New York, NY: Oxford UP, 1991–2000.

———. "Goethe in Paestum: a higher-critical look at the *Italienische Reise.*" Oxford German Studies 20/21 (1991–1992): 18–31.

Brenner, Peter J., ed. *Der Reisebericht: Die Entwicklung einer Gattung in der deutschen Literatur.* Frankfurt am Main: Suhrkamp, 1989.

———. *Der Reisebericht in der deutschen Literatur: Ein Forschungsüberblick als Vorstudie zu einer Gattungsgeschichte.* Tübingen: Niemeyer, 1990.

Brown, Jane K. *Goethe's Faust: The German Tragedy.* Ithaca, NY: Cornell UP, 1986.

Bumm, Peter. *August Graf von Platen: Eine Biographie.* Paderborn: Schöningh, 1990.

Busch, Frank. *August Graf von Platen. Thomas Mann: Zeichen und Gefühle.* Munich: Fink, 1987.

Butor, Michel. "Le voyage et l'écriture." *Romantisme* 4 (1972): 4–19.

Buzard, James. *The Beaten Track: European Tourism, Literature and the Ways to 'Culture' 1800–1918.* New York, NY: Oxford UP, 1993.

Byron. *A Critical Edition of the Major Works.* Ed. Jerome J. McGann. New York, NY: Oxford UP, 1986.

Cardinal, Roger. "The Passionate Traveler: Goethe in Italy." *Publications of the English Goethe Society,* New Series 67 (1997): 17–32.

Chard, Chloe. "Grand and Ghostly Tours: The Topography of Memory." *Eighteenth-Century Studies* 31.1 (1997): 101–8.

———. *Pleasure and Guilt on the Grand Tour: Travel Writing and Imaginative Geography 1600–1830.* Manchester: Manchester UP, 1999.

Chard, Chloe, and Helen Langdon, ed. *Transports: Travels, Pleasure, and Imaginative Geography, 1600–1830.* New Haven, CT: Yale UP, 1996.

Corbineau-Hoffmann, Angelika. *Paradoxie der Fiktion: Literarische Venedig-Bilder 1797–1984.* Berlin: de Gruyter, 1993.

Derks, Paul. *Die Schande der heiligen Päderastie: Homosexualität und Öffentlichkeit in der deutschen Literatur, 1750–1850.* Berlin: Rosa Winkel, 1990.

Destro, Alberto. "Reiste Heine wirklich nach Italien?" *"Ich Narr des Glücks": Heinrich Heine 1797–1856 — Bilder einer Ausstellung.* Ed. Joseph A. Kruse. Stuttgart: Metzler, 1997. 223–29.

Dove, Richard. *The "Individualität" of August von Platen.* Frankfurt am Main: Lang, 1983.

Dyserinck, Hugo. "Zum Problem der 'images' und 'mirages' und ihrer Untersuchung im Rahmen der Vergleichenden Literaturwissenschaft." *Arcadia* 1 (1966): 107–20.

Eissler, Kurt Robert. *Goethe: A Psychoanalytic Study 1775–1786.* 2 vols. Detroit, MI: Wayne State UP, 1963.

Enzensberger, Hans Magnus. "Eine Theorie des Tourismus." *Einzelheiten.* Frankfurt am Main: Suhrkamp, 1962. 147–68.

Fischer, Manfred S. "Literarische Seinsweise und politische Funktion nationenbezogener Images: Ein Beitrag zur Theorie der komparatistischen Imagologie." neohelicon 10: 2 (1983): 251–74.

Freud, Sigmund. "Eine Erinnerungsstörung auf der Akropolis." *Gesammelte Werke.* Ed. Anna Freud. Vol. 16. London: Imago, 1950. 250–57.

Gilman, Sander. "Goethe's Touch: Touching, Seeing, and Sexuality." *Inscribing the Other.* Lincoln, NE: U of Nebraska P, 1991. 29–49.

Goethe, Johann Caspar. *Reise durch Italien im Jahre 1740* (Viaggo per l'Italia). Trans. Albert Meier. Frankfurt am Main: Deutscher Taschenbuch, 1986.

Gould, Robert. "Problems of Reception and Autobiographical Method in the *Zweiter Römischer Aufenthalt* of Goethe's *Italienische Reise*." Carlton German Papers 22 (1994): 82.

Grimm, Gunther E., ed. *Italien-Dichtung I: Erzählungen*. Stuttgart: Reclam, 1988.

———. *Italien-Dichtung II: Gedichte von der Klassik bis zur Gegenwart*. Stuttgart: Reclam, 1988.

Grimm, Gunther E., Ursula Breymayer, and Walter Erhard. *"Ein Gefühl von freierem Leben": Deutsche Dichter in Italien*. Stuttgart: Metzler, 1990.

Grimm, Jakob, and Wilhelm Grimm. *Deutsches Wörterbuch*. Ed. Karl Euling. Vol. 11. Leipzig: Hirzel, 1936.

Haar, Carel ter. *Joseph von Eichendorff: Aus dem Leben eines Taugenichts-Text, Materialien, Kommentar*. Munich: Hanser, 1977.

Haile, H. G. "Prudery in the Publication History of Goethe's *Roman Elegies*." *German Quarterly* 49:3 (1976): 287–94.

Henel, Heinrich. "Epigonenlyrik: Rückert und Platen." *Euphorion* 55 (1961): 260–78.

———. "Erlebnisdichtung und Symbolismus." *Deutsche Vierteljahrsschrift für Literaturwissenschaft und Geistesgeschichte* 32 (1958): 71–98.

Hermand, Jost. *Der frühe Heine: ein Kommentar zu den "Reisebildern."* Munich: Winkler, 1976.

Hoffmeister, Gerhart, ed. *Goethe in Italy: 1786–1986*. Amsterdam: Rodopi, 1988.

Höhn, Gerhard. *Heine-Handbuch: Zeit, Person, Werk*. Stuttgart: Metzler, 1987.

Holub, Robert C. *Heinrich Heine's Reception of German Grecophilia: The Function and Application of the Hellenic Tradition in the First Half of the Nineteenth Century*. Heidelberg: Winter, 1981.

Huch, Ricarda. *Literaturgeschichte und Literaturkritik*. Ed. Wilhelm Emrich. Vol. 6. Cologne: Kiepenheuer & Witsch, 1969.

Klinkenberg, Ralf H. *Die Reisebilder Heinrich Heines: Vermittlung durch literarische Stilmittel*. Frankfurt: Lang, 1981.

Kriz, Kay Dian. "Introduction: The Grand Tour." *Eighteenth-Century Studies* 31.1 (1997): 87–89.

Link, Jürgen. *Artistische Form und ästhetischer Sinn in Platens Lyrik*. Munich: Fink, 1971.

Littlewood, Ian. *A Literary Companion to Venice*. New York, NY: St. Martin's, 1995.

Loeffler, Bertina Maria. *Reactionary Romanticism: The Figure of Italy and the Desire for Social Privilege in the Writings of Goethe, Ludwig Tieck, and Dorothea Schlegel.* Diss. UC San Diego, 1996. Ann Arbor, MI: UMI, 1996. 9705752.

Maierhofer, Waltraud. "Italia und Germania. Zum Frauen- und Deutschlandbild in Heines italienischen Reisebildern." *Aufklärung und Skepsis: Internationaler Heine Kongress 1997 zum 200. Geburtstag.* Ed. Joseph A. Kruse, Bernd Witte, and Karin Füllner. Stuttgart: Metzler, 1999. 153–78.

Manger, Klaus, ed. *Italienbeziehungen des klassischen Weimars.* Tübingen: Niemeyer, 1997.

Mann, Thomas. "August von Platen." *Adel des Geistes.* Stockholm: Bermann-Fischer, 1945. 503–17.

Marcus, Laura. *Auto/biographical Discourses: Theory, Criticism, Practice.* Manchester: Manchester UP, 1994.

Marianelli, Marianello. "Die Idee der Entwicklung im Spiegel von Goethes Italienischer Reise." *Goethe Jahrbuch* 99 (1982): 117–32.

Marks, Hanna H., ed. *Erläuterungen und Dokumente: Joseph von Eichendorff Das Marmorbild.* Stuttgart: Reclam, 1984.

Mayer, Hans. *Zur Deutschen Klassik und Romantik.* Pfullingen: Neske, 1963.

Mitchell, B. R., ed. *International Historical Statistics: Europe 1750–1988.* New York, NY: Stockton, 1992.

Nehring, Wolfgang. "Wilhlem Heinrich Wackenroder." *German Writers in the Age of Goethe, 1789–1832.* Ed. James Hardin and Christoph E. Schweitzer. Detroit, MI: Gale, 1989. 352–56.

Nicolai, Gustav. *Italien wie es wirklich ist. Bericht über eine merkwürdige Reise in den hesperischen Gefilden, als Warnungsstimme für Alle, welche sich dahin sehnen.* 2 vols. Leipzig: Wigand, 1834.

Niederer, Heinrich. "Goethes unzeitgemässe Reise nach Italien: 1786–1788." *Jahrbuch des Freien Deutschen Hochstifts* (1980): 55–107.

Och, Gunnar, ed. *Was er wünscht, das ist ihm nie geworden: August Graf von Platen, 1796–1835.* Erlangen: Universitätsbibliothek, 1996. 133–49.

Oswald, Stefan. *Italienbilder: Beiträge zur Wandlung der deutschen Italienauffassung 1770–1840.* Heidelberg: Winter, 1985.

Paglia, Camille. *Sexual Personae: Art and Decadence from Nefertiti to Emily Dickinson.* New York, NY: Vintage, 1991.

Pascal, Roy. *Design and Truth in Autobiography.* Cambridge, MA: Harvard UP, 1960.

Paulin, Roger. *Ludwig Tieck: A Literary Biography.* New York, NY: Oxford UP, 1985.

Pemble, John. *The Mediterranean Passion: Victorians and Edwardians in the South.* New York, NY: Oxford UP, 1987.

———. *Venice Rediscovered.* New York, NY: Oxford UP, 1995.

Peters, George F. *"Der große Heide Nr. 2": Heinrich Heine and the Levels of his Goethe Reception.* New York, NY: Lang, 1989.

Pikulik, Lothar. *Romantik als Ungenügen an der Normalität. Am Beispiel Tiecks, Hoffmanns, Eichendorffs.* Frankfurt am Main: Suhrkamp, 1979.

Porter, Dennis. *Haunted Journeys: Desire and Transgression in European Travel Writing.* Princeton, NJ: Princeton UP, 1991.

Pruys, Karl Hugo. *Die Liebkosungen des Tigers: eine erotische Goethe Biographie.* Berlin: edition q, 1997.

Requadt, Paul. *Die Bildersprache der deutschen Italiendichtung: Von Goethe bis Benn.* Bern: Francke, 1962.

Richter, Simon. "Winckelmann's Progeny: Homosocial Networking in the Eighteenth Century." *Outing Goethe and his Age.* Ed. Alice A. Kuzniar. Stanford, CA: Stanford UP, 1996. 33–46.

Rieff, David. "German Hatred (of Germans)." *Harper's Magazine* (May 1994): 30–35.

Rousseau, G. S. "Love and Antiquities: Walpole and Gray on the Grand Tour." *Perilous Enlightenment: Pre- and Post-modern Discourses: Sexual, Historical.* Manchester: Manchester UP, 1991. 172–99.

Rybka, Knut. *Eichendorffs Italienische Reise: Textarbeit zum "Taugenichts."* Frankfurt am Main: Lang, 1993.

Said, Edward. *Orientalism.* New York, NY: Vintage, 1979.

Sammons, Jeffrey L. "Heine als Weltbürger? A Skeptical Inquiry." *Modern Language Notes* 101 (1986): 609–27.

———. *Heinrich Heine: A Modern Biography.* Princeton, NJ: Princeton UP, 1979.

———. *Heinrich Heine, The Elusive Poet.* New Haven, CT: Yale UP, 1969.

———. "Platen's Tulip Image." *Monatshefte* 52 (1960): 293–301.

Schenk, Christiana. *Venedig im Spiegel der Décadence-Literatur des Fin de siècle.* Frankfurt am Main: Lang, 1992.

Scherer, Gabriela and Beatrice Wehrli, ed. *Wahrheit und Wort: Festschrift für Rolf Tarot zum 65. Geburtstag.* Bern: Peter Lang, 1996.

Schindler, Herbert. *Nazarener: Romantischer Geist und christliche Kunst im 19. Jahrhundert.* Regensburg: Pustet, 1982.

Schlegel, Friedrich. *Kritische Friedrich Schlegel Ausgabe*. Ed. Hans Eichner. Vol. 4. Vienna: Schöningh, 1959.

Schreiner, Sabine. *Sprachenlernen in Lebensgeschichten der Goethezeit*. Munich: Iudicium, 1992.

Schultz, Hartwig, ed. *Erläuterungen und Dokumente: Joseph von Eichendorff, Aus dem Leben eines Taugenichts*. Stuttgart: Reclam, 1994.

Schumann, Detlev. "Eichendorff's Verhältnis zu Goethe." *Literaturwissenschaftliches Jahrbuch im Auftrage der Görres Gesellschaft* (1968): 159–218.

Schütze, Jochen K. *Goethe-Reisen*. Vienna: Passagen, 1998.

Seidlin, Oskar. *Versuche über Eichendorff*. Göttingen: Vandenhoeck und Ruprecht, 1965.

Sengle, Friedrich. *Biedermeierzeit: Deutsche Literatur im Spannungsfeld zwischen Restauration und Revolution 1815–1848*. Vol. 3. Stuttgart: Metzler, 1980. 415–67.

Staël, Germaine de. *Corinne ou l'Italie*. ed. Simone Balayé. Paris: Gallimard, 1985.

Stauf, Renate. *Der problematische Europäer: Heinrich Heine im Konflikt zwischen Nationenkritik und gesellschaftlicher Utopie*. Heidelberg: Winter, 1997.

Sterne, Laurence. *A Sentimental Journey*. New York, NY: Penguin, 1986.

Stowe, William. *Going Abroad: European Travel in Nineteenth-Century American Culture*. Princeton, NJ: Princeton UP, 1994.

Tanner, Tony. *Venice Desired*. Cambridge, MA: Blackwell, 1992.

Vaget, Hans Rudolf. Introduction. *Erotic Poems*. By Johann Wolfgang von Goethe. New York, NY: Oxford UP, 1997.

Van Den Abbeele, Georges. *Travel as Metaphor from Montaigne to Rousseau*. Minneapolis, MN: U of Minnesota P, 1992.

Wackenroder, Wilhelm Heinrich. *Sämtliche Werke und Briefe: Historisch-kritische Ausgabe*. Ed. Silvio Vietto. Heidelberg: Winter, 1991.

Walter-Schneider, Margret and Martina Hasler. "Die Kunst in Rom: Zum 7. und 8. Kapitel von Eichendorff's Erzählung *Aus dem Leben eines Taugenichts*," *Aurora: Jahrbuch der Eichendorff Gesellschaft* 45 (1985): 49–62.

Wellek, René. "The Crisis of Comparative Literature." *Concepts of Criticism*. Ed. Stephen G. Nichols Jr. New Haven, CT: Yale UP, 1963. 282–95.

Werner, Michael. "Heines Reise von München nach Genua im Lichte ihrer Quellen." *Heine Jahrbuch* 14 (1975): 24–46.

Widmann, Carlos. "Sog des Südens." *Der Spiegel* (24 February 2001): 54–73.

Wilton, Andrew, and Iliana Bignamani, ed. *Grand Tour: The Lure of Italy in the Eighteenth Century.* London: Tate Gallery, 1996.

Zapperi, Roberto. *Das Incognito: Goethes ganz andere Existenz im Rom.* Trans. Ingeborg Walter. Munich: Beck, 1999.

Notes

Introduction

[1] René Wellek, "The Crisis of Comparative Literature," *Concepts of Criticism,* ed. Stephen G. Nichols, Jr. (New Haven: Yale UP, 1963), 282–95.

[2] Hugo Dyserinck, "Zum Problem der 'images' and 'mirages' und ihrer Untersuchung im Rahmen der Vergleichenden Literaturwissenschaft," *Arcadia* 1 (1966): 110–11.

[3] Peter Boerner, "National Images and their Place in Literary Research: Germany as seen by Eighteenth-century French and English Reading Audiences," *Monatshefte* 67 (1975): 360.

[4] Manfred S. Fischer, "Literarische Seinsweise und politische Funktion nationenbezogener Images: Ein Beitrag zur Theorie der komparatistischen Imagologie," *neohelicon* 10 (1983): 259.

[5] In 1990 Brenner published a 741-page volume, *Der Reisebericht in der deutschen Literatur: Ein Forschungsüberblick als Vorstudie zu einer Gattungsgeschichte,* in which he employs a bibliographic approach. He outlines the many literary periods and then briefly summarizes the research of a multitude of scholars covering each phase. Brenner concludes with an extremely comprehensive bibliography for the field, which includes all the secondary research he deems important for the many primary authors and eras included. Peter J. Brenner, *Der Reisebericht in der deutschen Literatur: Ein Forschungsüberblick als Vorstudie zu einer Gattungsgeschichte* (Tübingen: Niemeyer, 1990).

[6] Peter J. Brenner, "Die Erfahrung der Fremde," *Der Reisebericht: Die Entwicklung einer Gattung in der deutschen Literatur,* ed. Peter J. Brenner (Frankfurt am Main: Suhrkamp, 1989), 14. Brenner alludes to the genre's relationship to the larger category of autobiography as well as the role of subjectivity in such writings. Therefore, the generalized description of the traveler as liar seems questionable. Misrepresentation of self is not identical with misrepresentation of place. Brenner does not address the distinction. In terms of modern travel, the accessibility of even the most remote parts of the world would, I think, preclude gross misrepresentation of exotic locales. This anthology of essays offers an overview of the history of the *Reisebericht* from the Middle Ages to the present day.

[7] Wolfgang Neuber, "Zur Gattungspoetik des Reiseberichts," *Der Reisebericht: Die Entwicklung einer Gattung in der deutschen Literatur*, ed. Brenner, 51–52.

[8] Dennis Porter, *Haunted Journeys: Desire and Transgression in European Travel Writing* (Princeton: Princeton UP, 1991), 9.

[9] Harold Bloom, *The Anxiety of Influence: A Theory of Poetry* (New York: Oxford UP, 1973), 30.

[10] Bloom cites Goethe as "a great denier of influence" and one of the prime examples of the strong poet. Bloom, 56, 72.

[11] Edward Said, *Orientalism* (New York: Vintage, 1979), 3.

[12] William Stowe, *Going Abroad: European Travel in Nineteenth-Century American Culture* (Princeton: Princeton UP, 1994), 12–13. Stowe's is just one of several recent useful English-language works on travel narrative. See also James Buzard, *The Beaten Track: European Tourism, Literature, and the Ways to "Culture" 1800–1918* (Oxford: Claredon Press, 1993). This generation of critics is very much informed by the work of Michel Butor. See Michel Butor, "Le voyage et l'ecriture," *Romantisme* 4 (1972): 4–19.

[13] There is also great evidence of a general, public interest in the Grand Tour. For example, The Tate Gallery in London staged a massive exhibit in 1996 titled "The Grand Tour: The Lure of Italy in the 18th Century." The lavish catalogue published in conjunction with the exhibit includes references to Goethe's Italian journey and even to the Italian experiences of the Dowager Duchess Anna Amalie of Weimar. Andrew Wilton and Iliana Bignamani, ed., *Grand Tour: The Lure of Italy in the Eighteenth Century* (London: Tate Gallery, 1996). I am also reminded of the ongoing popularity of cinematic representations of Italian adventures, themselves usually based on literary texts. Recent examples include E. M. Forster's *A Room with a View*, Elizabeth [von Arnim]'s *Enchanted April*, and Henry James's *The Wings of the Dove*.

[14] Kay Dian Kriz, "Introduction: The Grand Tour," *Eighteenth-Century Studies* 31.1 (1997): 87.

[15] Chloe Chard, introduction, *Transports: Travel, Pleasure, and Imaginative Geography, 1600–1830,* ed. Chloe Chard and Helen Langdon (New Haven: Yale UP, 1996), 5.

[16] Chloe Chard, *Pleasure and Guilt on the Grand Tour: Travel Writing and Imaginative Geography 1600–1830* (Manchester: Manchester UP, 1999), 1–9.

[17] The apartment at 20 Via del Corso in Rome in which Goethe lived with Tischbein was dedicated as a museum of Goethe's Italian experiences on 1 June 1997. It is the only museum funded and managed by the German government outside of the Federal Republic.

[18] Georges Van Den Abbeele, *Travel as Metaphor: From Montaigne to Rousseau* (Minneapolis: U of Minnesota P, 1992), xvii–xviii. Van den Abbeele's argument overlooks various subcategories of travel, which, in contrast to vol-

untary and recreational travel, are not undertaken for pleasure or education: true nomadism lacks the self-referential focus of a homeland elsewhere. In the nomadic existence, home and abroad, familiar and foreign are conflated. The other extreme, exile, either by choice or by enforcement, implies a loss of the home, although the orientation may well remain focused on that place. It seems that Van den Abbeele's argument would accommodate exile, but would discount the more primitive model of nomadism. The works investigated in this study, although generally of the model of journey for pleasure or education, at times will exhibit characteristics of nomadism or exile.

Chapter 1

[1] Nicholas Boyle, *Goethe: The Poet and the Age,* vol. 1 (New York: Oxford UP, 1991), 445. This image continues to dominate the public's view: in 1982 Andy Warhol completed a series of boldly colored screenprints based on Tischbein's painting. The Warhol print decorates the jackets of the twelve-volume Suhrkamp English-language edition of Goethe's works. Subsequent references to this, at present, two-volume work will be made in the text, abbreviated as *B1* and *B2*. Volume 2 was published in 2000.

[2] Johann Wolfgang von Goethe, *Italienische Reise,* ed. Christoph Michel and Hans-Georg Dewitz (Frankfurt am Main: Deutscher Klassiker Verlag, 1993), 163. All further references to this edition of the *Italienische Reise* made in the text will be abbreviated as *IR* and, where applicable, will also include the date of Goethe's entry.

[3] Tischbein left this unfinished painting behind, undated and unsigned, while fleeing from the revolution in Naples in 1799. Karl von Rothschild purchased the painting in Italy in the 1840s and gifted it in 1877 to the Städelsche Kunstinstitut in Frankfurt am Main, where it remains today. Thus, it was not displayed in Germany until long after Goethe's death.

[4] Johann Wolfgang von Goethe, *Wilhelm Meisters Lehrjahre,* ed. Wilhelm Voßkamp and Herbert Jaumann (Frankfurt am Main: Deutscher Klassiker Verlag, 1992), 503.

[5] Johann Wolfgang von Goethe, *Dichtung und Wahrheit,* ed. Klaus D. Müller (Frankfurt am Main: Deutscher Klassiker Verlag, 1986), 19–20. All further references to this work will be made in the text, abbreviated as *DW*. An additional recollection in the text describes the change in his father as he recounted his Italian experiences to the children. *DW,* 40.

[6] Sabine Schreiner, *Sprachenlernen in Lebensgeschichten der Goethezeit* (München: Iudicium, 1992), 85.

[7] Thomas P. Saine, introduction, *Italian Journey,* by Johann Wolfgang von Goethe, eds. Thomas P. Saine and Jeffrey L. Sammons (Princeton: Princeton UP, 1989), 1.

[8] A selective German translation first appeared in 1972, the complete text in German in 1986. *Viaggio per l'Italia* is comprised, like most travel accounts of its day, of a large number of letters, in this case addressed to a fictitious nobleman.

[9] Johann Caspar Goethe, *Reise durch Italien im Jahre 1740 (Viaggo per l'Italia),* trans. and ed. Albert Meier (Frankfurt am Main: Deutscher Taschenbuch Verlag, 1986), 54–55.

[10] It is in reference to Goethe's relationship with his father that a psychoanalytic reading of the biography is most relevant and credible. See Kurt Robert Eissler, *Goethe: A Psychoanalytic Study 1775–1786,* 2 vols. (Detroit: Wayne State UP, 1963).

[11] Johann Wolfgang von Goethe, *Von Frankfurt nach Weimar: Briefe, Tagebücher und Gespräche vom 23. Mai 1764 bis 30. Oktober 1775,* ed. Wilhelm Große (Frankfurt am Main: Deutscher Klassiker Verlag, 1997), 207–8. Henceforth this volume shall be referred to in the text as *VFW.*

[12] These events are recounted at the close of the first volume of *Dichtung und Wahrheit. DW,* 849–52.

[13] Most interestingly, during Goethe's absence from Weimar, Jagemann began work on the *Gazetta di Weimar,* a weekly Italian serial (6 January 1787 to 27 June 1789). Jagemann published, edited, and wrote most of the articles in the *Gazetta* on topics, including politics and religion, among a wider range typical of the time's enlightened multidisciplinary interests. There is no proof that Goethe owned or later read the *Gazetta.* Those left behind in Weimar followed Goethe's progress along the southern peninsula with great enthusiasm. Katharina Gerhardt, "Christian Joseph Jagemann — ein Vermittler italienischer Sprache und Kultur im Klassischen Weimar." *Italienbeziehungen des klassischen Weimar,* ed. Klaus Manger (Tübingen: Niemeyer, 1997), 245–63.

[14] I refer to the work, in its totality, throughout this investigation as the *Italienische Reise.*

[15] Stefan Oswald, *Italienbilder: Beiträge zur Wandlung der deutschen Italienauffassung 1770–1840* (Heidelberg: Carl Winter, 1985), 96. Further references to this very useful work will be made parenthetically, abbreviated as *O.*

[16] Johann Wolfgang von Goethe, *Napoleonische Zeit: Briefe, Tagebücher und Gespräche vom 10. Mai 1805 bis 6. Juni 1816. Teil II.,* ed. Rose Unterberger (Frankfurt am Main: Deutscher Klassiker Verlag, 1994), 455.

[17] Robert Gould, "Problems of Reception and Autobiographical Method in the 'Zweiter Römischer Aufenthalt' of Goethe's Italienische Reise," *Carlton Germanic Papers* 22 (1994): 82.

[18] Italo Michele Battafarano, "Goethes Italienische Reise — Quasi ein Roman: Zur Literarizität eines autor-referentiellen Textes," *Wahrheit und Wort: Festschrift für Rolf Tarot zum 65. Geburtstag,* ed. Gabriela Scherer and Beatrice Wehrli (Bern: Peter Lang, 1996), 29.

[19] Jochen K. Schütze, *Goethe-Reisen* (Vienna: Passagen, 1998), 87.

[20] Laura Marcus, *Auto/biographical Discourses: Theory, Criticism, Practice* (Manchester: Manchester UP, 1994), 33.

[21] Roy Pascal, *Design and Truth in Autobiography* (Cambridge: Harvard UP, 1960), 36.

[22] Erich Trunz, commentary, *Autobiographische Schriften I*, by Johann Wolfgang von Goethe (Munich: C. H. Beck, 1981), 640.

[23] Marcus, 141. She cites Katherine Goodman.

[24] Peter Boerner, "Italienische Reise," *Interpretationen: Goethes Erzählwerk*, ed. Paul Michael Lützeler and James E. McLeod (Stuttgart: Reclam, 1985), 351.

[25] Brenner, *Der Reisebericht in der deutschen Literatur*, 275.

[26] Hans Mayer, "Italienische Reise," *Zur deutschen Klassik und Romantik* (Pfullingen: Neske, 1963), 64.

[27] I will return to the subject of the Nazarenes in my discussion of Eichendorff's role in the German Romantic image of Italy.

[28] Grimm, Breymayer, and Erhart's contribution lies in the larger context of the history of German writers traveling to Italy, rather than in their individual chapter on Goethe. Gunther Grimm, Ursula Breymayer, and Walter Erhart, *"Ein Gefühl von freierem Leben": Deutsche Dichter in Italien* (Stuttgart: Metzler, 1990).

[29] Heinrich Niederer, "Goethes unzeitgemäße Reise nach Italien: 1786–1788," *Jahrbuch des Freien Deutschen Hochstifts* (1980): 63

[30] Johann Wolfgang von Goethe, "Requiem, dem frohsten Manne des Jahrhunderts, dem Fürsten von Ligne," *Gedichte und Singspiele II: Gedichte, Nachlese und Nachlaß*, ed. Siegfried Seidel (Berlin: Aufbau, 1979), 537.

[31] This epigraph was included in the first editions of both 1816 and 1817. However, it was omitted in the publication of the *Zweiter Römischer Aufenthalt* in 1829.

Chapter 2

[1] Roberto Zapperi, *Das Inkognito: Goethes ganz andere Existenz im Rom*, trans. Ingeborg Walter (Munich: Beck, 1999), 39. Zapperi's entire second chapter is devoted to Goethe's use of the incognito. Further references to this work will be abbreviated as *Z*.

[2] Grimm, Breymayer, and Erhard, 61.

[3] Jochen K. Schütze, *Goethe-Reisen* (Vienna: Passagen, 1998), 25. All subsequent references will be abbreviated as *GR*.

[4] Jane K. Brown, "The Renaissance of Goethe's Poetic Genius in Italy," *Goethe in Italy, 1786–1986: A Bicentennial Symposium*, ed. Gerhart Hoffmeister (Amsterdam: Rodopi, 1988), 83.

[5] Lilian Furst, "Goethe's *Italienische Reise* in its European Context," *Goethe in Italy*, 122–23.

[6] Richard Block argues that Goethe senior left a void that the son sought to fill through his own Italian journey. Block reads Winckelmann, who came chronologically between father and son, as a stand-in for the father. Goethe can only overcome the ghost of his father by extending his journey beyond Naples. During the son's entire stay in Italy, he runs the risk of total annihilation by the forces of influence at play. "The father's absence, which shadows Goethe throughout most of his Italian journey as a very real presence, is what will eventually hook a Goethe readership." Richard O. Block, *The Spell of Italy: The Goethe-Effect and the German Literary Imagination*, diss., Northwestern U, 1998, 155.

[7] On 7 September 1786, Goethe reports meeting a young harper and his daughter south of Munich, also on their way to Bolzano. He devotes a lengthy page and a half to his description of the captivating girl, reminiscent of Mignon in *Wilhelm Meisters Lehrjahre*. By 1786 Goethe had set aside the manuscript of *Wilhelm Meisters Theatralische Sendung*, in which both Mignon and the Harper already figured. *IR*, 16–18.

[8] Grimm, Breymayer, and Erhard, 63.

[9] This is part of the collection at the Goethe-Schiller Archives in Weimar. It recounts his purchases of clothes and wigs, food, shelter, and even refers to "women," which Zapperi interprets as evidence of Goethe's visits to Italian prostitutes. Zapperi, 140–41.

[10] Roger Cardinal, "The Passionate Traveler: Goethe in Italy," *Publications of the English Goethe Society*, New Series 67 (1997): 27.

[11] This passage from the travel report is particularly reminiscent of the well-known passage in *Dichtung und Wahrheit* in which Goethe describes the prevalence of things Italian in his parents' home. *DW*, 19–20.

[12] At that time Naples had approximately twice the population of Rome. In 1750 Rome had a population of 156,000 while Naples had a reported 305,000 inhabitants. In 1790 Rome had 163,000 inhabitants, however the population in Naples had grown at a much faster rate: the census of 1796 recorded 427,000 inhabitants. B. R. Mitchell, ed., *International Historical Statistics: Europe: 1750–1993* (New York: Stockton Press, 1998), 74–76.

[13] His interest in geology has less to do with any curiosity about the origins of the earth than might be expected. His theories on the *Urphänomen* are based more directly on his *Farbenlehre*.

[14] Paestum, the southernmost point of Goethe's journey, besides the island of Sicily, is situated approximately 100 miles south of Naples. Today the Greek

ruins of Paestum, most especially the three temples, are considered to be superior in quality to those found on the island of Sicily.

[15] Jane K. Brown, *Goethe's Faust: The German Tragedy* (Ithaca: Cornell UP, 1986), 221, 232.

[16] Nicholas Boyle, "Goethe in Paestum: a higher-critical look at the *Italienische Reise*," *Oxford German Studies 20/21* (1991–1992): 30.

[17] Goethe later reports that the duke did not make the journey.

[18] Saine and Sammons, "Notes," *Italian Journey*, by Goethe, 462, note 60.

[19] See Zapperi's reading of the IR for a detailed analysis of the ongoing relationship of Goethe and the duke during the poet's absence from Weimar and a description of Goethe's expert manipulation of the situation to return on his own terms to Germany. *Z*, chapter 7.

[20] This variant is found in Goethe, *IR*, 1155–57.

[21] Moritz's *Reisen eines Deutschen in Italien* (Travels of a German in Italy) was published in three volumes from 1792 to 1793.

[22] These could be Moritz, Fritz Bury, Johann Georg Schütz, or possibly Angelika Kauffmann. Michel and Dewitz, "Commentary," *Italienische Reise*, by Goethe, 1414.

[23] August von Goethe is buried in the Protestant Cemetery in Rome, site of the Pyramid of Cestius, which his father mentions in the *Italienische Reise* and sketched while in Rome. Ironically, his tombstone does not include his name, but rather states in Latin: "Goethe. The son, who preceded his father." For an interesting account of three generations of Goethes in Rome see: Andreas Beyer, "Reisen — Bleiben — Sterben: Die Goethes in Rom," *Italienbeziehungen des klassischen Weimar*, ed. Manger, 63–84.

[24] Eissler, 2: 1019. Roberto Zapperi refutes this long accepted view, postulating that Goethe frequently visited prostitutes while abroad. *Z*, 140–41.

[25] Johann Wolfgang von Goethe, *Italien — Im Schatten der Revolution: Briefe, Tagebücher und Gespräche vom 3. September 1786 bis 12. Juni 1794*, ed. Karl Eibl (Deutscher Klassiker Verlag: Frankfurt am Main, 1991), 387–88. Further references are abbreviated *ISR*. Zapperi believes that Goethe's supposed fear of venereal disease was merely a fiction maintained to maintain his privacy. *Z*, 152–53.

[26] Two months later, Goethe learns that Maddalena Riggi's fiancé has broken off their engagement. Goethe visits her frequently, and upon his departure, she is grateful for his ongoing attention and concern. What is interesting about Goethe's attraction to the young woman from Milan is the overlooked fact that on his own trip to Italy, Goethe's father fell in love and briefly corresponded with a young woman in Milan named Maria Merati.

[27] In his title and throughout the published account, Goethe refers to the "Carneval," but in this reference to the event a year earlier he misspelled it as "Carnaval."

[28] Michel and Dewitz, "Commentary," *Italienische Reise,* by Goethe, 1426.

[29] Grimm, Breymayer, and Erhard, 92.

[30] Marianello Marianelli, "Die Idee der Entwicklung im Spiegel von Goethe's Italienische Reise," *Goethe-Jahrbuch* 99 (1982): 121.

Chapter 3

[1] *Tristia ex Ponto,* I: 3: verses 1–4 and 27–30. The editors of the *Frankfurter Ausgabe* report that Goethe expressed his identification with Ovid six months after returning to Weimar, specifically in a letter to Herder in Rome dated 27 December 1788. Goethe commissioned the German translation of Ovid's elegy included in his text from Friedrich Wilhelm Riemer in 1829. Michel and Dewitz, commentary, *Italienische Reise,* by Goethe, 1449.

[2] Within the eighteen months following his return to Weimar, Goethe did publish a series of informative essays on various Italian topics in *Wieland's Der Teutsche Merkur.* Of these ten relatively short essays, Goethe addressed the content of five in his later *Italienische Reise.* Topics included the Italian means of telling time, *Volksgesang,* various works of art, and theories of art. In 1789 Goethe also published a deluxe edition of *Das Römische Carneval,* which, as mentioned above, would also later be included in the *Italienische Reise.* His essay concerning Cagliostro was published in 1792.

[3] Karl Eibl, commentary, *Gedichte 1756 – 1799,* by Johann Wolfgang von Goethe (Frankfurt am Main: Deutscher Klassiker Verlag, 1987), 1094.

[4] H. G. Haile, "Prudery in the Publication History of Goethe's *Roman Elegies,*" *The German Quarterly* 49:3 (1976): 287–88.

[5] Hans Rudolf Vaget, introduction, *Erotic Poems,* by Johann Wolfgang von Goethe (New York: Oxford UP, 1997), xx–xxi.

[6] Since 1815 the *Elegien* have been published with a motto, also published with the poems in *Die Horen:* Nos venerem tutam concessaque furta canemus, Inque meo nullum carmine crimen erit. ("Sicheren Liebesgenuß und gestatteten Raub nur besing' ich;/ Nirgends in meinem Gedicht wird ein Verbrechen gelehrt.") This motto is a citation from Ovid's *Ars amatoria* I, 33 f. Goethe, *Gedichte 1756–1799,* 393 and 1099.

[7] The *Frankfurter Ausgabe* (Goethe, *Gedichte 1756–1799*) includes two parallel texts for the *Römische Elegien,* Goethe's 1788 manuscript and the first publication in *Die Horen* in 1795. I cite the latter, the version generally used in scholarship today, but will remark when significant differences exist. All parenthetical references to the poetry, include elegy number, where applicable, and line number.

[8] Chard, "Grand and Ghostly Tours: The Topography of Memory." *Eighteenth-Century Studies* 31.1 (1997): 101–2.

[9] Sander Gilman, "Goethe's Touch: Touching, Seeing, and Sexuality," *Inscribing the Other* (Lincoln: U Nebraska P, 1991), 48.

[10] Karl Hugo Pruys, Die Liebkosungen des Tigers: eine erotische Goethe-Biographie (Berlin: edition q, 1997).

[11] Karl Eibl recounts the history of the connection between the two words in a palindrome: "Schon in der Antike wurde das zu einem anscheinend recht verbreiteten Palindrom benutzt: 'Roma tibi subito motibus ibit Amor.'" Eibl, commentary, *Gedichte: 1756–1799*, 1099–1100.

[12] Goethe comments on the repeated presence of this song in the *Italienische Reise* on 17 September 1786. *IR*, 53.

[13] On 25 February 1787 in the *Italienische Reise*, Goethe tells of the typical Neapolitan's conception of Germany and the Germans. It refers to snow, mountains, and wooden buildings. *IR*, 199.

[14] Goethe, *Gedichte: 1756–1799*, 398, 400. Its last six lines are identical to the closing lines of the published version.

[15] Eibl, commentary, *Gedichte: 1756–1799*, 1104.

[16] Eibl, commentary, *Gedichte: 1756–1799*, 1121–22. Northern travelers, including Heine, often commented on the presence of fleas in the Italian inns. These lines also refer to Hadrian's biography, *Scriptores historiae augustae*. Hadrian is reported to have said that he preferred the arduous travails and climate of Britian to the fleas of Rome.

[17] Although Goethe spelled the name Faustine in the poem, commentators refer to Faustina, probably because of the repeated attempts to link the character to an actual Italian woman.

[18] An additional sixty-seven epigrams remained unpublished at the time of Goethe's death, but are extant today.

[19] The *Venezianische Epigramme* are published in the *Frankfurter Ausgabe* in the same volume of Goethe's poetry as the *Römische Elegien*, *Gedichte: 1756–1799*.

[20] Goethe often thought of returning to Italy throughout the second half of his life. The closest he came to making a return trip, an extended journey in the style of the first, was in 1795 and 1796. Concrete plans were made, itineraries were mapped out, traveling clothes were purchased. Goethe planned to collaborate with Meyer on an all-encompassing book on Italy, an artist's description of Italy, its culture and history as outgrowths of its natural surroundings (*B2*, 297). Meyer set out ahead and waited in Italy for Goethe. But in the end family responsibility, political developments, and poetic priority intervened. In late 1795 Goethe's third child died shortly after birth. Napoleon's armies continued their expansion through Europe, entering Italy in 1796. Boyle speculates that Schiller too influenced Goethe's ultimate decision

against a protracted visit to Italy, suggesting that there were more pressing poetic or literary projects than a book on Italy, for example, *Faust* (*B2*, 548). Christiane and August traveled with Goethe to Frankfurt, where they waited for him, unsure of his plans. He traveled as far as the Gotthard Pass. For the third time, he ascended the mountain to look into Italy, but ultimately renounced another journey south, a prudent decision in terms of his own personal safety, and instead returned to his family and to life in Weimar.

Chapter 4

[1] This substitution is explored at length by Lothar Pikulik. Lothar Pikulik, *Romantik als Ungenügen an der Normalität. Am Beispiel Tiecks, Hoffmanns, Eichendorffs* (Frankfurt am Main: Suhrkamp, 1979). As reviewed by Brenner, *Der Reisebericht in der deutschen Literatur*, 330.

[2] The authorial signature of some of the eighteen pieces comprising Herzensergießungen is not all together clear. Various reference works consulted assign anywhere from only three to as many as five of the selections to Tieck. Scholars agree that Tieck authored *Sehnsucht nach Italien*, the first portion of interest to this discussion. The status of the second, *Brief eines jungen deutschen Malers in Rom an seinen Freund in Nürnberg*, is less certain, but is generally considered to be the work of Tieck's pen. (*The Dictionary of Literary Biography* reports that Tieck claimed responsibility for this selection in 1798, but then stated in 1814 that Wackenroder had written it.) Wolfgang Nehring, "Wilhelm Heinrich Wackenroder," *Dictionary of Literary Biography*, vol. 90, *German Writers in the Age of Goethe, 1789–1832*, ed. James Hardin and Christoph E. Schweitzer (Detroit: Gale Research, 1989), 355.

[3] Roger Paulin, *Ludwig Tieck: A Literary Biography* (Oxford: Clarendon P, 1985), 36.

[4] Tieck in Wilhelm Heinrich Wackenroder, *Sämtliche Werke und Briefe: Historisch-kritische Ausgabe*, ed. Silvio Vietto (Heidelberg: Winter, 1991), 1: 59. All further references will be abbreviated in the text as *TW*.

[5] Tieck's conception of the nomadic, wandering traveler is not unrelated to the wanderers of Goethe's early career, notably Werther and the travelers of "Wandrers Sturmlied" and "Der Wandrer."

[6] In Tieck's novel *Franz Sternbalds Wanderungen* (1798), Dürer is the teacher of the protagonist who sets out to further his education in Italy.

[7] Johann Wolfgang von Goethe, *Ästhetische Schriften 1771–1805*, ed. Friedmar Apel (Frankfurt: Deutscher Klassiker Verlag, 1998), 475.

[8] As in the case of the *Herzensergießungen*, the authorial status of much of the *Phantasien* has been debated at length. This later volume contains contributions from both writers, although Tieck likely penned the majority.

[9] Art historians, including Keith Andrews and Herbert Schindler, have debated the origin of the term Nazarene as a description of this group of paint-

ers and their style: its roots are to be found either in the painters' preferred coiffure or in the predominantly religious content of their work. These painters wore their hair long and parted in the middle to emulate Albrecht Dürer as depicted in his most famous self-portrait. As early as the seventeenth century, Italians described such hair, synonymous with the predominant image of Jesus Christ, as "alla nazarena," or in the Nazarene style. Thus, most historians agree that "i nazareni" was most likely a slightly pejorative term used by contemporary Romans to describe these eccentric German artists. Eventually, other Germans in Rome reported this term in their correspondence home, and the label stuck. The use of the term Nazarene as a description of their specific style of painting first appears much later in the nineteenth century.

[10] Herbert Schindler, *Nazarener: Romantischer Geist und christliche Kunst im 19. Jahrhundert* (Regensburg: Friedrich Pustet, 1982), 82.

[11] Keith Andrews reiterates that many of the German artists living in Rome at the time of the publication of *Herzensergießungen* speculated that Goethe was its anonymous author. These painters, a generation older than the Nazarenes who had yet to arrive in Rome, perhaps could arrive at what now seems such a preposterous conclusion because Goethe's primary work on Italy would not be published until 1816. They either had not yet read Goethe's *Einleitung in die Propyläen* or failed to read it as a reaction to *Herzensergießungen*. Keith Andrews, *The Nazarenes: A Brotherhood of German Painters in Rome* (Oxford: Clarendon, 1964), 14.

[12] Traditionally, Meyer's text is included in Goethe's collected writings. Johann Heinrich Meyer, "Neu-Deutsche Religios-Patriotische Kunst," *Über Kunst und Altertum* I 2 (1817) in *Ästhetische Schriften 1816–1820*, ed. Hendrik Birus (Frankfurt am Main: Deutscher Klassiker Verlag, 1999), 105–29.

[13] Johann Wolfgang von Goethe, *Zwischen Weimar und Jena — Einsam-Tätiges Alter I: Briefe, Tagebücher und Gespräche vom 6. Juni 1816 bis zum 26. Dezember 1822, Teil I*, ed. Dorothea Schäfer-Weiss (Frankfurt am Main: Deutscher Klassiker Verlag, 1999), 86. Further citations will be abbreviated *ZWJ*.

[14] Bertina Loeffler shows how Goethe's resistance to post-revolution change indeed allies him politically, if not aesthetically, with the early Romantics; thus, Goethe's *Italienische Reise* is his claim for artistic immortality. In a similar fashion Tieck, in William Lovell (1792), and Dorothee Schlegel, in Florentin (1801), also depict and in a sense exploit the aesthetic image of Italy as a means to fulfill their desire for social privilege. Bertina Maria Loeffler, *Reactionary Romanticism: The Figure of Italy and the Desire for Social Privilege in the Writings of Goethe, Ludwig Tieck, and Dorothea Schlegel*, diss., UC-San Diego, 1996.

[15] Friedrich Schlegel, "Über die deutsche Kunstausstellung zu Rom, im Frühjahr 1819, und über den Gegenwärtigen Stand der deutschen Kunst in Rom," *Ansichten und Ideen der Christlichen Kunst,* ed. Hans Eichner (Vi-

enna: Schöningh, 1959), 258. This essay appeared in the *Wiener Jahrbuch der Literatur,* vol. 7, July–September 1819.

[16] Paul Requadt, *Die Bildersprache der deutschen Italiendichtung: Von Goethe bis Benn* (Bern: Francke, 1962), 107.

[17] All these poems included in the novel appear without titles; however, Eichendorff included them in his 1837 collection of poetry with the titles that I refer to above.

[18] Joseph von Eichendorff, *Dichter und Ihre Gesellen,* ed. Brigitte Schillbach and Hartwig Schultz (Frankfurt am Main: Deutscher Klassiker, 1993), 325–26. All further parenthetical citations are abbreviated in the text as *DG.*

[19] Richarda Huch, "Die Romantik," *Literaturgeschichte und Literaturkritik,* ed. Wilhelm Emrich (Berlin: Kiepenheuer & Witsch, 1969), 382.

[20] Detlev Schumann, "Eichendorff's Verhältnis zu Goethe," *Literaturwissenschaftliches Jahrbuch im Auftrage der Görres Gesellschaft,* ed. Hermann Kunisch (Berlin: Duncker und Humblot, 1968), 183. Most interesting is Schumann's observation that the acoustic emphasis of Eichendorff's poem stands in sharp contrast to the visual agenda pursued by Goethe.

[21] Teodolinda Barolini, "Giovanni Boccaccio," *European Writers — The Middle Ages and the Renaissance,* vol. 2, *Petrarch to Renaissance Short Fiction,* ed. William T. H. Jackson and George Stade (New York: Scribners, 1983), 510.

[22] Wolfgang Frühwald and Brigitte Schillbach, commentary, *Ahnung und Gegenwart. Erzählungen I,* by Joseph von Eichendorff (Frankfurt am Main: Deutscher Klassiker Verlag, 1985), 758. All further references to *Das Marmorbild* will be abbreviated as *MB* and those to *Aus dem Leben eines Taugenichts* will be abbreviated as *ALT.* Both works are contained in this volume of Eichendorff's work.

[23] Hanna Marks, ed., *Erläuterungen und Dokumente: Joseph von Eichendorff, Das Marmorbild* (Stuttgart: Reclam, 1984), 41.

[24] An extant earlier textual variant indicates that Eichendorff's, at least original, intention in "Mailand," was the Italian city and not the landscape of the month of May. Frühwald and Schillbach, commentary, *MB,* 778.

[25] Joseph Freiherr von Eichendorff, "Der deutsche Roman des achtzehnten Jahrhunderts in seinem Verhältnis zu Christentum," *Geschichte der Poesie,* ed. Hartwig Schultz (Frankfurt am Main, Deutscher Klassiker Verlag, 1990), 464–68.

[26] Requadt, 108.

[27] As cited by the Grimms: "erst seit dem ende des 18. jahrhunderts mit enger beziehung auf das gefühlsleben schrecklich grauenvoll; schauder, angst, entsetzen, furcht, beklemmung, unbehagen, befangenheit, abneigung u.a. verursachend." Jakob Grimm and Wilhelm Grimm, *Deutsches Wörterbuch,* ed. Karl Euling (Leipzig: Hirzel, 1936) vol. 11/3: 1057. The development of this us-

age is contemporaneous with the rise of the popularity of the Gothic novel in Germany.

[28] Perhaps the ending gesture of the third portion of *Dichtung und Wahrheit*, which appeared in 1814, planted the seed in Eichendorff's mind for an Italian journey. Goethe's narrative breaks off with the decision, albeit unfulfilled, to visit Italy.

[29] Hartwig Schultz, ed., *Erläuterungen und Dokumente: Joseph von Eichendorff, Aus dem Leben eines Taugenichts* (Stuttgart: Reclam, 1994), 50.

[30] The first edition of the novella mentioned Wien only in the last paragraph of chapter 2, instead referring to "W"; however, in 1841 Eichendorff changed the abbreviated references to "Wien." Frühwald and Schillbach, commentary, *ALT*, 807.

[31] Eichendorff's figuration of the mountaintop castle is surely also informed by the European tradition of the Gothic novel most prevalent in English literature of the late eighteenth century. One thinks immediately of Horace Walpole's *Castle of Otranto* (1764) and Anne Radcliff's romances, most notably *The Mysteries of Udolpho* (1794) and *The Italian* (1797). For Walpole, the Gothic setting was synonymous with the Medieval. The later exponents of the genre embraced a more timeless situation, in which the term Gothic came to describe the mysterious, macabre plot elements.

[32] Goethe spelled the name incorrectly (Pallagonia) in his account found in the second part of the *Italienische Reise*.

[33] Seidlin's emphasis on the emblem rather than the symbol in Eichendorff's work remains of importance. In his conservative approach though, his description of Eichendorff's Rome as the presumably Christian "Gottesstadt" is questionable. Oskar Seidlin, *Versuche über Eichendorff* (Göttingen: Vandenhoeck und Ruprecht, 1965), 16. (This essay originally appeared in the *Journal of English and Germanic Philology* 52 [1953].) Throughout *Taugenichts* the city remains curiously devoid of the Christian content normally associated with it. Eichendorff's single religious reference beyond the church towers and angels described during the protagonist's approach to the city is the *Marienbild*. Finally, the Rome to which the married Taugenichts plans to return also lacks any Christian reference, renowned only for its *Wasserkünste*. Ultimately, the Taugenichts is a *Sonntagskind*, who is at home in a universal and natural religious space and is often underway on Sundays and significantly, not in church. The Rome of his childhood fantasies is vastly more religious than the Rome he actually visits.

[34] Knut Rybka, *Eichendorffs Italienische Reise: Textarbeit zum "Taugenichts"* (Frankfurt am Main: Peter Lang, 1993), 220.

[35] Rybka, 31.

[36] Frühwald and Schillback, commentary, *ALT*, 821.

[37] Margret Walter-Schneider and Martina Hasler investigate the role of the arts and classify Rome as the locus of classical art in *Taugenichts*. They see the protagonist's experiences in Rome as a critique of German Classicism, yet they fail to situate the *tableau vivant* and *Marienbild* in their historical contexts. In addition, they do not mention the Nazarene school by name. Margret Walter-Schneider and Martina Hasler, "Die Kunst in Rom: Zum 7. und 8. Kapitel von Eichendorffs Erzählung 'Aus dem Leben eines Taugenichts,'" *Aurora: Jahrbuch der Eichendorff Gesellschaft* 45 (1985), 49–62.

[38] Schumann, 159–218. Numerous commentators cite Eichendorff's apparent orientation on Goethe's description of his own birth from *Dichtung und Wahrheit* in his own autobiographical writings (*Kapitel von meiner Geburt, Unstern*), albeit with an ironic twist. Despite the favorable constellations, destiny will prove to be other than expected.

[39] Throughout his book Rybka draws some of the same parallels that I do between Eichendorff and Goethe. I have credited Rybka throughout this chapter when he has offered insight beyond my own. Significantly, he does not investigate the important search for the father figure, the parallels between Wien and Weimar, the connection of Goethe's visit to the Palace of Palagonia to the Taugenichts's trip to the mountaintop, and the similarities between Overbeck's painting and the Madonna in the *Taugenichts*. In addition, Rybka falters in his impulse to accomplish too much. Rybka alternates between close intertextual analysis and a more structuralist approach, going so far as to calculate percentages of word occurrence and parallel sentence structures in various of Eichendorff's texts, a strategy that does little to support his primary argument. His ultimate conclusion that Eichendorff's Italian journey is a *Sprachreise* seems only loosely connected to his main contention that Werther is the real traveler in both Goethe's and Eichendorff's narratives. Rybka, 267.

[40] Rybka, 118.

[41] Eichendorff, "Auch ich war in Arkadien!" *Dichter und Ihre Gesellen*, 103. These brief introductory paragraphs have been restored to the text in the Deutscher Klassiker Verlag edition of Eichendorff's work. Further references are abbreviated as *A*.

[42] Hans Magnus Enzensberger, "Eine Theorie des Tourismus," *Einzelheiten* (Frankfurt am Main: Suhrkamp, 1962), 149, 156.

Chapter 5

[1] The gradual loss of Venice's political power actually began in the sixteenth century with the rise of the Turks. Venice's prized isolation was in jeopardy once the port was opened for international travel.

² France ruled Venice from 1805 to 1815. With Napoleon's defeat Venice returned to Austrian control until 1866 when the Venetians voted to join Italy after Austria's defeat by Prussia.

³ Interest in literary representations of Italy has never waned. Publications ranging from scholarly investigations to literary companions for travelers continue to appear. Recent titles include: Christiana Schenk, *Venedig im Spiegel der Décadence-Literatur des Fin de siècle* (Frankfurt am Main: Peter Lang, 1987); Tony Tanner, *Venice Desired* (Cambridge, Mass.: Blackwell, 1992); Angelika Corbineau-Hoffmann, *Paradoxie der Fiktion: Literarische Venedig-Bilder 1797–1984* (Berlin: de Gruyter, 1993); John Pemble, *Venice Rediscovered* (New York: Oxford, 1995); Ian Littlewood, *A Literary Companion to Venice* (New York: St. Martin's, 1995).

⁴ Byron, *A Critical Edition of the Major Works*, ed. Jerome J. McGann (New York: Oxford, 1986), 153 (Canto IV: 18).

⁵ In fact, attempts at a complete modern critical edition of Platen's work have fallen short. Only the first volume of the edition appeared, containing the poetry. The second volume, which was to contain Platen's prose and dramatic works, was never published. August von Platen, *Lyrik,* ed. Kurt Wölfel and Jürgen Link (Munich: Winkler, 1982). All further references will be made parenthetically, abbreviated as *P*.

⁶ Although these later works lie beyond the scope of this chapter, they certainly invite further inquiry. More attention to Platen's overall response to Italian culture might also include a reading of his historical drama set in Venice, *Die Liga von Cambrai* (*The League of Cambrai,* 1833).

⁷ Peter Bumm, *August Graf von Platen: Eine Biographie* (Paderborn: Schöningh, 1990), 58. All subsequent references to this work in the text will be abbreviated as *PB*.

⁸ Platen's diary describes the scene of the meeting and indicates that literature was not a topic of discussion during the visit: "Von Goethes Person wage ich kaum etwas zu sagen." Platen, *Die Tagebücher des Grafen August von Platen: Aus der Handschrift des Dichters,* ed. G. von Laubmann and L. von Scheffler, vol. 2 (Stuttgart: Cotta, 1900), 494. Further references will be abbreviated *PT*.

⁹ Jürgen Link, commentary, *P*, 856–57.

¹⁰ Goethe, *Gedichte 1800–1832,* ed. Karl Eibl (Frankfurt am Main: Deutscher Klassiker Verlag, 1988), 408. In 1821 Platen responds directly to this poem in his "Das Sonett an Goethe" (*P*, 370).

¹¹ Goethe did complete a seldom-considered cycle of seventeen love sonnets in 1808, titled simply *Sonette*.

¹² Johann Peter Eckermann, "Neue Ghaselen von August Graf von Platen," *Über Kunst und Alterthum IV 3 (1824) in Ästhetische Schriften 1821–1824* by Goethe, ed. Stefan Grief and Andrea Ruhlig (Frankfurt am Main: Deutscher Klassiker Verlag, 1998), 591.

[13] Karl Gödeke, afterword, *Gesammelte Werke des Grafen August von Platen in einem Band,* August von Platen (Stuttgart: Cotta, 1839), 438. Karl Gödeke included Grimm's remarks in his commentary to this one-volume edition of Platen's work in 1839, which was reissued in an unrevised form until 1893. He does not cite his source for Grimm's comments. Bumm speculates that Grimm may have been influenced by Eckermann's earlier review. *PB*, 163.

[14] Johann Peter Eckermann, *Gespräche mit Goethe in den letzten Jahren seines Lebens,* ed. Christoph Michel and Hans Grüters (Frankfurt am Main: Deutscher Klassiker Verlag, 1999), 167. This brief remark was the cause of much speculation after its first publication because of the series of stars, instead of the poet's name. The public concluded that Goethe made the remark about Heine. Eckermann corrected the misunderstanding in a publication of 1836. Platen's name was not printed in the text until its third edition in 1867. Eckermann, *Gespräche,* 1172. As Derks explains, Eckermann mistook the date of his conversation with Goethe. Goethe seems to be addressing Platen's satirical works here, the first of which, *Die verhängnisvolle Gabel,* did not appear until 1826. Eckermann's *Tagebücher* later revealed that the discussion regarding Platen took place on 11 February 1831. Paul Derks, *Die Schande der heiligen Päderastie: Homosexualität und Öffentlichkeit in der deutschen Literatur, 1750–1850* (Berlin: Rosa Winkel, 1990), 591–93.

[15] Thomas Mann, "August von Platen," *Adel des Geistes* (Stockholm: Bermann-Fischer, 1945), 503–17. The connections between Mann's *Tristan* (1902) and *Der Tod in Venedig* (1911), and the figure of Platen and his famous sonnet "Tristan" are well known. One is also reminded of Platen's earlier influence on Meyer and Nietzsche: Meyer's "Venedig" ("Venedig, einen Winter lebt' ich dort," 1881) and Nietzsche's "Venedig" ("An der Brücke stand / jüngst ich in brauner Nacht," 1888).

[16] Heinrich Henel, "Epigonenlyrik: Rückert und Platen," *Euphorion* 51 (1961): 268, 271.

[17] Also of importance in Platen scholarship is Henel's selection of Platen's poetry, published as *Gedichte* in 1968. In a departure from previous editions of Platen's work, Henel organizes the poetry thematically rather than by genre: August von Platen, *Gedichte,* ed. Heinrich Henel (Stuttgart: Reclam 1968). Although Henel's edition has made Platen's work more accessible to a wider audience, the editors of the 1982 collected edition conclude that Henel's use of thematic categories attenuates the poet's attention to genre as presented in his *Ausgabe letzter Hand* (*P*, 691).

[18] Jürgen Link, *Artistischer Form und ästhetischer Sinn in Platens Lyrik* (Munich: Fink, 1971), 243.

[19] Friedrich Sengle, "August Graf von Platen (1796–1835)," *Biedermeierzeit: Deutsche Literatur im Spannungsfeld zwischen Restauration und Revolution 1815–1848,* vol. 3 (Stuttgart: Metzler, 1980), 415.

[20] Richard Dove, *The "Individualität" of August von Platen: Subjectivity and Solipsism at the Close of the Kunstperiode* (Frankfurt: Lang, 1983), 27.

[21] Frank Busch, *August Graf von Platen. Thomas Mann. Zeichen und Gefühle* (Munich: Fink, 1987), 15.

[22] Robert Aldrich, *The Seduction of the Mediterranean: Writing, Art and Homosexual Fantasy* (New York: Routledge, 1993), 41–68.

[23] One major drawback of Bumm's study is his avoidance of academic footnotes. He includes an apparatus at the end of each of the book's three major sections, divided by chapters, in which he cites his sources in a sort of running paragraph without division or numbers. His ongoing references to Platen's correspondence and diaries are included in this unfortunate fashion, which makes the task of locating his sources very difficult.

[24] Platen omitted "Der Canalazzo trägt auf breitem Rücken," "Ich liebe dich, wie jener Formen eine," and "Was läßt im Leben sich zuletzt gewinnen." Significantly a previously unpublished sonnet ("Wenn tiefe Schwermut meine Seele wieget") is added to the end of the cycle.

[25] In addition, Koch and Petzet also include a variant of the first sonnet as found in an 1824 manuscript, which Platen had written for Frau von Schelling: "Der Morgen lächelte zu meinem Glücke."

[26] Corbineau-Hoffmann, 176.

[27] Bumm believes that Platen's Italian was not nearly as fluent as some have speculated: "Platens Italienisch kann 1834 nur so gut gewesen sein, wie es die eigene grobe Übertragung mehrerer seiner Gedichte für Leopardi beweist." And this after seven years in Italy. *PB*, 74.

[28] Chloe Chard, "Crossing Boundaries," *Transports*, 138.

[29] In a time before photography, many travelers on the Grand Tour commissioned portraits of themselves situated in exotic surroundings and collected engravings of the ruins they visited and the works of art they admired. All of these things served later as evidence of the traveler's presence in the foreign land and as validation of their experience.

[30] The complete title was eliminated after the first publication of the cycle. In the collections of 1828 and 1834, the cycle was subsumed into the author's larger grouping of sonnets, introduced only by the heading "Venedig."

[31] She does, however, misread Platen's second, that is alternative ending, in which it appears that departure is avoided or at least delayed.

[32] I will refer to excerpts from the *Sonette aus Venedig* parenthetically throughout this chapter. Where applicable, the Roman numeral refers to the sonnet's position in the cycle as originally published in 1825 (see appendix) and the Arabic numeral to the line number.

[33] All Roman numeral references to Goethe's *Römische Elegien* refer to the 1795 edition of the cycle. All parenthetical references include number of the elegy (Roman numeral) and line number where applicable.

[34] Although Veronese painted several allegories of Venice, the most admired is the ceiling painting *Il Trionfo di Venezia* (The Triumph of Venice, 1579–82), located above the Doge's throne in the *Sala del Maggior Consiglio* of the *Palazzo Ducale*, in which Venice is crowned with the laurel by winged Victory. See figure 3.

[35] There exists a long-established tradition of such an allegorization of Venice. In a broader sense, Italy, too, was often described in female terms. One such example in which such an embodiment of the nation is linked to poetry can be found in the figure of Madame de Staël's *Corinne*. De Stäel writes: "Corinne est le lien de ses amis entre eux; elle est le mouvement, l'intérêt de notre vie; nous comptons sur sa bonté; nous sommes fiers de son génie; nous disons aux étrangers: — regardez-la, c'est l'image de notre belle Italie; elle est ce que nous serions sans l'ignorance, l'envie, la discorde et l'indolence auxquelles notre sort nous a condamnés." Germaine de Staël, *Corinne ou l'Italie,* ed. Simone Balayé (Paris: Gallimard, 1985), 57.

[36] See Jeffrey L. Sammons's lengthier discussion of the tulip as a symbol within Platen's oeuvre. Jeffrey L. Sammons, "Platen's Tulip Image," *Monatshefte* 52 (1960): 293–301. He calls attention to the catalogue effect of Platen's description of Venetian art and the overall effect of sublimation of the homoerotic associated with this flower in Platen's poetry.

[37] The Austrian censors banned the *Sonette aus Venedig,* obviously for their strong anti-Austrian sentiment concerning the occupation of Venice. Jochen Heymann, "Venedig sehen und sterben: August von Platens erste Italienreise und die venezianische Volksdichtung," *Was er wünscht, das ist ihm nie geworden: August Graf von Platen, 1796–1835,* ed. Gunnar Och (Erlangen: Universitätsbibliothek, 1996), 147 n. 10.

[38] This celebration took place on Ascension Day and for it the Doge rode out to sea in the Bucentaur. Goethe saw the last Bucentaur displayed in the Arsenal of Venice and reported on it on 5 October 1786 (*IR,* 85–86).

[39] Platen arrived in Munich on 19 November. At first he followed his instinct that it would be wise to assume a low profile as he was aware of his late return to Germany. To the contrary though, Platen soon became more active in certain circles of society so much so that his name was published in the list of visitors in the daily papers. He seems to have known that trouble would be awaiting him in Erlangen and chose to avoid it as long as possible. After his arrival there around the turn of the year, Platen was arrested on 2 January 1825 and jailed in a military complex in Nuremberg. After ten days he was transferred to house arrest; he would remain confined to the home of a friend until 23 March. *PB,* 358–59.

[40] G. S. Rousseau, "Love and Antiquities: Walpole and Gray on the Grand Tour," *Perilous Enlightenment: Pre- and Post-modern Discourses: Sexual, Historical* (Manchester: Manchester UP, 1991), 172–99. He cites the example of a heterosexual who stayed in Italy so long that it was assumed he must be homosexual, 190.

[41] Simon Richter, "Winckelmann's Progeny: Homosocial Networking in the Eighteenth Century," *Outing Goethe and his Age,* ed. Alice A. Kuzniar (Stanford: Stanford UP: 1996), 33.

[42] Paintings: Titian's *Assumption of Mary, Tobias with the Angel,* and *St. John in the Desert;* Veronese's *St. Sebastian,* and Palma Vecchio's *St. Barbara.*
    Sculpture: Campagnia's *Sleeping Christ.*

[43] Veronese's *The Family of Darius before Alexander.*

[44] Veronese's *The Triumph of Venice.*

[45] Camille Paglia, *Sexual Personae: Art and Decadence from Nefertiti to Emily Dickinson* (New York: Vintage, 1991), 168.

[46] It is tempting to speculate on what his lengthier description of Campagna's *Sleeping Christ* might have been. The reader will recall his attention to the anthropomorphization of sculptural forms in the ninth sonnet: "Doch um noch mehr zu fesseln mich, zu halten, / So mischt sich unter jene Kunstgebilde / Die schönste Blüte lebender Gestalten" (IX: 12–14).

[47] Staël, *Corinne,* 67–68.

Chapter 6

[1] Heinrich Heine, "Reise von München nach Genua," *Reisebilder III, IV,* ed. Alfred Opitz (Hamburg: Hoffmann und Campe, 1986), 62. All further references will be cited parenthetically to this volume of the *Düsseldorfer Heine Ausgabe,* which contains all three Italian travel pieces. They will be abbreviated as follows: R for *Reise nach München nach Genua,* B for *Die Bäder von Lucca,* and S for *Die Stadt Lucca.* References to the companion commentary volume will be indicated by *RB.*

[2] His publisher, Julius Campe, who himself had visited Italy, recommended a transalpine journey to the young writer in a letter of 26 December 1827. Heinrich Heine, *Briefe an Heine 1823–1826,* ed. Renate Francke (Berlin: Akademie Verlag, 1974), 38. This edition, the *Säkularausgabe,* is the primary source for Heine's correspondence. A bout of illness apparently prevented him from leaving in the spring of 1828. It is unclear just how spontaneous Heine's decision was to go to Italy. As to the actual circumstances, three days were required for receiving the necessary travel documentation in his passport; in addition, Heine was obligated to complete a number of editorial projects in Munich before his departure. Commentary, *RB,* 839.

[3] Its first two, very short chapters had been serialized in Cotta's *Morgenblatt* in November 1829 under the title *Italienische Fragmente.* The title of the

volume imparts the sense that the time for travel and its corresponding literary genre has expired, not only for the author personally, but perhaps even more consequentially, as an acceptable mode of representation and discourse. The second edition (1834) was retitled *Reisebilder: Vierter Teil.*

[4] The final installment of Goethe's project was not published until after Heine's return to Germany from Italy; however, it was available in 1829, a year before the first of Heine's essays was published in book form.

[5] Lucca was not a completely unusual stop for traveling poets; Shelley visited in 1818 and Byron in 1822. At closer look though, Lucca's early nineteenth-century history reflects the tumultuous nature of European politics, a subject of increasingly great interest to Heine. During Napoleon's reign it was ruled as a principality by one of Napoleon's sisters, Elisa Baciocchi. With his defeat in 1815, it fell to Spanish rule until it was ceded to Tuscany in 1847. In 1860 it would be incorporated into the unified Kingdom of Italy.

[6] There has been some speculation about Heine's original intentions. Did he plan to go further south than Genoa? How long did he foresee staying in Italy? Werner has convincingly shown that Heine had planned only to go as far as Genoa. Michael Werner, "Heines *Reise von München nach Genua* im Lichte ihrer Quellen," *Heine Jahrbuch* 14 (1975): 28. Heine wrote that a bad flu might prevent him from returning home that winter, although this proved not to be the case. Letter to Cotta, 11 November 1828. Heinrich Heine, *Briefe 1815–1831,* ed. Fritz H. Eisner (Berlin: Akademie Verlag, 1970), 347.

[7] Jost Hermand, *Der frühe Heine: Ein Kommentar zu den "Reisebildern"* (Munich: Winkler, 1976), 11–12.

[8] Ralf H. Klinkenberg, *Die Reisebilder Heinrich Heines: Vermittlung durch literarische Stilmittel* (Frankfurt: Lang, 1981), 66.

[9] Hermand, 13–14.

[10] Brenner, *Der Reisebericht in der deutschen Literatur,* 361. Although Brenner does not provide statistics, his claim is credible if one considers the amount of research, in total, on all of Heine's travel essays.

[11] It seems that the most often discussed of the *Reisebilder* is without question *Die Harzreise.* This is a text not without pertinence to the present investigation because of its connection to Goethe. Most prominent is Heine's silence in the text about his visit to Goethe's home in Weimar on 1 October 1824. In fact, the absence of any serious reference to their encounter in Heine's work is perhaps the most cited explanation for his troublesome relationship with the figure of Goethe. See, for example, Jost Hermand's well-known study of *Die Harzreise* as a parody of Goethe's *Werther,* which itself has met with some disagreement. Hermand, "Die Harzreise. Unmut gegen Goethe," *Der frühe Heine,* 59–80.

[12] A prime example is the lengthy exegesis on Napoleon found near the end of the *Reise von München nach Genua.* Heine never visited Marengo, the battle-

field where Napoleon achieved his greatest Italian victory on 14 June 1800. Heine, *RB*, 68–74.

[13] Jeffrey L. Sammons, *Heinrich Heine: A Modern Biography* (Princeton: Princeton UP, 1979), 6.

[14] Heinrich Heine, "Die Nordsee. Dritte Abteilung." *Briefe aus Berlin. Über Polen. Reisebilder I/II (Prosa)*, ed. Jost Hermand (Hamburg: Hoffmann und Campe, 1973), 147.

[15] Letter from Karl Immerman to Heine, 1 February 1830, *Briefe an Heine*, 52–53.

[16] George F. Peters, *"Der große Heide Nr. 2": Heinrich Heine and the Levels of His Goethe Reception* (New York: Peter Lang, 1989), 55.

[17] Peters does draw attention to a variant of the twenty-sixth chapter of that text, which reveals a much more deeply perceived inferiority complex vis-à-vis Goethe. Here Heine plays with the similarity between the names *Gott* and *Goethe*, and offers a prayer to both. His final version of the chapter offers a more cynical view of Goethe and less introspective look at himself. Peters, 122–25.

[18] He correctly interprets the eagle that the narrator comes upon in the third chapter of *Die Stadt Lucca* as "what arguably represents Heine's strongest published anti-Goethean declaration, although the Weimar poet is not mentioned by name." Peters, 96. The text in question is found in *S*, 164–65.

[19] Michael Werner convincingly reveals the extent to which Heine's account of his journey is far less an account of actual experiences, but rather is derived from much reading and research. Werner offers a list of twenty titles that inform Heine's first essay on Italy. These texts were either referred directly to by Heine in the essays and correspondence, or were signed out of the library at Göttingen. Werner, 25.

[20] This is, in a way, analogous to the most cutting criticisms of the organized religion found in *Die Stadt Lucca*, which are uttered by Mathilde rather than the narrator.

[21] Letter to Eduard von Schenk, early September 1828, Heine, *Briefe*, 339.

[22] Günther Oesterle, "Heinrich Heine's *Reise von München nach Genua* — 'ein träumendes Spielgelbild' vergangener und gegenwärtiger Zeiten," *Italienische Reise. Reisen nach Italien*, ed. Italo Michele Battafarano (Gardolo di Trento: Reverdito, 1988), 270.

[23] Jeffrey L. Sammons, "Heine as *Weltbürger*? A Skeptical Inquiry," *Modern Language Notes* 101 (1986), 622.

[24] Renate Stauf, *Der problematische Europäer: Heinrich Heine im Konflikt zwischen Nationenkritik und gesellschaftlicher Utopie* (Heidelberg: Winter, 1997), 61.

[25] Guillaume van Gemert, "Heinrich Heine und der Wandel des Italienbildes: Die Reise von München nach Genua im Spiegel kontemporärer Auslandsreisen deutscher Dichter," *Italienische Reise. Reisen nach Italien*, 300–301.

[26] Waltraud Maierhofer, "Italia und Germania. Zum Frauen- und Deutschlandbild in Heines italienischen *Reisebildern*," *Aufklärung und Skepsis: Internationaler Heine Kongress 1997 zum 200. Geburtstag*, ed. Joseph A. Kruse, Bernd Witte, and Karin Füllner (Stuttgart: Metzler, 1999), 159. Maierhofer establishes Heine's female depictions in relation to various visual portrayals of women, including the works of the Nazarene painters. They are an amalgam of both ancient models, such as those found in Greek sculpture, and the more modern idealizations propagated by the Nazarenes and their strict Catholic beliefs.

[27] Letter to Moses Moser, 6 September 1828. Heine, *Briefe 1815–1831*, 340.

[28] Gerhard Höhn, *Heine Handbuch* (Stuttgart: Metzler, 1987), 154.

[29] Jeffrey L. Sammons, *Heine: A Modern Biography*, 148.

[30] Heine, Letter to Eduard von Schenk, Early September 1828. Heine, *Briefe*, 339.

[31] Robert C. Holub, *Heinrich Heine's Reception of German Grecophilia: The Function and Application of the Hellenic Tradition in the First Half of the Nineteenth Century* (Heidelberg: Winter, 1981), 55.

[32] The most comprehensive analysis of the Platen-Heine feud remains Paul Derks's lengthy chapter "Parodie eines antiken Übermuts." His excellent chronology traces the genesis of the feud, the publications of the texts in question, including reviews and responses, the aftermath, and the political implications of the scandal. Derks, 479–613.

[33] In addition, while Heine traveled around northern Italy in the fall of 1828, his path came perilously close to crossing that of his rival. During the previous spring while in Florence, Platen had made the acquaintance of the influential art historian Carl von Rumohr. In October Heine also met Rumohr while visiting the Uffizi Gallery. Derks reports that Platen thought Heine feared running into him because of a possible challenge to a duel. Derks interprets this as evidence of Platen's own similar fear. Derks, 522.

[34] Block, 236–37.

[35] Alberto Destro, "Reiste Heine wirklich nach Italien?" *"Ich Narr des Glücks": Heinrich Heine 1797–1856 — Bilder einer Ausstellung*, ed. Joseph A. Kruse (Stuttgart: Metzler, 1997), 229.

[36] Chard, *Pleasure and Guilt on the Grand Tour*, 1–39.

Conclusion

[1] Gustav Nicolai, *Italien wie es wirklich ist. Bericht über eine merkwürdige Reise in den hesperischen Gefilden, als Warnungsstimme für Alle, welche sich dahin sehnen,* 2 vols. (Leipzig: Otto Wigand, 1834), 1.

[2] David Rieff, "German Hatred (of Germans)," *Harper's Magazine* (May 1994): 30.

[3] Carlos Widmann, "Sog des Südens," *Der Spiegel* (24 February 2001): 54–73.

[4] Sigmund Freud, "Eine Erinnerungsstörung auf der Akropolis," *Gesammelte Werke,* ed. Anna Freud, vol. 16 (London: Imago, 1950), 256.

Index

Aix-la-Chapelle, Treaty of, 2
Aldrich, Robert, 119
Andrews, Keith, 198–99
Anna Amalia, Duchess of Saxon-
  Weimar, 18, 73
Archenholz, Johann Wilhelm von,
  works by: *England und Italien*,
  31–32
Arnim, Ludwig Joachim von, 87
Augustine of Hippo, Saint, works
  by: *Confessions*, 22
autobiography, 19, 22–24, 92–94,
  146–48

Baedeker, Karl, 110, 122
baroque: art and architecture, 24,
  45, 99; German literature, 93,
  115, 118
Battafarano, Italo Michele, 21
Bellini, Giovanni, 127, 134
Biedermeier, 94, 122
Block, Richard O., 171, 194
Bloom, Harold, 6
Boccaccio, Giovanni, 88–89
Boerner, Peter, 4, 23–24
Boyle, Nicholas, 18, 26, 42, 53,
  57–58, 72, 197–98
Brenner, Peter J., 5–6, 23–24, 146
Brentano, Clemens, 86
Breymayer, Ursula, 25, 57
Brown, Jane K., 30–31, 42
Bumm, Peter, 119–20, 122, 135
Burkhardt, Jacob, works by:
  *Die Kultur der Renaissance
  in Italien*, 163
Busch, Frank, 119
Butor, Michel, 190
Buzard, James, 190
Byron, George Gordon, Lord, 109

Byron, George Gordon, Lord,
  works by: *Childe Harold's
  Pilgrimage*, 113

Cagliostro (Joseph Balsamo), 45
Campo Formio, Treaty of, 113
Cardinal, Roger, 33
Carl August, Duke of Saxon-
  Weimar, 18–19, 49, 51, 57, 66,
  73
Carré, Jean-Marie, 3–4
Catallus, 60
Chard, Chloe, 7–8, 63–64, 123,
  172
Classicism, German, 13, 41, 56–
  57, 60, 86, 118, 154, 167,
  169–71, 173–74
Corbineau-Hoffmann, Angelika,
  121, 126
Cornelius, Peter, 81, 84
Culler, Jonathan, 9

Derks, Paul, 119, 204, 210
Destro, Alberto, 171
Dewitz, Hans-George, 23
Dove, Richard, 118
Dürer, Albrecht, 2, 79–82, 198
Dyserinck, Hugo, 4

Eichendorff, Hermann von (son of
  Joseph von Eichendorff), 107–9
Eichendorff, Joseph von: as a late
  Romantic, 86; his criticism of
  Werther, 92–93
Eichendorff, Joseph von, works by:
  Ahnung und Gegenwart, 93,
  106; "Auch ich war in
  Arkadien!" 107–9; *Aus dem
  Leben eines Taugenichts:*

composition and publication
history of, 93; *Dichter und ihre
Gesellen*, 87–89; *Der deutsche
Roman des achtzehnten
Jahrhunderts in seinem
Verhältnis zum Christentum*,
92; "Gotterdämmerung," 90;
Das Marmorbild, 89–93;
"Rückkehr," 87–88;
"Sehnsucht," 88–89
Einem, Herbert von, 23
Eissler, Kurt Robert, 53
ekphrastic poetry, 127
Enzensberger, Hans Magnus, 109
Erhard, Walter, 25, 57

Fiorillo, Johann Domenik, 79
Fischer, Manfred S., 4
Forster, Georg, works by:
Ansichten vom Niederrhein, 163
Fouqué, Friedrich de la Motte, 89
Frederick II, Emperor, 2, 67
French Revolution, 1, 3, 66, 68
Freud, Sigmund, 6, 177

Germans in Italy, history of, 1–3,
176–77
ghazal, 115
Gilman, Sander, 64
Goethe, Christiane (née Vulpius)
(wife of J. W. von Goethe), 10,
26, 62, 72
Goethe, Johann Caspar (father of
J. W. von Goethe), 15–18, 32,
35, 37–38, 52
Goethe, Johann Caspar, works by:
Viaggio per L'Italia, 16–17
Goethe, Johann Wolfgang von:
aborted journeys to Italy, 17–
18; incognito in Italy, 29–31;
Italian influences in childhood,
15–16; and the Italian
language, 16; preparations for
his Italian journey, 18–19, 26;

relationship to father, 16–17,
38; return to Weimar, 21, 49;
second trip to Italy, 72–75;
sexual experiences in Italy, 52–
54, 64
Goethe, Johann Wolfgang von,
works by: "Amor ein Land-
schaftsmaler," 56; *Aus Meinem
Leben. Dichtung und Wahrheit*,
15, 22–23; *Campagne in
Frankreich*, 40; "Cupido, der
lose eigensinnige Knabe," 56;
Egmont, 56; *Faust, Part I*, 56,
106; *Faust, Part II*, 41;
Hermann und Dorothea, 18;
Iphigenie auf Tauris, 14, 37,
41, 56; *Italienische Reise*:
composition and publication
history of, 19–22; "Kennst du
das Land?" 14–15, 148, 157,
164; *Die Leiden des jungen
Werthers*, 30, 67–68, 106;
Metamorphose der Pflanzen, 24;
Propyläen, 80–83; *Reisetagebücher für die Frau von Stein*,
19; "Requiem, dem frohsten
Manne des Jahrhunderts, dem
Fürsten von Ligne," 27–28;
Das Römische Carneval, 54–56;
Römische Elegien: composition
and publication history of, 60–
62; figure of Faustina in, 73–
74; self-censorship in, 61;
Torquato Tasso, 56; *Über Kunst
und Altertum*, 83–85;
Venezianische Epigramme, 73–
74; *West-Östlicher Divan*, 10,
150, 167; *Wilhelm Meisters
Lehrjahre*, 14–15; *Wilhelm
Meisters Theatralische Sendung*,
15; *Wilhelm Meisters
Wanderjahre*, 15
Goethe, Julius August Walther von
(son of J. W. von Goethe), 52

Goethe Museum in Rome, 173, 190
Gould, Robert, 21
Grand Tour, 2, 8, 136, 172
Grimm, Gunther E., 25, 57
Grimm, Jakob, 115; critique of Platen's work, 116, 204
Guyard, Marius-François, 3

Hackert, Philipp, 22, 43
Haile, H. G., 61
Hamilton, Lady Emma (née Hart), 7, 38, 164
Hamilton, Sir William, 7, 38
Happel, Eberhard G., 88
Hasler, Martina, 202
Heine, Heinrich: defense of Goethe, 150; feud with Platen, 170–71; and German Classicism's orientation on Greece, 169–70; and the Italian language, 158; and the Romantics, 159, 169–70; and sensualism, 167; trip to Italy, 143–44; and women in Italy, 165–66
Heine, Heinrich, works by: *Die Bäder von Lucca:* publication history of, 144; *Buch der Lieder,* 146; *Die Harzreise,* 144; *Die Nordsee,* 144, 147–49; *Reise von München nach Genua:* publication history of, 144; *Die Romantische Schule,* 150; *Die Stadt Lucca:* publication history of, 144
Henel, Heinrich, 118, 120, 204
Herculaneum, 2, 40, 42
Herder, Johann Gottfried, 19, 24, 42, 49
Hermand, Jost, 149–50
Hoffmann, E. T. A., 86, 89, 94, 104
Holub, Robert C., 169–71

Homer, works by: *The Odyssey,* 44–46
homosexuality in Italy, 119, 135
Huch, Ricarda, 88
Hummel, Johann Erdmann, paintings by: *Gesellschaft in einer italienischen Locanda [die Fermata],* 104

imagology, 3–4
imitation (*Nachahmung*), 153, 169

Jagemann, Christian Joseph, 18

Kaufmann, Angelika, 22, 53, 74
Kavaliersreise, 2–3, 9, 174–75
Kniep, Christoph Heinrich, 43, 45
Koch, Max, 120
Koeppen, Wolfgang, works by: *Der Tod in Rom,* 176

Langer, Ernst Theodor, 17
Lessing, Gotthold Ephraim, 13
Ligne, Field Marshall Charles Joseph (Prince of), 27
Link, Jürgen, 118, 120, 126
Loeffler, Bertina Maria, 199

MacCannell, Dean, 9
Maierhofer, Waltraud, 164–65
Mann, Thomas, works by: "August von Platen," 117; *Der Tod in Venedig,* 176
Mayer, Hans, 24
Menzel, Wolfgang, works by: *Die Deutsche Literatur,* 150
Meyer, Johann Heinrich, 20, 80, 197
Meyer, Johann Heinrich, works by: "*Neudeutsche religios-patriotische Kunst,*" 83–85
Michel, Christoph, 23
Morgan, Lady (née Sydney Owenson), works by: *Italy,* 152

Moritz, Karl Philipp, 21, 37
Moritz, Karl Philipp, works by:
    *Reisen eines Deutschen in
    England,* 51–52
Murray, John, 110

Napoleonic Wars, 3, 77, 122
Nazarene painters, 25, 78, 81–86,
    198–99
Neuber, Wolfgang, 6
Nicolai, Gustav, works by: *Italien
    wie es wirklich ist,* 175–76
Niederer, Heinrich, 25–26
Novalis (Friedrich von
    Hardenberg), 86–87

Oswald, Stefan, 20, 25, 27, 54,
    163, 171
Overbeck, Friedrich, 81, 84
Overbeck, Friedrich, paintings by:
    Italia und Germania, 76, 82–
    83, 89, 103, 175
Ovid, 51, 60

Paestum, 37, 41–42, 56
Paglia, Camille, 137
Paulsen, J. J. H., 26
Pemble, John, 136
Peters, George F., 150–51
Petzet, Erich, 120
Pikulik, Lothar, 198
Platen, August von: death of, 177;
    feud with Heine, 170–71;
    reputation at fin de siècle, 117;
    and sexuality, 119, 135–38;
    visits to and stays in Italy, 114,
    139–40; youth of, 114
Platen, August von, works by:
    Neue Ghaselen, 116; *Sonette aus
    Venedig:* publication history of,
    119–21, 179–80; *Die Tage-
    bücher des Grafen August von
    Platen,* 121, 123–24, 132, 136,
    140; "Tristan," 139

Platen-Gesellschaft, 117
Pompeii, 3, 37, 40–42, 56
Porter, Dennis, 6
Propertius, 61
Pruys, Karl Hugo, 64

Raphael, 77, 80–82
Reiffenstein, Johann Friedrich, 37
Requadt, Paul, 87, 93
Restoration, 3, 136, 149, 163
Richter, Simon, 136
Rieff, David, 176
Riggi, Maddalena, 54
Rilke, Rainer Maria, 117, 176
Romanticism, German: conception
    of travel in, 33, 77, 78, 110;
    trope of *Sehnsucht* in, 92, 110;
    trope of *Wandern* in, 78; versus
    German Classicism, 25–28, 57,
    59, 78, 86, 89, 151
Rousseau, G. S., 136
Rousseau, Jean Jacques, 22, 110,
    119
Rybka, Knut, 103, 106–7

Said, Edward, 7
Sammons, Jeffrey L., 147, 162,
    167, 206
Schiller, Friedrich von, works
    edited by: *Die Horen,* 61, 67;
    *Musenalmanach für das Jahr
    1796,* 73
Schindler, Herbert, 82
Schlegel, August Wilhelm von,
    116
Schlegel, Dorothea von, 82
Schlegel, Friedrich von, works by:
    "Über die deutsche
    Kunstausstellung zu Rom, im
    Frühjahr 1819, und über den
    gegenwärtigen Stand der
    deutschen Kunst in Rom," 85–
    86
Schultz, Hartwig, 95

Schumann, Detlev, 106
Schütze, Jochen K., 22, 30, 44, 58–59
Seidel, Philipp, 18, 26, 30, 54
Seidlin, Oskar, 201
Sengle, Friedrich, 118, 122
Seume, Gottfried, works by: *Spaziergang nach Syrakus im Jahre 1802,* 109, 163
sonnet: Goethe's use of, 116; Petrarchan, 116; Platen's use of, 115; Romantic appropriation of, 115
Spitzweg, Carl, paintings by: *Engländer in der Campagna,* 142, 156–57, 175
Staël, Germaine de, works by: *Corinne ou l'Italie,* 139, 149, 152, 206
Stauf, Renate, 163–64
Stein, Charlotte von, 18, 19, 96
Sterne, Laurence, works by: *A Sentimental Journey,* 7
Stowe, William, 190

Tieck, Ludwig, 78–81, 87, 109
Tieck, Ludwig, works by: *Herzensergießungen eines kunstliebenden Klosterbruders,* 78–81, 84; *Phantasien über die Kunst,* 81
Tischbein, J. H. W., 22, 29–30, 37, 39–40
Tischbein, J. H. W., paintings by: *Goethe in der Campagna di Roma,* 12–14, 102–3, 191
Titian (Tiziano Vecellio), 125, 128–30, 138
tourism, history of, 1–3, 8, 109, 122–23, 174–75
travel literature: and autobiography, 23; criticism of genre, 3–8; development of genre in German, 5, 24, 153, 163, 172

Vaget, Hans Rudolf, 61
Van Den Abbeele, Georges, 9
Venetian painting: contrasted with Florentine painting in the Renaissance, 136–37
Venice: female personification as *La Serenissima,* 129, 131, 137; history of, 113–14; homosexuality in, 135
Venusberg, 89
Veronese, Paulo, 128, 138
Veronese, Paulo, paintings by: *Il Trionfo di Venezia,* 112, 128, 131
Vesuvius, 38–40, 47
Volkmann, Johann Jacob, works by: *Historisch-kritischen Nachrichten von Italien,* 31, 47

Wackenroder, Wilhelm Heinrich, 78–79
Wackenroder, Wilhelm Heinrich, works by: *Herzensergießungen eines kunstliebenden Klosterbruders,* 78–81, 84; *Phantasien über die Kunst,* 81
Walter-Schneider, Margret, 202
Wellek, René, 3–5
Werner, Michael, 208, 209
Wieland, Christoph Martin, works edited by: *Der teutsche Merkur,* 196
Wienbarg, Ludolf, works by: *Holland in den Jahren 1831 und 1832,* 163
Winckelmann, Johann Joachim, 24, 194
Winckelmann, Johann Joachim, works by: *Geschichte der Kunst des Altertums,* 3, 119
Wölfel, Kurt, 120

Zapperi, Roberto, 30, 33, 51
Zelter, Karl Friedrich, 20, 84–85